SOUTHEASTERN COMMUNITY COLLEGE

NORTH CAROLINA

P9-DZA-943

Forerunners
of Black Power

SOUTHEASTERN COMMUNITY COLLEGE LIBRARY

Forerunners
of Black Power

The Rhetoric of Abolition

Edited by

Ernest G. Bormann
University of Minnesota

PRENTICE-HALL. INC.
Englewood Cliffs, New Jersey

© 1971 by
Prentice-Hall, Inc.
Englewood Cliffs, New Jersey

All rights reserved.
No part of this book may be reproduced
in any form or by any means
without permission in writing from the publisher.

C–13–326835–7
P–13–326827–6

Library of Congress Catalog Card No.: 70–133572

Current printing (last digit)
10 9 8 7 6 5 4 3 2 1

Printed in the United States of America

PRENTICE-HALL INTERNATIONAL, INC., *London*
PRENTICE-HALL OF AUSTRALIA, PTY. LTD., *Sydney*
PRENTICE-HALL OF CANADA, LTD., *Toronto*
PRENTICE-HALL OF INDIA PRIVATE LIMITED, *New Delhi*
PRENTICE-HALL OF JAPAN, INC., *Tokyo*

Contents

Part IV

Female Antislavery Speakers, 174

Part V

Establishment Spokesmen for Antislavery, 198

Preface

Teaching by example is an old tradition. Students learn about speech and communication best when they test the advice and theory they get from lectures, textbooks, and discussions against real and varied samples of actual discourse. By considering not only the rhetorical options they must make but also the choices that were made by speakers and publicists whose efforts have withstood the test of history, students become more critical and demanding of the efforts of others and of themselves. In the final analysis, the development of a feel for excellence and responsibility in public discourse can be developed in no other way.

Forerunners of Black Power: The Rhetoric of Abolition is designed to meet the need for both models of persuasive campaigns and examples of essays in speech criticism to complement the emphasis on methods and general principles in courses in speech communication. The essays and selections in this volume provide a focus for courses in public speaking, written composition, speech fundamentals, discussion, argumentation, persuasion, and rhetorical criticism. They are a good model of a persuasive campaign for courses in the history of public address and in speech criticism. They are a useful collection of documents for courses in history, American studies, and humanities.

The book brings together into a unified pattern some of the outstanding speeches and tracts relating to the abolition of the "peculiar institution" of nineteenth-century America. These speeches represent unique documents in American social and intellectual history. They also illustrate one of the most exciting and successful persuasive reform campaigns in the history of American public address.

Included in this collection are speeches by black speakers. With the exception of some by Frederick Douglass and Booker T. Washington, speeches by leading nineteenth-century black orators are difficult to find in contemporary anthologies. The book also contains speeches by early prominent women speakers in the United States. Just as the women's liberation movement grew out of the current civil rights agitation, so did the women's rights movement of the nineteenth century grow out of the antislavery reform.

The radical rhetoric surrounding the race issue in the United States today and the revolutionary agitation of the New Left present contemporary reform materials of great importance to today's student. The involved participant in today's affairs will often have difficulty in analyzing contemporary radical persuasion from any sort of perspective. A sound perspective for study requires a sense of history and an understanding of a culture's rhetorical traditions. That today's speeches provide a highly useful and exciting focus for the student of speech communication is a truism, but to plunge immediately into some of the more explosive materials may lead to relatively unthinking and emotional responses. Students may enjoy highly emotional exchanges of opinion, but such sessions are seldom educational. This volume is designed to present the student with a collection of radical speeches devoted to a highly successful persuasive campaign in American history which is far enough in the past to allow the student to develop some perspective and yet so closely related to the present that it is exciting and relevant. The student who has worked through the first sections of the book is well prepared to speak and write on contemporary speakers and writers with a more useful perspective.

The book begins with an essay that provides the historical background against which the abolitionists spoke and describes the leading rhetorical features of the movement. The introductory essay is followed by fifteen selections divided into five parts. Each part is preceded by a note that describes the text and the situation. Each speech is introduced with a biographical sketch of the speaker. The concluding essay sketches the developments of persuasion relating to civil rights and black power in America from the end of the Civil War to the present. The rhetorical threads described and illustrated in the introductory essay are followed through from the post-Civil War period to the present.

ERNEST G. BORMANN
Minneapolis

The Rhetoric
of Abolition

Few reform efforts in American history can challenge the abolition movement of the years from 1830 to 1860 in terms of entertainment, excitement, and violence. Few reforms have been supported by so many inspired, dedicated, involved, and admirable people and few by as many crackpots, radicals, neurotics, and fanatics as the antislavery movement.

A number of tendencies long resident in the American experience, as well as the intellectual and moral climate in Great Britain during the first third of the nineteenth century, served to stimulate the emergence of the historical movement aimed at the *immediate* emancipation of the slaves which is usually called *abolitionism*. My concern will be with the verbal expression of the cluster of attitudes, feelings, and ideas associated with antislavery in the nineteenth century, that is, with the *rhetoric* of abolition.

By rhetoric, I mean the use of verbal symbols to describe the world, the culture, God, and the universe in such a way as to provide meaning for two or more people. The rhetoric of a pair of lovers may be interesting, is probably to some extent idiosyncratic, and may be trivial. The rhetoric of a reform movement like abolition, on the other hand, is not only interesting but is profoundly woven into the accumulating cultural patterns of the United States. The echoes of that rhetoric continue to provide harmonic overtones for the symphony of inherited meanings which swirls around every citizen of the United States as contemporary America debates racial justice and Black Power.

Many Americans had written about and spoken against slavery before 1830. The most important flurry of antislavery rhetoric prior to the rise of the abolitionists came at the time of the Revolutionary War. James Otis denounced the institution of slavery in his pamphlet *The Rights of the British Colonies Asserted and Proved* in 1764. A few years later Nathaniel Appleton came out strongly for the freedom of the slaves. In 1775 Thomas Paine denounced slavery in round terms in an essay entitled *African Slavery in America*.

1

Among the founders of the Articles of Confederation and the Federal Constitution antislavery sentiment was strong. Jefferson's thoughts on the subject
are widely known, and many leading Southerners of the late eighteenth century looked to the elimination of the institution. Congress excluded slavery
from the Northwest Territory in 1787. By 1804 every Northern state had
either abolished slavery or passed laws for the gradual emancipation of slaves.
In 1808 the international slave trade was outlawed, and the Missouri Compromise of 1820 prohibited slavery in the territory north of 36' 30° in the
Louisiana Purchase.

Antislavery societies were organized as early as 1775 when the Pennsylvania Abolition Society was formed. They soon spread throughout the new
country both North and South. The various societies sent delegates to a
national meeting of the American Convention of Delegates from Abolition
Societies. The national body, however, was a weak coalition of organizations
with little agreement on methods to be used to achieve emancipation.

A stronger force in the antislavery field was the American Society for
Colonizing the Free People of Colour of the United States. The Colonizing
Society was organized in 1816 and represented the culmination of efforts
that began back in the times of the Revolutionary War. By 1833, when the
American Anti-Slavery Society was organized, there were ninety-seven local
colonization societies in the North and 136 in the South, yet in the years
from 1820 to 1833, the colonization efforts had resulted in placing fewer than
three thousand Negroes in Africa.

The abolition movement in the 1830's was, in some respects, a continuation of the antislavery sentiment of the earlier times. The antislavery efforts
of the abolitionists, however, blazed forth with such zeal and intensity that
in a few years the movement established itself as one of the great reform
efforts of our history. The abolitionists condemned slavery as a sin, and while
the earlier antislavery societies had been gradualists in their approach, the
abolitionists made immediate emancipation their slogan. The antislavery
movement of the 1830's was different enough in activity, clarity of purpose,
and in rhetoric to justify setting it aside as a unique rhetorical movement.

Arthur and Lewis Tappan of New York City are exemplars of the radical
reformers who dedicated their property and their lives to the cause of reform-
ing mankind. The Tappan brothers were wealthy merchants who sustained
with time and money the cause of temperance, Sunday schools, tract and
Bible distribution, Sabbath observance, and education. They were part of the
interconnected power structure that controlled a huge empire of benevolent
societies. Many of the societies were relatively new, the product of the years
from 1820 to 1830, but they had by the end of that decade already grown

into immense institutions spreading over the entire country. The eight largest societies were dedicated to promoting home and foreign missions, distributing Bibles and religious tracts, promoting Sunday schools, propagating temperance, and saving the sinful sailors. In addition to the big eight, many lesser groups were dedicated to such causes as saving prostitutes, outlawing the wearing of corsets, and promoting manual labor education.

Although the benevolent empire was nondenominational, it was dominated by "New School" Presbyterians of the persuasion of the Great Revival. The leaders of the societies were relatively few and included, in addition to the Tappans, such people as Thomas Smith Grimké, Gerrit Smith, Anson Phelps Stokes, and William Jay. The abolition movement became one of the benevolent reforms and, perhaps, the most dramatic and effective of them all. The abolitionists began on the English model (as did the other benevolent associations) and formed a national society.

The national society sought to mobilize public opinion in behalf of its doctrines and searched for the most effective means to form new local societies, gain converts, and raise money. After some trial and error the abolitionists discovered that the paid professional lecturer was the most effective technique for their purposes.

Once the public advocates had established a large number of local antislavery societies and nurtured them, the movement turned more and more to substantial written tracts containing detailed arguments filled with factual materials and to the columns of reform newspapers to propagandize their efforts. In the second phase of the effort, volunteers recruited by the flaming reform speakers, self-taught in the arts of antislavery rhetoric by boning up on the tracts and newspapers, began to build a larger following by word of mouth. The campaign to petition state and federal legislatures in behalf of abolition brought the persuasive efforts of friends and acquaintances to bear on the unconverted and built the movement until it became a political force of power.

As the number of local volunteers grew, the regional and national antislavery societies began to wither away. By the end of the year 1838 the bulk of the state antislavery societies had become defunct, and the American Anti-Slavery Society itself was losing strength and effectiveness. In 1839 John Quincy Adams emerged as the leader of the petition forces in Congress, and the squabbling and disorganization within the ranks of the national society caused him to write a public indictment of the American Anti-Slavery Society which was a nearly fatal blow to an organization already starving for lack of financial support.

William Lloyd Garrison and his followers had captured the national society by 1840, and it degenerated into a minor association of the more radical of the reformers. The power base of the antislavery movement had shifted to the struggle for petitions, and its center had moved from Boston and New York to Washington, D.C. In the House of Representatives the elderly former President, John Quincy Adams, conducted a speaking campaign unique in the annals of American public address for the rights of petition and for a moderate and practical mode of emancipating the slaves. Theodore Weld hurried out of retirement on his farm to sift the materials in the Library of Congress and develop the briefs for Adams. In addition to Weld's silent help, Adams was supported by a little group of vocal antislavery Whigs including Joshua Giddings of Ohio, William Slade of Vermont, and Seth M. Gates of western New York in the House of Representatives.

The debate in Congress reached a climax when Joshua Giddings introduced a series of antislavery resolutions based upon the case of an American vessel called the *Creole*, which had been seized by some slaves who had sailed the ship to the British port of Nassau. The *Creole* case raised the issue of the status of slaves on an American vessel on the high seas. The Whig colleagues of Giddings censored him for breaking the gentlemen's agreement in Congress not to raise the issue of slavery. Giddings resigned his seat and returned to Ohio to run for reelection. When his constituency returned him to Congress with a large majority, the question of the ability of the Whig party to discipline its members was settled, and from that time until the Civil War the insurgent Whig antislavery bloc in Congress became the center for a new political movement in national affairs.

With the rise of the Congressional antislavery speakers and the emphasis on political action, the abolitionist impulse worked its way into the Whig party, eventually divided that party, furnished leadership for the new Republican party, and contributed to Lincoln's election to the presidency and, ultimately, to the crowning achievement of abolition, the Emancipation Proclamation.[1]

While the emphasis shifted from oral discourse to written persuasion to face-to-face interpersonal efforts and back to legislative debate and political stump speaking, all three techniques were part of the arsenal of abolition from its beginnings until the Civil War.

[1]For my analysis of the structure of the persuasive campaign for abolition, I am indebted to Gilbert Barnes' classic study, *The Antislavery Impulse, 1830–1844* (New York: Appleton-Century Co., 1933). Barnes makes a convincing case for the move from speeches to tracts to house-to-house canvasses for petition signatures to the Congress, and then to the political parties in the campaign for abolition.

The abolition speech played a major role in the propaganda efforts of the movement in several ways. Often the antislavery agent gave the same set of lectures over and over as he moved from town to town, and he was able to hone his rhetoric to a fine edge. On occasion too, the antislavery agent wrote up his speeches and edited them into the Anti-Slavery Tract.

In the selections of the rhetoric of the abolitionists that follow, I have included a number of items that represent the joint oral-written tradition. The line between a speech and an antislavery tract or an essay in an anti-slavery newspaper is difficult to draw. Even the items published as speeches were heavily edited, and the essays or tracts were often derived from a speech or a series of lectures. The important thing for the student of the rhetoric of abolition to understand, however, is that whether published as speeches or essays the discourse participates in the same rhetorical traditions.

Within the abolition movement speech practices varied. Some of the differences among the speakers were idiosyncratic and can only be fully understood on the basis of biographical information and individual case studies of the speakers involved. Much of the variation, however, is systematic and is related to the fact that groups of speakers participated in a common world view, a common approach to the question of persuasion, and a common rhetorical theory.

The speakers for abolition divide into two main rhetorical camps—those who practiced the rhetoric of agitation and those who participated in the rhetoric of conversion. Both groups were heavily influenced by the Puritan preaching heritage and spoke for abolition of slavery in language reminiscent of the sermons of the Puritan divines of the eighteenth century.

The early Puritan preachers told their audiences in painstaking and graphic detail that man was a mean, miserable creature who had grieved God mightily. Their sermons hammered the theme that man was marked by the sin of Adam and would inevitably fall short of the perfection of God. Even those few elected by God and called to the invisible church were unworthy of such election and received salvation only because of God's perfect grace and not because they deserved it. But even as they assured their auditors that man was by nature a mean and unworthy creature, they also told their congregations that one soul saved was more precious than all the treasures of this world. The Puritan rhetoric placed man in the center of the universe and made the final judgment of a man's life the central drama of the human condition.

The Puritan sermon dwelt also on the notion that the way to salvation was long and hard. Their archetypal metaphor was the image of the Pilgrim making his slow progress through the trials and temptations of the world.

Even as he emphasized the essential meanness of human nature and the difficulty of making progress toward salvation, the Puritan divine put great pressure on his audience to seek salvation *immediately*. The minister often urged the congregation in the Puritan meeting house to take advantage of the present opportunity, to act immediately lest they miss the nick of time that might be their only way to heaven. Part of the strenuous effort to seek salvation and do good works that exemplified so much of the Puritan culture can be attributed to the great time pressure the rhetoric of the Puritan sermon put upon the congregation to act *now* or be forever damned.

By the 1830's the view of man that had permeated the rhetoric of the Puritans a century before was largely changed. The new revivalists whose words fed the religious enthusiasms of the 1820's were preaching immediate conversion and free grace. They told their audiences that man was perfectible, that he was a free agent and morally responsible for his behavior. They saw God's millennial plan for man as a great blueprint to achieve perfection for man and that, very shortly. Predictions of the second coming of Christ and the concurrent end of the world were often made and widely believed. Indeed, a large number of people believed the prediction of William Miller that the world would end on October 22, 1844. Angelina Grimké Weld, herself the first important female antislavery speaker, wife of the preeminent evangelist for abolition, Theodore Dwight Weld, was pregnant at the time and wondered on occasion if she were perhaps the chosen vessel.

The early eighteen hundreds in the United States were years of great optimism, of faith in the perfection of man, of considerable confidence that the millennium was at hand and that God had chosen North America as its seat on this earth. Among those who believed in the cluster of optimistic, millennial, free-will, and free-grace propositions there was a great drive to move into the world and help perfect man and society for the great day. The slogan of the reformers was "Faith without works is dead."

While the reformers differed from their Puritan forebears in their optimism and belief in free grace, they embraced the inheritance from Puritan rhetoric that time was pressing. Their sense of destiny led them to believe that violent exertions and sacrifices on their part would result in great good works in a very short period of time.

The agitator and the evangelist thus both participated in the same rhetorical tradition. The essential difference was that the strategy of the agitator was to sting, goad, and disturb the audience, while the aim of the antislavery evangelist was to convert the listener to the gospel of immediate abolition and to recruit people for active work in the antislavery cause.

Although the lines are not always clearly drawn, the agitators of abolition were led by and tended to cluster around William Lloyd Garrison and the Boston antislavery forces, while the evangelists for abolition were associated with the benevolent empire and the headquarters of the American Anti-Slavery Society in New York City.

In addition to the Tappans, Elizur Wright, National Secretary of the society, and Henry B. Stanton played important roles in the rhetoric of conversion. None of these, however, was as important to the rhetorical efforts of the larger and more influential part of the abolition movement as was Theodore Dwight Weld.

Weld, born in Connecticut in 1803, came from a long line of Puritans. He numbered among his ancestors Dwights, Edwardses, and Hutchinsons. Both of his grandfathers were ministers, and his father, Ludovicus Weld, was a graduate of Harvard and a pastor of the Congregational Church.

When Weld was a young teenager, he managed a hundred-acre farm and collected enough money to go to Phillips Academy, where he studied so hard that he developed a severe inflammation of the eyes. The doctors thought he might regain his eyesight if he rested regularly in a dark room for seven years. Weld was full of animal spirits and restless. He could not follow the doctor's advice, and he cast about for something to do. He always had a poor memory. When grown to manhood he was so forgetful that he often had to go to the window to see what season of the year it was. While at Phillips Academy he had attended a series of lectures on the art of improving the memory, and he continued to read on the subject. He decided to take to the road as an itinerating lecturer on mnemonics.

The seventeen-year-old Weld proved to be an able lecturer and toured the country for the next three years. With his eyes much improved, Weld, at twenty, enrolled at Hamilton College in New York in time to be caught up in the Great Revival when it swept through the region. Charles Grandison Finney was one of the most notable and controversial evangelists of the time when he converted Weld. Most controversial were Finney's "new measures" for gaining converts, which consisted of protracted meetings, an anxious seat for the penitents, and a band of assistants who moved among the people to help with the work. Weld joined Finney's Holy Band and worked with such zeal at the revival that his health failed again, and he spent the winter of 1827 on a whaling vessel bound for Labrador.

The sea restored his health, and Weld enrolled at the Oneida Institute, a manual labor school permeated with evangelical religion, perfectionism, and reform. Too much was going on, however; too many opportunities beckoned for a man of Weld's ability, temperament, and training for him to continue long as a student. Few times in the history of the United States, before or since, were more congenial for a professional speaker. The spoken word was exalted above the written. The mails were slow, the press inefficient, and the general level of literacy was such that the direct and magnetic propagation of ideas by public speech was much the more exciting and efficient way to get things done. Weld was a thoroughly trained professional speaker. He was tough, resolute, fearless, and had great physical stamina. Despite his poor memory, he had the intellectual powers and imagination to dazzle his audience with his descriptive skill, his narrative power, and his verbal eloquence.

In Weld's day the role of professional rhetorician was played by *agents*. A wide variety of organizations, institutions, and societies employed people whose duties were to forward the goals of the group. Agents lectured, lobbied at legislatures, and tried to persuade people in conversations to support their causes. President Gale of Oneida knew of Weld's persuasive skills, and he soon had him traveling the country to raise money for the school.

When Finney accepted the Tappans' invitation to take a church in New York, he promised to try to turn some of their contributions toward Oneida Institute. (Finney had studied with President Gale when he gave up the law and prepared for his career as an evangelist.) Lewis Tappan enrolled his two sons in the school and became converted to the manual labor plan. The Tappans, with characteristic zeal, organized a Society for Promoting Manual Labor in Literary Institutions. By now, too, the Tappans had their eyes on Weld, and when they offered to make him the agent of their new manual labor society, he accepted.

Weld reveled in the agency life. He liked the adventure, excitement, and frantic vigorous activity. He was filled with zeal and burning desire to do something to improve the world and justify his life.

During his manual labor agency, Weld also lectured on temperance and discussed the evils of slavery. Toward the end of his year he visited Western Reserve College in Ohio and discussed the problem of the antislavery reform with Professors Elizur Wright and Beriah Green. When Weld returned to New York, he was a convert to the doctrine of immediate abolition.

One of Weld's duties as agent for the manual labor reform was to select a site for a manual labor seminary to train ministers for evangelical religion. Weld selected Lane Seminary in Cincinnati, Ohio. The understanding was that whatever school Weld selected would be given substantial financial support by the Tappans. To Lane, Weld brought a number of his friends—one might almost say disciples—from Oneida. In addition, he recruited several acquaintances from his itinerating in the South, including Marius Robinson and William Allan.

The Tappans secured Lyman Beecher, the foremost Eastern revivalist, for the Presidency of Lane and, with the help of Weld, hoped to make the school not only a force for evangelical religion but also the center for antislavery and manual labor reform in the west.

Although asked to join the Lane faculty as professor of rhetoric, Weld decided to return as a student. He was, however, no ordinary student, and even though Beecher was one of the most famous religious leaders in the country, he was not the leader of Lane Seminary in the eyes of Weld's followers. Beecher himself wrote that Weld "took the lead of the whole institution. The young men had, many of them, been under his care, and they thought he was a god."

Weld soon set to work to abolitionize the student body. He started first with the southern students and converted William T. Allan of Alabama. Most of the antislavery sentiment at Lane, as in the country at large, was channeled into the Colonization Society. When Weld had sufficient students on his side, he challenged the colonization partisans to a public debate. Despite faculty opposition the debates were held. The result was one of the great forensic events in the history of reform speaking. The debates lasted for eighteen evenings, with eighteen speakers delivering major addresses. The first nine evenings considered the question of whether or not the people of the slave-holding state sought to abolish slavery immediately. For the first two evenings William Allan argued for immediate emancipation. Weld closed the discussion of the question of immediate emancipation. On the ninth evening a unanimous vote was given for the affirmative. The last nine nights considered the usefulness of the American Colonization Society.

As a result of the debates, the bulk of the students were converted to immediate abolition and formed a society to propagate the new doctrine. They moved into the black community and began teaching and doing good works. They also began to lecture in favor of their new doctrine. Their activity aroused the ire of a substantial segment of the community, and pressure was put on the trustees to stop the students from continuing the antislavery promotions and the work in the black sections of Cincinnati. Beecher was in the East on a fund-raising trip over the summer when the crisis broke. He temporized for a time but was forced to take a stand when school resumed in the fall. He chastised the students and accused Weld and

Allan as ringleaders, threatening them with expulsion. Weld walked out of Lane and took over fifty "Lane Rebels" with him. Nine or ten enrolled at other schools, and four recanted and requested entrance at Lane.

The Tappans, disgusted with Beecher, gave Lane no further support and turned instead to a small school in Oberlin, Ohio. When the trustees of Oberlin College agreed to student freedom of discussion and the admission of qualified Negroes, and when Charles Finney agreed to come as professor of theology, Weld urged the Lane Rebels to enroll, and about twenty did so in 1835. Weld himself never returned to school but took instead, in October, 1834, a full-time agency for the new American Anti-Slavery Society.

Weld's agency was the prototype for all of the subsequent itinerating of the evangelical agents in the West. In a sense he invented the abolition agency. Not only did he perfect the techniques, the arguments, and the appeals, but he selected and indoctrinated the new trainees, gave them the tricks of the trade, and drilled them in the case for immediate abolition. Weld's agency thus illustrates the best of the persuasive efforts of a host of evangelical antislavery agents.

Weld used the same tactics to propagate abolition that he had developed to get a hall and hearing for his memory lectures, that he had modified when he helped Finney with the revivals in New York, and that he had perfected on his manual labor agency. Going into a new community, he would search out a minister who might allow his church to be used for an antislavery meeting. Often his first few meetings would arouse opposition and, on occasion, riots and violence.

Reporting to Wright, who was by now national secretary of the Anti-Slavery Society in New York, Weld wrote from Putnam, Ohio, in March, 1835, that he had lectured five times in Concord, seven times in Oldtown, nine times in Bloomingburg, and fourteen times at Circleville. He had a public debate with a physician and a Baptist deacon at Oldtown, and at Circleville he had debates three evenings with a lawyer. Indeed, Weld handled the debaters so handily that his opponents accused the abolitionists of setting them up as foils.

At Circleville he faced the kind of fierce opposition that he often had to handle. During the second lecture a mob gathered and threw stones and eggs through the windows. One of the stones struck Weld on the head and stunned him. His supporters hung cloaks up at the windows to protect the audience from the missiles. The threats of the mob were so loud that the trustees of the church would not allow him to lecture in the vestry room again. He then found a large room fitted for a store. Again the crowd threw stones and clubs against the shuttered windows. Weld was uninjured that night but faced even larger and more violent demonstrations for the next several nights. After he had lectured seven times, however, the commotion quieted, and for the latter part of the course he had "a smooth sea." Not only that, but "God owned his truth—confounded those which rose up against him—filled gainsayers with confusions, and *now* Circleville may be set down as a strong abolitionist center."[2]

Through the year 1835 Weld pursued his agency, repeating the story of Circleville over and over, meeting the mobs and the local debaters, besting them during the course of protracted meetings in the manner of Finney's "New Measures," and calling at the close for those converted to immediate abolition to stand. Thus he made his way in the tradition of the itinerating evangelists.

Theodore Weld was an event. He broke the monotony of the frontier routine. Excitement followed in his wake. He aroused controversies and mobs. He projected an image of a doer of mighty deeds who asserted that God was at his elbow and inspired his words. Those who accepted the latter image must have found him a credible and persuasive speaker. As Weld moved through Ohio and Pennsylvania, he left behind him in most of the villages and towns an active local antislavery society.

Weld moved from Pennsylvania to New York. His triumphant tour continued until he came to Troy, and there, for one of the few times in his career, Weld was defeated. He was repeatedly mobbed, and on one occasion a group rushed up the aisles of the church where he was speaking to pull him from the pulpit. Despite his best efforts Weld was unable to tame the mobs at Troy and get a hearing. He kept his agency for a short time longer with some success, but he had once again wasted his great physical stamina with such prodigality that his health and his voice were both gone. He was to speak in public again only many years later but never again with such concentrated energy and with such great effect. For all intents and purposes, the premier practitioner of the arts of the benevolent agent in the early nineteenth century was to give up his profession after 1836. He did, however, take up another function of rhetorician when he moved to the New York headquarters and wrote the essence of his antislavery lectures into powerful tracts for distribution throughout the country.

Late in August, the year of his great agency, Weld went to Oberlin and

[2]Gilbert W. Barnes and Dwight L. Dumond, eds., *Letters of Theodore Dwight Weld, Angelina Grimké Weld and Sarah Grimké, 1822–1844*, 2 vols. (New York: Appleton-Century Co., 1934), p. 207. The letters of the Welds and Sarah Grimké were published in two volumes, but the pages were numbered consecutively. Subsequent references will be to *Weld-Grimké Letters* and the page numbers.

recruited thirteen of the Lane Rebels, including William Allan, James Thome, John Alvord, Huntington Lyman, and Sereno Streeter to join him as agents. Henry B. Stanton was already at work as an agent in Rhode Island. Later Weld returned to claim still more of his following until thirty of fifty-four who signed the statement of the Lane Rebels were itinerating for abolition.

Weld and his men were so effective that the national society decided to invest almost all of its resources into increasing the number of agents to seventy, the number of the Biblical apostles, and, at Weld's insistence, they agreed to send them into the rural areas. Weld took on the task of recruiting the new agents. Again the core of Oneida men who had been at Lane and moved to Oberlin helped him. With the new men recruited, the Lane Rebels took to the field, while the neophytes congregated in New York, where for twenty days, eight hours a day, Weld in his "screech owl" voice indoctrinated them in the methods of evangelical conversion to abolition. For four days he developed his Bible argument for them. The band of antislavery agents that took the field the next year were, for the most part, practitioners of the rhetoric of conversion as it was fashioned by Weld and the Lane Rebels.

On balance, Weld was the leading rhetorician using both the written and oral mode of the evangelical tradition. One reason that Weld's name is not as widely known as Garrison's is that Weld systematically resisted all efforts to puff his reputation. Garrison, on the other hand, basked in the limelight and stepped forward after the Civil War to accept the accolades of the victorious forces of emancipation. In addition, well before the Civil War, Weld became disillusioned with the internal bickering and showboating of the leaders of the antislavery forces and retired from active participation to teach school. Garrison, on the other hand, was one of the leading figures involved in the battle for control of the antislavery societies and for the resulting publicity.

The foremost orator in the camp of the agitators, however, was not Garrison but a blue-blooded scion of one of the best families of Boston, a graduate of Harvard Law School by the name of Wendell Phillips. Garrison was an able speaker, but his rhetorical skills were better adapted to pamphleteering and editorial writing.

Wendell Phillips, son of a mayor of Boston, was educated at the Boston Latin School and then at Harvard College and Law School. He was launched upon what seemed a promising career in the law when he was attracted to the reform efforts of the Garrisonians. He saw Garrison mobbed in the streets of Boston in October, 1835. Later he married a reform-minded young woman and soon became part of the antislavery forces. He came to sudden prominence when he spoke with considerable effect at a meeting in Faneuil Hall in

December, 1837, called by outraged citizens of Boston to pass resolutions condemning the killing of Elijah P. Lovejoy, an abolitionist minister and editor, in Alton, Illinois. The meeting was packed by those opposing the resolutions, and the state's attorney of Massachusetts, Mr. Austin, rose in the gallery and gave an impassioned speech against them. In the ensuing melee, with considerable difficulty, Phillips, a relatively unknown speaker, subdued the crowd long enough to deliver his famous "Murder of Lovejoy Speech." From that time on until the Civil War, he was one of the leading speakers for abolition. When Weld retired from active speechmaking, Phillips became the best orator of the movement.

Wendell Phillips presented a much different platform image from that of Weld, who systematically cultivated a rough-hewn and unkempt Western appearance. Phillips was always a gentleman in manner and demeanor. He delivered the most stinging rebukes to his audiences in a relatively calm and gentlemanly way. His delivery was so markedly at variance with his inflammatory language and sentiments that it was often commented on by his listeners. One contemporary critic described Phillips as follows:

> He handles and throws out the most stinging sentences with the most playful, easy air of nonchalance;—sentences that burn in and leave a scar,—sentences that sear the heart and brand a man.... When he utters such ejaculations as "The United States Constitution is a covenant with Hell," he does not gnash his teeth like a modern Sir Giles Overreach, as the stereotype agitator is presumed to do; no, he is as "bland as a couple of summer mornings," as it has been expressed.[3]

Phillips' genre was the lecture platform. He spent his entire long career as a reform lecturer, going far and wide throughout the country. A product of an age of lecturing, he grew up with the Lyceum movement, which was an adult education and uplift impulse that organized local clubs to arrange a program of lecturers for which tickets were sold. In the heyday of the abolition agitation, a number of Eastern lecturers such as Wendell Phillips and Theodore Parker made lecture tours under the auspices of the lyceums.

Even after the war and the Emancipation Proclamation, Phillips continued his speaking in behalf of various reforms such as women's rights and temperance.

Both the followers of Weld and of Garrison introduced to the public platform, in significant numbers, the black orator. An important feature of the rhetoric of both wings of the movement was the graphic, detailed, and revolting description of the evils of slavery. One of the ways in which the

[3]Edward G. Parker, *The Golden Age of American Oratory* (Boston: Whittemore, Niles, and Hall, 1857), pp. 395–96.

credibility of the descriptions was enhanced was by presenting the testimony of a man or woman who had experienced slavery first-hand. Telling your experience was an old evangelical technique utilized by the circuit-riding Methodists, the frontier Baptists, and Presbyterians to encourage conversions to Christianity, and that practice was adapted in the 1830's to the problem of bringing the antislavery case to the American people. In the Lane Debates one of the speakers who made the greatest effect was a black former slave, James Bradley, who testified about the atrocities associated with slavery.

Many former slaves were brought to platforms in abolition meetings either as inarticulate exhibitions of the inhumanity of slavery or, in those instances when native ability fitted them for the task, as speakers. Foremost among the latter was the man who called himself Frederick Douglass and who became the greatest black agitator for abolition in our history.

Under the impetus of the abolition reform a host of other black men and women took the platform and spoke to largely white audiences on the evils of slavery. Probably not until the civil rights movements of the post-World-War-II era have such a high proportion of black speakers spoken with such eloquence and effect to so many white audiences as in the decades from 1830 to the Civil War. In addition to Frederick Douglass, such black speakers as Charles Remond, Robert Purvis, Samuel Ward, Henry Garnet, Soujourner Truth, and Harriet Tubman became prominent.

The Garrisonians served as a magnet to attract a host of revolutionaries and reformers, some of whom were sincere, dedicated, and able, and others who were crackpots and zealots. Garrison incorporated a host of other reform measures into his platform and into his agitations. Among others, he embraced the cause of women's rights.

During colonial times and in the early years of the republic, women had been largely denied the platform not only because woman's role in society was clearly specified to be a private one but also because of the religious inhibitions resulting from the interpretation of Saint Paul's Biblical injunction against women speaking in public.

Indeed, the restrictions on what a good woman could do were partly responsible for the rise of reform zeal and the woman reform speaker in the nineteenth century. Good women in the early years of the country were largely confined to the home. The educational system prepared them for little else except music, drawing, sewing, and the domestic sciences. Most of the professions were closed to women. Many nice women did not attend theatres or other social events that had a taint of immorality. They could, however, in good conscience, go to public lectures, prayer meetings, and sermons. As the benevolent reform movement gained momentum in the 1830's, more and more ladies attended reform meetings. At first these were often female parlor meetings and discussions. The period saw the rise of the female antislavery societies of which the Boston Female Anti-Slavery Society was an exemplar.

Many women found the reform oratory in its heyday exciting, stimulating, and rewarding. Particularly in New England, where people had little opportunity for culture, adult education, and entertainment other than that provided by the exciting speakers of the day, the women found public speeches an outlet from the routine and boredom of their usual circle.

With their husbands, brothers, and other male relatives, they began to attend these meetings. Not only did some find themselves in full accord with the idealistic goals of the reformers but they found also an outlet for their desire to improve mankind. The procedures of the meeting were exciting and stimulating. There were songs such as "Freedom's Summons," the "Temperance War Song," and "I Am an Abolitionist—I Glory in the Name." Usually there were prayers calling down God's blessing and help on the reform efforts. But most of all there were the speeches full of violence, sex, pathos, melodrama, righteous indignation, round epithets, and castigation of the slavocracy.

Women learned in the 1830's how to organize and conduct their own meetings and how to address them. Gradually they began to address mixed audiences, first to storms of opposition from the general public as well as the clergy, and finally as an accepted right.

Unique in the annals of abolition, not only because she was the first of the great female antislavery speakers, not only because she was the daughter of a South Carolina slaveowner and became the wife of Theodore Weld himself, but also because she was torn between the Garrisonian wing and the New York faction of the movement, was Angelina Grimké.

Angelina's older sister, Sarah, had emigrated from her native Charleston to Philadelphia before her. Sarah became a convert to Quakerism and rejected her life as a southern belle. Angelina followed, and the two sisters came to view slavery as a great evil. They both attended the antislavery convention in New York City in November, 1836. Because they were Southerners, they were viewed as exceptionally valuable converts to the cause. Just as the ex-slave could speak with extraordinary ethos on the subject, so could the converted Southerner testify with more than usual credibility. Thus, during the Lane debates, the conversions of William T. Allan of Alabama and Huntington Lyman of Louisiana to the doctrine of immediate abolition were viewed as particularly significant events. James Gillespie Birney owed his prominence in antislavery circles not only to his skill and zeal as publicist, speaker, and organizer but also because he was once a slaveholder and could speak with considerable authority upon the evils of slavery.

Angelina and Sarah Grimké moved to Boston where they were swept up into the circle of the Garrisonians, which contained among others the women of the Boston Female Anti-Slavery Society including such leading figures of the movement as Maria Chapman, Lydia M. Child, and Anne Weston. Soon the Grimké sisters were holding parlor meetings for groups of women. Their popularity was such that the meetings were moved to larger halls and churches. They continued to speak to women audiences, but gradually their reputation aroused the curiosity of men. By June, 1837, the Grimkés were speaking "promiscuously" to mixed audiences.

Sarah was dedicated and zealous but not a very good speaker. When Theodore Weld heard of a projected series of lectures that would have the sisters alternate their speeches, he urged Sarah to accept her limitations and give way to Angelina's superior speaking ability. The high point of Angelina's career came when she testified before a committee of the Massachusetts legislature. To a hall so packed that she was passed over the heads of the spectators to reach the front of the room, she delivered several hours of moving testimony. Even then, however, she was engaged to Theodore Weld, and after their wedding she retired from the lecture platform.

On the evening of May 16, 1838, Angelina Grimké Weld gave her last public abolition address during the dedication ceremonies for Pennsylvania Hall built by Philadelphia reformers to consecrate free speech, liberty, and the rights of man. Many leading abolitionists congregated for the occasion. At the same noisy meeting, Abby Kelley began a long and violent career as antislavery agitator in the Garrisonian tradition. A host of women spoke for abolition in addition to Angelina Grimké and Abby Kelley. Many also lectured on temperance and agitated for women's rights. In addition to those already mentioned, the leading orators of abolition included Lucretia Mott, Lucy Stone, Antoinette Brown, Sallie Holley, Susan B. Anthony, and Elizabeth Cady Stanton.[4]

Among the Garrisonians there were a number of second-order speakers

[4]See Lillian O'Connor, *Pioneer Women Orators* (New York: Columbia University Press, 1954). I have followed quite closely the analysis of Doris Yoakum, "Woman's Introduction to the American Platform," in William N. Brigance, ed., *A History and Criticism of American Public Address* (New York: McGraw-Hill Book Co., 1943), I, 153–92.

who were active and effective. Included among the lesser talents were such men as Stephen Foster, Parker Pillsbury, David Lee Child, Samuel May, Amos Phelps, George Bourne, John A. Collins, and Charles Sumner.

A reform movement such as abolition requires organization to succeed. A chaotic impulse may influence events by blindly striking out or by surfacing in unusual unexpected violence like black rioting in the cities in the 1960's, but a reform movement requires more than the impulse. In addition to a program of action, an ideology, and administrative skills, an organization requires meetings that provide interaction among the members until leadership emerges. Spokesmen must then establish channels of communication so they can indoctrinate people into the party line, encourage them in adversity, and inform them in times of triumph. Most important for our concerns is that among the leadership of any successful reform movement there must be rhetoricians who provide both the insider and outsider with a meaningful interpretation of the movement. I briefly sketched the leading rhetoricians of the abolition movement above. Before examining the details of the rhetoric they provided, we need to pause to examine the functions of rhetoric for a reform movement.

Writers on General Semantics such as Wendell Johnson and S. I. Hayakawa often argue that the word is not the thing.[5] Many scholars then go on to assume that since the word is not the thing, any discrepancy between words and things must necessarily be resolved in the direction of things and that words are to be discounted as misleading, trivial, or unimportant unless they stand in a close and accurate relation to things. Thus, some historians argue that although the period from 1840 to 1860 saw a great political debate in the United States over the extension of slavery in the territories, that debate was trivial because the "real" issues were economic interests in conflict between the North and the South. Other historians suggest that although the abolitionists often argued from theological grounds that slavery was a sin and that to save his eternal soul every person must work for its elimination, the "real" reason the abolitionists fought for antislavery was because they were members of a displaced social elite, descendents of old and socially prominent New England families victimized by a status revolution when leadership in the North was seized by merchant princes, manufacturing tycoons, and buccaneers of high finance. The abolitionists, from this view, were not so much trying to free the slaves as reasserting traditional class

[5]S. I. Hayakawa, *Language in Thought and Action* (New York: Harcourt, Brace & World, Inc., 1964); Wendell Johnson, *People in Quandaries: The Semantics of Personal Adjustment* (New York: Harper and Row, Publishers, 1946).

values back home. The words the abolitionists spoke are thus discounted as being essentially unimportant to the "reality" of the situation.[6]

When one makes a rhetorical analysis, however, he starts from the opposite assumption, namely, that when there is a discrepancy between the word and the thing, the most important cultural artifact for understanding the events may not be the things but the words. The words used by the abolitionists and their enemies provide the basis for one of the more important explanatory structures in the study of abolitionism.

A brief historical example from more contemporary times illustrates the importance of words rather than things most graphically. When the Democratic National Convention was held in Chicago in 1968, there was a great influx of people of many shades of political opinion to demonstrate against the war in Vietnam. During the course of that convention the Chicago police, the National Guard, and the demonstrators milled about, shouted, threw things, and, on occasion, hit one another. The perspective of time has allowed the intense emotions generated on that occasion to cool, and the evidence collected in a more objective fashion indicates that what happened on that occasion was, as historical precedent would suggest, chaotic and unpatterned. Spurred to mob frenzy, the demonstrators charged about without discipline or plan. The police rioted. In short, the events were characterized by a breakdown of organization; both the leaders of the police and the National Guard and those of the demonstration lost control of the situation, and the result was chaos.

However, a great body of highly structured rhetoric grew up around those chaotic events which read highly charged meanings into them. Some of the rhetoricians viewed the chaos and, as though it were some huge milling Rorschach test, saw in it the pattern of outside conspirators carefully planning and executing a violent confrontation that resulted in provoking, by obscenities and violence, a police response in order to destroy the institutions of the country. Other rhetoricians saw the chaos as deliberately controlled and planned by the Mayor of Chicago or the President of the United States as an attempt to frustrate the idealistic efforts of the best young people of the country to improve society. Some saw the demonstrators as neurotic or psychotic, undisciplined, crude, sexually loose, ill-mannered, boorish, and dangerous. Others saw them as the most intelligent, best educated, most idealistic

---

[6]For a clear and insightful survey of various historical explanations of abolition, see the "Introduction" in Richard O. Curry, ed., *The Abolitionists: Reformers or Fanatics?* (New York: Holt, Rinehart and Winston, Inc., 1965), pp. 1–9. For a brief presentation of the "status revolution" thesis, see David Donald, "Abolition Leadership: A Displaced Social Elite," in the same volume, pp. 42–48.

young people in the country's history. (The latter apparently knew little of the history of the Lane Rebels and the abolition reform.) Some saw the Chicago police and their officers and Mayor Daley as brutal, piggish, psychotic, fascistic, searching out innocent young ladies to hit on the head with a billy club. Others saw the Mayor and the police as fearless and dedicated men who under extreme provocation acted to enforce law and order to protect lives in a highly explosive situation with great justification and considerable restraint.

The words certainly did not match the events on the occasion of the 1968 Democratic Convention. I contend, however, that in this instance, as so often is the case, the words were much more important than the chaos. The words not only changed the course of future events because of the way the people participating in the various rhetorics subsequently voted, but the very quality of the lives of those who appropriated the meanings of a given rhetoric was changed and intensified. Those who accepted the military-industrial-establishment-conspiracy rhetoric hated Mayor Daley, loved the idealistic young angels out to save the world, felt abhorrence at the thought of the prince of devils manipulating events from Washington and brutally repressing the forces of good on the convention floor. Those who believed in the Yippie-Communist-conspiracy school of rhetoric hated a long-haired, unwashed, obscenity-howling, feces-throwing stereotype and felt a thrill of justification at the thought of the noble forces of good moving in to beat back these minor minions of the prince of devils, whether for them he resided at Peking, Hanoi, or Havana.

The words supplied meanings for the speakers, writers, listeners, and readers. The words structured their world, gave them a self-image and a group to identify with, provided them with icons fashioned from meanings to love and to hate. The words stimulated by the chaos of Chicago gave people a picture of what they called "reality" and enabled them to distinguish the reality (their rhetoric) from the descriptions of the world they found in the enemy's rhetoric. The enemy's rhetoric could then be discounted as "mere words" while their own rhetoric was sanctioned because it told it "as it really was" or because it was a description of "reality."

Rhetoric, as I define it, therefore, relates primarily to the study of the words and how they work to shape meanings for individuals, groups, and nations. When careful scholarly study reveals a discrepancy between words and things, such discrepancy plays a part in rhetorical analysis, but the emphasis remains on the words and how they work.

Let us turn, then, to a rhetorical analysis of the abolition movement. Every reform in American history has faced several similar rhetorical problems. First, a reform movement must mobilize popular support in behalf of its program. Gaining converts poses important subsidiary problems. The effective reform rhetoric must discuss things gone wrong, which their efforts will make right. The discussion of "reality" is usually indexed for the listener or reader by expressions like "the facts show" or "the truth is" or "what is really behind the scenes is" or "the way it really is." In addition to pointing out the evils of reality, a reform rhetoric must indicate the historical *meaning* of the effort. Where does the movement stand in the history of the culture? Is it part of a culminating ongoing progression towards an ever better society? Is it part of a purging process to cleanse and restore the society to an earlier, better time? Is it outside the culture, alien and pure, while the culture is rotten? Every effective reform rhetoric provides a complete and plausible answer to such questions.

The second major task of a reform rhetoric is to indoctrinate the converts and weld the true believers into a highly committed and cohesive group. A sense of *esprit de corps* requires an insider rhetoric which furnishes each member with a sense of fulfillment and meaning for his life. In the face of the inevitable failures and difficulties, the loyal followers must be sustained and encouraged by suitable words.

The two major schools of the rhetoric of abolition met the tactical rhetorical problems with speeches, tracts, and newspapers that provided some similar and some strikingly different answers.

The agitators associated with William Lloyd Garrison met the first problem of mobilizing popular support with a rhetoric that failed miserably. While they provided much the same description of reality as the Weld group, their analysis of the nature of the movement and its place in the cultural history was much different from the speakers of the evangelical tradition. The tactic of the agitators was to goad, sting, insult, and attack the favored values and world view of the neutral or hostile listener or reader. Garrison and Phillips attacked the Sabbath, the churches, and, finally, the Constitution and the Union. At the beginning of his career Garrison was already rehearsing the rhetoric of agitation when he delivered a Fourth of July address in the Park Street Church in Boston. He said in part:

> What has Christianity done by direct effort for our slave population? Comparatively nothing. She has explored the isles of the ocean for objects of commiseration; but amazing stupidity! she can gaze without emotion on a multitude of miserable beings at home, large enough to constitute a nation of freemen, whom tyranny has heathenized by law.... The blood of souls is upon her garments, yet she heeds not the stain. The clanking of the prisoner's chains strike upon her ear, but they cannot penetrate her heart.

Shortly after attacking the hallowed institution of the church, Garrison turned on the nation itself.

> Every Fourth of July our Declaration of Independence is produced, with a sublime indignation, to set forth the tyranny of the mother country, and to challenge the admiration of the world. But what a pitiful detail of grievances does this document present, in comparison with the wrongs which our slaves endure? In the one case it is hardly the plucking of a hair from the head; in the other, it is the crushing of a live body on the wheel—the stings of the wasp contrasted with the tortures of the Inquisition. Before God I must say that such a glaring contradiction as exists between our creed and practice the annals of six thousand years cannot parallel. In view of it I am ashamed of my country. I am sick of our unmeaning declamation in praise of liberty and equality; of our hypocritical cant about the inalienable rights of man. I would not for my right hand stand up before a European assembly, and exult that I am an American citizen, and denounce the usurpations of a kingly government as wicked and unjust; or, should I make the attempt, the recollection of my country's barbarity and despotism would blister my lips, and cover my cheeks with burning blushes of shame.[7]

As Garrison's agitation continued, the themes of his early Fourth of July address were developed with greater richness, greater powers of invective, but with little basic change in tactics. By the spring of 1842, his attack on the Union was direct and unbending. In January, 1843, the agitators had their way at the annual meeting of the Massachusetts Anti-Slavery Society, and the following resolution "wrapped up," according to Edmund Quincy who was in attendance, "by Garrison in some of his favorite Old Testament Hebraisms" was passed: "That the compact which exists between the North and the South is a covenant with death and an agreement with hell—involving both parties in atrocious criminality—and should be immediately annulled."[8]

On the Fourth of July, 1854, after the passage of the Kansas-Nebraska Act, which he viewed as the repeal of the Missouri Compromise, Garrison spoke at Framingham, Massachusetts. During the course of his speech he burned several documents, including a copy of the Fugitive Slave Law and then, holding up a copy of the Constitution, he burned it and said, "So perish all compromises with tyranny! And let all people say, Amen."[9]

Not only did the agitators alienate the uncommitted but when divisions appeared with the antislavery forces over questions of policy and of belief and Garrison's leadership was challenged, the agitators turned the very same

[7]Quoted in Archibald H. Grimké, *William Lloyd Garrison, The Abolitionist* (London: Funk and Wagnalls, 1891), p. 64.

[8]Quoted in Grimké, pp. 310–11.

[9]Quoted in Grimké, p. 354.

style of righteous overstatement against their former allies. The rhetoric of agitation served, therefore, as a divisive force within the movement as well as a repelling agent for those whom the movement might have radicalized.

Gilbert Barnes, who wrote a brilliant study of *The Antislavery Impulse, 1830–1844,* concluded that Garrison's intemperate attacks on the churches which did supply the main muscle for the antislavery impulse made him "an enemy of the antislavery impulse itself."[10] Barnes argued, "Another handicap of the new society was the unfortunate repute of William Lloyd Garrison.... Over the entire agitation his name cast 'a vague and indefinite odium' which hampered its growth from the beginning."[11]

The response of the speakers and writers practicing the rhetoric of conversion was in some respects similar to that of the agitators, but in its essential features the tactic was much different. To understand the differences one must have some knowledge of the rhetorical theory of the great evangelist of the revival of the 1820's, Charles Grandison Finney. Finney's rhetorical theory, which he outlined in his *Lectures on Revivals of Religion,* rested upon one basic axiom and its psychological corollary.[12] The basic criterion, for Finney, by which to judge preaching was *effect.* (This contrasts with the Garrisonian preoccupation with the criterion of adherence to *principle.*) The psychological corollary to the axiom of effect was that the proper measures are those that work to achieve the largest number of conversion experiences which are sudden, deep, and brief. A speaker who followed Finney's theory and practice could therefore judge his excellence by counting the number of converts that resulted from a protracted period of speaking.

Finney was trained as a lawyer and saw his task much the same as that of an advocate striving for a verdict from a jury. He was much more persuasive than the agitators. The abolitionists like Weld and the Lane Rebels argued at length with carefully structured speeches cast in the old firstly, secondly, thirdly style of the Puritan sermon. They always had a lecture or two or a part of a given speech devoted to answering objections to their position. They quoted testimony, historical and legal precedent, specific examples, and statistical information in support of their case.

When Henry B. Stanton argued for memorials against slavery before the Committee of the House of Representatives of Massachusetts, he exemplified the more persuasive tactic of the rhetoric of conversion. Stanton spoke for

[10]Barnes, p. 98.

[11]Gilbert Barnes, "The Western Revival Origins," in Curry, ed., pp. 17–18.

[12]For an excellent edition of Finney's lectures, see William G. McLoughlin, ed., *Lectures on Revivals of Religion, by Charles Grandison Finney* (Cambridge, Mass.: Harvard University Press, 1960).

three days, giving a summary of the Lane Rebel's famous course of lectures. He began the second day of his testimony as follows:

> I am aware, Mr. Chairman, that it is customary on occasions like this, to commence by descanting upon the *importance* of the subject under discussion. This is common place. I dislike to stoop to it on the present occasion, lest my reason for so doing should be regarded as trivial. Yet, I will run the hazard. In courts of justice, the advocate often trembles, as he rises to address the jury, when the pecuniary interests of his client are at stake; then what should be my feelings, when I rise to address you, not in behalf of the pecuniary interests of one client, but in behalf of the liberties and the lives, the interests, temporal and eternal, of thousands? Ay more;—the questions here discussed are not confined in their bearings to the slaves in the District of Columbia; nor in this nation. The cause of freedom throughout the world; the honor of God's law, will be deeply affected by your deliberations. The interests here involved are co-extensive with human hopes and human happiness; wide as the universe, lasting as eternity, high as Heaven. Then, sir, the slave, the master, this Commonwealth, the nation, the world, Jehovah himself, demand that we deliberate patiently, cautiously, impartially. And, gentlemen, your constituents will pardon you for so doing. No subject is more discussed by them, than that now before you; and the intensity of their feelings, not less than their immediate concernment, requires this deliberation at your hands.

> *   *   *

> And I ask the indulgent attention of the Committee, because I believe, that as you shall decide so the Legislature will act. Your number is unusually large; you justly have the confidence of the House, and to you they look to mature this subject for their action. Upon you, therefore, rests the responsibility for a decision. Hear me then for my cause, and bear with me, because I plead not only for the suffering, but the dumb.

When one contrasts Stanton's handling of the problem of introducing his thesis to a suspicious if not hostile audience with the manner of the agitator, the differences between the rhetoric of conversion and of agitation become clearer. Stanton wishes to persuade them to act on the memorials before the committee. He does not lash out at them and bait them by calling them such things as slaves of the slave power.

When Stanton comes to discuss the program of the abolitionists, he is at pains to indicate that it is not a radical or dangerous scheme.

> And now, Mr. Chairman, what do the petitioners ask you to request Congress to do? I answer;—merely to repeal these odious statutes immediately and to enact others, if necessary, in their stead. By immediate abolition, they do not intend that the Slaves of the District should be "turned loose:"—nor, that they should be, as a *sine qua non* to abolition, immediately invested with all political rights such as the elective franchise. But, simply, that Congress should immediately restore to every slave, the ownership of his own body, mind and soul. That they should no longer permit them to be "deemed, held, and sold,

as chattels personal, to all intents, constructions and purposes whatsoever";
but should give the slaves a fee simple in their own blood, bones, and brains.

Finally, the difference between the approach to the potential convert is illuminated by comparing Garrison's charge of hypocrisy in his Fourth of July oration quoted before with Stanton's handling of the same theme before the committee of the Massachusetts Legislature.

> It is expedient that slavery at the Capitol should be abolished, because its toleration brings into contempt our nation's boasted love of equal rights, justly exposes us to the charge of hypocrisy, paralyzes the power of our free principles, and cripples our moral efforts for the overthrow of oppression throughout the world. The citizens of this nation have deep responsibilities, as republicans, as Christians, as citizens of the world. Our character and reputation are moral capital, loaned us by God, to be invested for the political and moral renovation of the human race. The Reformers of South America and Europe, have anxiously looked to us as the pioneer nation in the cause of human liberty, and hoped that our experiment would demonstrate even to tyrants, that man is capable of self-government. But, by cherishing in the heart of the republic such a system of cold-blooded oppression, as the sun has rarely seen, we have rolled back the tide of reform in other nations, and cut the sinews of struggling humanity.[13]

The agitators and the evangelists both had to describe the things that were wrong and needed to be changed if they wished to mobilize popular support for the cause. The institution of slavery as it existed comprised the things to be described, interpreted, explained, and judged. Both wings of the abolition movement utilized the same approach for the description of the brute facts. Their favorite device was the authoritative testimony of eyewitnesses. One reason that all abolitionists prized a speaker like Frederick Douglass or Angelina Grimké or James Birney was because as a former slave, daughter of a slaveholder, or as a former slaveholder, respectively, each could testify to incidents and examples of the evils of the system.

Examples of cruelty were told again and again by the antislavery speakers and recounted in antislavery newspapers and tracts. The violence of the system was catalogued with the same sensationalism that characterizes today's television fare. The brutality of owners and overseers was documented in speech after speech. Simon Legree was a favorite character in antislavery lectures long before Harriet Beecher Stowe gave him a name and put him in a novel. The sexual violations of the slave were told in detail, sometimes by innuendo and sometimes explicitly. Frederick Douglass often told how Covey the "slavebreaker" locked up a young woman with a hired male to breed and

[13]*Liberator*, March 18, 1837, p. 46.

how joyful Covey's wife was when the woman gave birth to twins. The speakers told of the sexual exploitations of young attractive black women and mulattos by white men, of the separation of families, and other horrifying narratives.

Theodore Weld and his wife, with the help of her sister, Sarah Grimké, searched thousands of Southern newspaper ads regarding runaway slaves, noted scars and other evidence of physical mutilation and brutality, and requested all friends of the cause who had personal knowledge of the horrors of slavery to write them their testimony. In his letter of request Weld asked for:

> A multitude of facts never yet published, facts that would thrill the land with horror.... Shall such facts lie hushed any longer, when from one end of heaven to the other, myriad voices are crying, "O Earth, Earth, cover not their blood." The old falsehood that the slave is *kindly treated*, shallow and stupid as it is, has lullabied to sleep four-fifths of the free North and West; but with God's blessing this sleep shall not be unto death. Give facts a voice, and cries of blood shall ring till deaf ears tingle.[14]

The result of the research of the Welds was one of the great antislavery tracts of all time, *Slavery As It Is: The Testimony of a Thousand Witnesses.* Harriet Beecher Stowe, who as a girl in Cincinnati had heard the Lane debates, claimed that she had *Slavery As It Is* in her sewing basket all the while she was writing the most popular rhetorical tract of the movement in the form of a novel called *Uncle Tom's Cabin.*

The facts of the case, of and by themselves, did not constitute a total rhetoric. Did the facts represent evils of this world to be reformed as evils are by the institutions of the culture, or did they represent sins in the eyes of God? If slavery was a sin, then it was a matter not just of temporal importance but of vital concern to each man, for his immortal soul might well be in danger throughout eternity. (Certainly the question of the sinfulness of slavery was something for the devout slaveholder to ponder.) All of the abolitionists were in general agreement that slavery was a sin, but it was the evangelical rhetoric that wrung the last bit of meaning from the connotations of sin and applied the powerful persuasive techniques of the searching sermon to its propagation. A searching sermon was one that forced the listener to face up to his sin. No matter where he tried to hide, the preacher searched him out and made him put himself on trial before his own conscience, search his life, compare his behavior to the Christian standard, and then admit that he was a sinner and in need of help.

[14]Quoted in Barnes, *The Antislavery Impulse,* p. 139.

As Gilbert Barnes discovered of the antislavery agents in the West:

> ... these young men preached the antislavery cause as a revival in benevolence
> ... they carried over into the antislavery cause the zeal of the Great Revival
> itself. ... They preached immediate emancipation; but in their hands it was
> more than the jesuitical "gradualism in a British cloak" of the New York
> philanthropists: it was an immediatism of repentence from sin. By making the
> sin of slavery "the standard to which the abolitionist is to rally," these agents
> made the antislavery cause "identical with religion; and men and women are
> exhorted by all they esteem holy, by all the high and exciting obligations of
> duty to man and God, ... to join in the pious work of purging the sin of
> slavery from the land."[15]

The Southern defenders of the slave system developed, of course, their
own rhetoric, and the Southern description and interpretation of things was
that slavery was good for the Negro, that the slave was well treated, and
that the condition of the black in the South was far better than the plight
of the white laborer (wage slave) in the North. The Southern rhetoric
asserted that the majority of Northern antislavery speakers had never seen
slavery as it really existed and therefore did not know what they were talking
about. When the evangelical antislavery agents made the sin of slavery their
main judgment, they threw the whole argument relating to the interpretation
of the institution (the things) into the tangle of Biblical exegesis. The
Southern rhetoricians searched the Scriptures and discovered that slavery was
of divine origin and sanctioned by the Bible itself.

Theodore Weld's most important series of lectures was devoted to the
Bible argument. He taught his Bible argument to the agents he commissioned as part of the seventy and subsequently wrote it up and published
it as a tract.

The agitators stressed the sinful aspects of slavery much less than the
evangelicals. They often used the term *moral* to express the opposite of the
concept *sin*. As Wendell Phillips put it, "Those who cling to moral effort
are the true champions of the fight."[16] The agitators argued on moral grounds
that slavery was a great wrong. The Garrisonians' decision to declare war on
the churches divided their efforts from the organized religion of the day
while the evangelicals continued their strong connection with the churches.
Perhaps the separation of the agitators from organized religion accounted for
the different nuance of their rhetoric; perhaps the emphasis is partially accounted for, too, by the fact that Garrison's views of religion were changing,

---

[15]Barnes, "Western Revival Origins," p. 18.
[16]Quoted in Philip S. Foner, *Frederick Douglass* (New York: The Citadel Press,
1964), p. 40.

and he may not have been as convinced of the reality of sin and of eternal damnation as were the evangelicals.

No matter how the propagandists of abolition interpreted the agreed-upon facts, the explanation of the existence of slavery was the last link in the chain of argument. The evangelicals tended to account for slavery as part of man's sinful nature, and some, like Charles Grandison Finney, argued that the first step in emancipation was to convert the slaveholder to true Christianity. When the Lane Rebels enrolled at Oberlin and were wrestling with their consciences as to the advisability of becoming agents of abolition, Finney argued they ought to become evangelists instead and convert the country, and that would accomplish abolition and all the other reforms as well.

Both the agitators and the evangelicals, however, agreed that whether or not man's inherent sinfulness was at the bottom of the problem, there was an undemocratic movement afoot conspiring to sustain and increase the slave power. The slavocracy influenced the Northern institutions because of political power within the Congress of the United States and because of its economic leverage with Northern business interests.

When Stanton argued his case for freeing the slaves in the District of Columbia, he asked how slavery could exist. His answer was only because it was sustained by law and the laws supporting it came from the power of the slave conspiracy. While the evangelicals stressed the sin of slavery, the agitators stressed the interpretation that the slave conspiracy had control over all elements of society. In an argument foreshadowing the contemporary theme that America is a racist society, the agitators of abolition saw the church, the economic institutions, and the government as racist. Every action against them and every resistance to their efforts they interpreted as further evidence of either the direct power of the conspiracy or of its ability to intimidate or frighten the masses.

One tactic of the rhetoricians of abolition relates to both the tasks of mobilizing public opinion and of building dedication for the movement among the recruits. The question of the identity of the movement required a rhetoric that placed it in the context of the culture of the times. I discuss the tactic here as part of the overall strategy of gaining converts and mobilizing opinion because it was, to my mind, more important in that regard. Nonetheless, the group identity developed by the speakers in annual meeting after annual meeting of local, state, and national societies played an extremely important role in development of group loyalty.

In regard to developing the group's self-image, the agitators differed markedly in their approach from the evangelicals. The agitators took the position that their movement was a revolutionary effort standing against and outside the cultural stream of the American experience. They saw themselves as pure and uncorrupted, as standing outside the essentially polluted culture. The agitators became no-government men and argued against ecclesiastical and civil institutions as being beyond reform. Their answer to the problem of union with the slaveholder was disunion. Garrison and Phillips burned and cursed the Constitution and denied that the tradition of the founders was a worthy one. Garrison took the typical stance when agitating against the admission of Texas to the Union when he said at Concord, Massachusetts:

> "But who are we," will men ask, "that talk of such things? Are we enough to make a revolution?" No sir; but we are enough to *begin* one, and, once begun, it never can be turned back. I am for revolution were I utterly alone. I am there because I *must* be there. I *must* cleave to the right. I cannot choose but obey the voice of God.... Do not tell me of our past Union, and for how many years we have been one. We were only one while we were ready to hunt, shoot down, and deliver up the slave, and allow the slave-power to form an oligarchy on the floor of Congress![17]

When the Liberty Party was formed to operate within the traditional political channels and focused upon the issue of slavery in the District of Columbia on the grounds that according to the National Constitution the question of slavery within the states was beyond the bounds of political remedy but that slavery within the District was within the Jurisdiction of the National Congress, Garrison responded:

> We have a very poor opinion of the intelligence of any man, and a great distrust of his candor or honesty, who tries to make it appear that no pro-slavery compromise was made between the North and South, at the adoption of the Constitution. We cherish feelings of profound contempt for the quibbling spirit of criticism which is endeavoring to explain away the meaning of language, the design of which as a matter of practice, and the adoption of which as a matter of bargain, were intelligently and clearly understood by the contracting parties.[18]

The evangelists for abolition, on the other hand, saw their efforts as a continuation of the best of the American experience. Henry Stanton in his testimony before the Massachusetts legislature argued heavily from historical precedent relating to the power of the national government to abolish slavery in the District of Columbia and defended the Constitution. He fixed responsibility for the sustaining of slavery on laws passed by the Congress

[17]Quoted in Grimké, pp. 317–18.
[18]Quoted in Grimké, pp. 322–23.

and argued that Congress had the right and duty to take legal remedies to eliminate slavery in the District.

> Were there time, I would detail a long catalogue of facts, showing, that if there was any compact between North and South, besides the *written* compact, it was not a *pro-slavery*, but an ANTI-SLAVERY compact. True to the pledge, the North returned from the Convention, and commenced the work of abolition. Numerous abolition societies were formed in Pennsylvania, Connecticut, Rhode Island, New York, New Jersey, and even in Maryland and Virginia. And numerous addresses and sermons denouncing slavery were put forth by the Pinckneys, the Jays, the Franklins, the Rushes, the Edwards, the Hopkins, and the Stiles of that day. Patrick Henry and Thomas Jefferson were not silent. And, by the great mass of the country, it was hoped, believed, and understood, that long, long ere this, the last vestige of slavery was to have rotted in a dishonored grave. Then, Sir, I go for the Compact![19]

But more than the outward forms of government, the evangelicals participated in some of the great sustaining cultural myths that celebrated the American experience and gave it meaning. They saw the country as the great experiment in guaranteeing the natural rights of man. They saw America as a model for all those around the world fighting against despotism. Their view was essentially optimistic; they wanted to save America for God and the world in order to better the human condition everywhere. Their view was westward; the great valley of the Ohio must be saved for evangelical religion and free soil.

Theodore Weld, writing from the West, expressed the basic evangelical position in these words: "Here is to be the battle field of the world. Here Satan's seat is. A mighty effort must be made to dislodge him *soon*, or the West is undone."[20]

The rhetoric of conversion, by placing the movement into the general cultural context, accepting the main positive myths of American self-identity, using the frame of America's values as the basis for ruthless and critical self-examination of the corruption of the sin of slavery, and then urging the need to cut out the corruption and propitiate the sin, thereby saving the noble American experiment, proved to have a powerful, persuasive appeal to the uncommitted. The evidence is clear that the rhetoric of conversion was much more successful at mobilizing popular support for abolition than was the tactic of agitation. In the year of Weld's great agency, he, along with a handful of Lane Rebels, converted hosts of people to the crusade and established many new local antislavery organizations. Weld himself converted many lawyers who became nationally prominent political leaders, including

[19]*Liberator*, March 18, 1837, p. 46.
[20]*Weld-Grimké Letters*, pp. 66–67.

Joshua Giddings, Henry B. Stanton, and Seth M. Gates. In May, 1835, before Weld's agency, there were 220 local antislavery organizations, forty-seven of which were in Massachusetts, forty in New York, and thirty-eight in Ohio. By May, 1836, there were 527 local societies with 133 in Ohio and 103 in New York, the states where Weld and his men itinerated. There were eighty-seven in Massachusetts.

As the agitators lost influence, divided, quarreled, and repelled potential recruits through the decade of the 1840's, the movement, powered by the rhetoric of conversion that argued it was working within the frame of the culture, particularly within the political channels, grew in power. Finally, even Garrison, who had roundly castigated the Liberty Party, came to give cautious approval to the Free Soil Party.

The second major rhetorical problem that both the agitators and evangelists of abolition had to face related to the building of a sense of community and commitment among the members who joined the movement. The antislavery forces used two tactics to built *esprit de corps.* The first tactic was common to both wings of the movement and consisted of appeals designed to make the movement the most important force in the individual's life. The second was to create clear, compelling goals for the abolitionists to achieve.

The movement built its self-image by rhetorical assertions that the cause itself was the greatest of all causes, by the individual's personal pledge to suffer for the cause, and by the appeal to the myth of supernatural sanction.

Again and again the insiders told one another that their cause was the most important in the world. When Garrison left the paper *Journal of the Times* in 1829, to edit *The Genius of Universal Emancipation,* he wrote:

> Hereafter, the editorial charge of this paper will devolve on another person. I am invited to occupy a broader field and to engage in a higher enterprise; that field embraces the whole country—that enterprise is in behalf of the slave population. . . . To my apprehension, the subject of slavery involves interests of greater moment to our welfare as a republic, and demands a more prudent and minute investigation than any other which has come before the American people since the Revolutionary struggle—than all others which now occupy their attention.[21]

Weld wrote to his friends in a similar vein:

> The cause we are wedded to is the cause of *changeless eternal right.* God has decreed its ultimate triumph, and if the signs of the times are not mockers, the victory shout will ring around the world before the generation that now is, goes to the dead.[22]

[21]Quoted in Grimké, p. 59.
[22]*Weld-Grimké Letters,* p. 100.

To further buttress their assertion that the movement was the most important in secular affairs, both the agitators and the evangelicals told one another again and again that the antislavery movement was the most important force in their lives and one for which they would be willing to suffer social ostracism, physical abuse, and even death.

Theodore Weld, writing from the scene of his only major defeat as an agent, at Troy, New York, when he thought the mobs might indeed kill him, expressed this determination as follows:

Poor outside whitewash! the tempest will batter it off the first stroke; the masks and veils, and sheep clothing gone, gone at the first blast of fire. God gird us all to do valiantly for the helpless and innocent. Blessed are they who die in the harness and are buried on the field or bleach there.[23]

Writing from jail in Baltimore, where he had been imprisoned for writing an attack on a slave trader, Garrison put it this way:

Is it supposed by Judge Brice that his frowns can intimidate me, or his sentence stifle my voice on the subject of African oppression? He does not know me. So long as a good Providence gives me strength and intellect, I will not cease to declare that the existence of slavery in this country is a foul reproach to the American name; nor will I hesitate to proclaim the guilt of kidnappers, slave abettors, or slaveowners, wheresoever they may reside, or however high they may be exalted. . . . It is my shame that I have done so little for the people of color; yea, before God, I feel humbled that my feelings are so cold, and my language so weak. A few white victims must be sacrificed to open the eyes of this nation, and to show the tyranny of our laws. I expect and am willing to be persecuted, imprisoned, and bound for advocating African rights; and I should deserve to be a slave myself if I shrunk from that duty or danger.[24]

No greater show of group loyalty is possible than the offer to be a martyr for the cause. The rhetoric of martyrdom was strong in both wings of the abolition movement.

Finally, the movement was justified to the followers with the myth of supernatural sanction. While the evangelicals made the appeal to God a prominent part of their rhetoric, the agitators also, but to a lesser degree, built commitment to the movement with that tactic.

The key term in the myth of supernatural sanction was *sin*. In the early instructions accompanying the commission to be an agent for the American Anti-Slavery Society, the speakers were instructed as follows:

Insist principally on the SIN OF SLAVERY, because our main hope is in the consciences of men, and it requires little logic to prove that it is always safe

[23] *Weld-Grimké Letters*, p. 310.
[24] Quoted in Grimké, pp. 82–83.

to do right. To question this, is to impeach the superintending Providence of God.[25]

Since slavery was a sin and the abolitionists were battling on the side of God, they had more than merely human reasons for committing themselves to the movement. They were God's chosen people and his instrumentality, which meant that they were inevitable and must win. One can recall the power of the more contemporary civil rights appeal that "We shall overcome." One is more tightly drawn to a mighty cause so right, so sanctioned by God himself that it will win and establish a better world.

For many of the evangelicals in the movement, battling the sin of slavery was an opportunity to avoid the guilt of doing nothing and then participating in the sin. Put more positively, committing themselves to abolition was a method of achieving eternal salvation. Their motto was "Faith without works is dead." To be converted and not to take up the cudgels in the fight against sin was to be, in fact, unsaved. What better place to work and demonstrate your faith than against the greatest sin of all—the sin of slavery.

The essence of any organization is that it have a common purpose. The statement of goals of any reform movement is a rhetorical move that adds direction and focus to the organization's activities and that, most importantly, provides a greater or lesser force for cohesion. When the goal is clear, the program unequivocal, the ideological pull of the movement is strongest on its members. Contemporary political parties tend not to use the potential attractiveness of the goals for building party loyalty to any great degree. The platform of the major parties tends, today, to be so general and vague that the parties can accommodate membership with a wide shade of opinion. Under the vague rhetoric of the platform almost anyone may work for the party. Victory in the election then becomes the major goal, and the platform tends to get lost in the shuffle of the campaign. A reform movement like abolition often utilizes the opposite tactic. By taking an extreme stand, expressing its goal in unequivocal language, and making its doctrine clear by frequent reiteration the spokesmen increase the level of commitment to the movement even though they may pay the price of restricting the movement to a relatively small group of highly dedicated people.

The antislavery movement divided several times because of the rhetorical handling of the goals problem. The evangelicals divided from the agitators on the question of goals, and both wings suffered some loss of support from the general public as well as from the members because of the way the goals

25 *Weld-Grimké Letters*, p. 125.

were debated and formulated. Strategically, the rhetoric of the goals of the movement related to two questions: What precisely did the stated goal of *immediate abolition* mean? Should the movement incorporate as goals other reforms such as temperance, peace, women's rights, as well as abolition?

The difference between abolition in 1833 as opposed to the prior anti-slavery efforts was the question of time. The first object of the attack of the abolitionists was the Colonization Society and its goal of gradualism in free-ing of the slaves. From the time of the Puritan founders, as we have seen, the rhetoric of New England always contained great time pressure upon the seeker after salvation. Involvement, activity, immediacy have been God-words for the persuaders and agitators of our history. As a result, Americans have been an impatient people. They hope for results "immediately if not sooner." Weld exuberantly predicted success for his new gospel shortly after he was converted to immediate emancipation. "Mark my word," he wrote, "*two years* will make an overturning from the bottom."[26]

The agitators were absolutely clear and unequivocal about the meaning of immediate abolition. For them it signified literally freedom *now*. As much as any other factor of their rhetoric, the original interpretation of the goal reveals the difference between the basic rhetorical stances of the two groups most clearly. The evangelicals admitted the practical difficulties in immedi-ately freeing the slaves and tried to interpret their goals to accommodate the problems. Recall Stanton's explanation of abolition in the quotation before as, not turning the slaves loose nor as investing them with all political rights including the vote but simply to restore to the black man the ownership of his own body. The evangelicals adopted the slogan "immediate emancipation, gradually accomplished." One is reminded of the Supreme Court's concept of school integration in the 1950's as being accomplished with "deliberate speed."

Garrison was a young man of twenty-four working with Benjamin Lundy on the *Genius of Universal Emancipation* when the English parliamentary debates over slavery were published in the United States. The more radical of the English abolitionists thought well of Lundy and sent him their papers and pamphlets. Garrison studied the abstract absolutes of the British anti-slavery rhetoric at the climax of the movement in Great Britain and adopted them as his own. He saw literal immediate abolition not as a policy but as a principle and therefore bound to succeed anytime or anyplace. Garrison continued to advocate literal immediatism of emancipation throughout his

[26]*Weld-Grimké Letters*, p. 100.

career. As he put it, "Duty is ours and events are God's.... All you have to do is set your slaves at liberty."[27]

The evangelicals had considerable difficulty trying to explain that by immediate emancipation they did not mean what Garrison meant. Their notion that immediate emancipation simply meant that the freeing of the slaves should start immediately, even if the process would take a matter of time, caused confusion within the ranks as well as among the potential converts.

Subsequently the evangelicals came to Garrison's position when James Thome and Horace Kimball went to the West Indies to study how immediate abolition was working in practice. They brought back a wealth of information which Weld hammered into another effective rhetorical tract called *Emancipation in the West Indies*. The result of the study of the West Indies' precedent caused the New York headquarters to revise the motto from "immediate emancipation, gradually accomplished," to a clear and unequivocal call for immediate freedom. Whatever the practical shortcomings of Garrison's call for literal immediacy, it was, rhetorically, the more powerful appeal.

The second question of strategy relating to goals was as important as the nature of the meaning of *immediate*. Should the movement have many goals, or should it concentrate on the one goal of freeing the slave? Theodore Weld was adamant that only one goal drive the reform movement. As the agitators embraced more and more reforms, involved themselves in more controversies (Garrison arguing the sabbath question with Lyman Beecher, arguing for women's rights, peace, temperance, and a number of other reforms), Weld urged that the main reform effort must be dedicated to one and only one goal. Dividing up the goals confused the followers and the general public, brought converts with a different set of goals to the movement, and dissipated the energy available for the antislavery reform.

Whereas Garrison's great rhetorical stroke was to discover the power of the concept of immediate abolition, absolute, simplistic, and unwavering, the evangelicals had the clearer eye when it came to the strategy of staying with one goal rather than chasing after many.

In summary, the agitators told themselves and their potential converts that they stood above and outside the mainstream of the culture. They rejected the compact of the Constitution, the notion of government itself; they saw the church as being corrupted by the slave power, and themselves as standing irrevocably for principle and for right. They told themselves that they were courageous, dedicated, and willing to die if need be for the greatest

[27]Barnes, *The Antislavery Impulse*, p. 103.

cause in the history of America and, indeed, in the history of all mankind. Their description of the facts of slavery was similar to the evangelicals', although their interpretation of the facts tended to stress that they resulted from a thoroughly racist and corrupt culture rather than from the natural sinfulness of man. Their efforts at gaining converts tended toward goading their audiences with attacks on popular personalities, on revered institutions, and on values that the listeners cherished. While the evangelists carefully adapted their ideas to the audience's psychology, the agitators took high moral ground, a firm grasp on principle, and dared the audience to join them.

The evangelical conversion rhetoric viewed the movement as part of the continuing cultural tradition. They handled the problem of accounting for the evils of slavery and still supporting elements within that society by a clear division of that which was sound from that which was sinful. They supported the original compact between the states, argued that the founders felt that slavery was waning and would shortly die, suggested that America was the great experiment in human freedom and the hope of all freedom-loving people around the globe, and that slavery must be purged to make the experiment work and keep America free from the charge of hypocrisy. The problem lay not with the basic dream and structure of American society but with the legal system and social mores. That the government contained evil conspirational slave power advocates they admitted, that the church contained Pharisaical elements they also admitted, but that both government and church could be saved for God and man they also contended. They emphasized the sin of slavery, saw it as essentially a question of religious conversion, and applied to the problem the tried and proven formulas of Finney's new measures. They argued that their movement was sanctioned by the true God and was, indeed, in the tradition of saving one's soul for eternal life. Abolition was the greatest and mightiest endeavor to which a man could dedicate his life. They, no less than the agitators, were ready to suffer all and die for the cause.

The issue of the advantage of utilizing the rhetorical tactics of the agitator versus the use of the more persuasive rhetoric of the evangelicals was something debated by the proponents of both. The agitators were adamant that they would not bend their principles one iota to please the corrupt, the apathetic, and the evil. They would go down to defeat and even death before they would compromise or sugar their message to make it sweeter for their audiences. They justified their agitation on the grounds that hot words melted the ice of apathy and that the lubberly public would continue for another two hundred years living contentedly with slavery unless stinging words were used to goad them to search their sleeping consciences. They argued that people who would never have heard about or considered abolition were forced to do so simply because their harsh style caused a furor, made headlines, caused violent counterefforts, forced the racist institutions to take repressive measures, and by thus confronting the establishment of the time, their tactics worked to achieve the abolition of slavery.

The argument of the agitators had some merit in light of the historical record. Garrison, Phillips, Foster, and the rest were widely talked about. They became famous or infamous, depending upon the region and the audience. They served to keep the issue before the American people. In sum, however, their entire rhetoric was much less successful than that of the evangelicals. The agitators did not gain support from outsiders for their cause. The evangelicals, on the other hand, converted enough people to sustain the petition drive and subsequently to help form and support the Liberty, Free Soil, and ultimately the Republican political parties. Finally, the agitators did not manage to build a sense of community and a dedication to a common cause among the true believers within the movement. Factions continually arose among the agitators. Cliques developed, and leaders fell out and bitterly attacked one another among the Garrisonians. Typical was the falling out between Frederick Douglass and Garrison, which degenerated into a bitter quarrel even involving charges about the personal life of Douglass. Symbolically, after the Civil War and the Emancipation Proclamation, after the two old agitators had both basked in the glory of their achievement, even Wendell Phillips and William Lloyd Garrison fought and would not talk to one another for a time.

In 1830, given the mood and temper of the West and North, the evangelical rhetoric proved more effective at building and cohering a reform movement than did the rhetoric of agitation.

The Haschish
John Greenleaf Whittier*

Of all that Orient lands can vaunt
Of marvels with our own competing,
The strangest is the Haschish plant,
And what will follow on its eating.

What pictures to the taster rise,
Of Dervish or of Almeh dances!
Of Eblis, or of Paradise,
Set all aglow with Houri glances!

The poppy visions of Cathay,
The heavy beer-trance of the Suabian;
The wizard lights and demon play
Of nights Walpurgis and Arabian!

The Mollah and the Christian dog
Change place in mad metempsychosis;
The Muezzin climbs the synagogue,
The Rabbi shakes his beard at Moses!

The Arab by his desert well
Sits choosing from some Caliph's daughters,
And hears his single camel's bell
Sound welcome to his regal quarters.

The Koran's reader makes complaint
Of Shitan dancing on and off it;
The robber offers alms, the saint
Drinks Tokay and blasphemes the Prophet.

Such scenes that Eastern plant awakes;
But we have one ordained to beat it,
The Haschish of the West, which makes
Or fools or knaves of all who eat it.

The preacher eats, and straight appears
His Bible in a new translation;
Its angels negro overseers,
And Heaven itself a snug plantation!

The man of peace, about whose dreams
The sweet millennial angels cluster,
Tastes the mad weed, and plots and schemes,
A raving Cuban filibuster!

The noisiest Democrat, with ease,
It turns to Slavery's parish beadle;

*From *The Writings of John Greenleaf Whittier* (Boston: Houghton, Mifflin and Co., 1892), vol. 3, *Anti-Slavery Poems: Songs of Labor and Reform*, 173–75.

The shrewdest statesman eats and sees
Due southward point the polar needle.

The Judge partakes, and sits erelong
Upon his bench a railing blackguard;
Decides off-hand that right is wrong,
And reads the ten commandments backward.

O potent plant! so rare a taste
Has never Turk or Gentoo gotten;
The hempen Haschish of the East
Is powerless to our Western Cotton!

Part I
Evangelical Religion
and Antislavery

The speakers for abolition in the evangelical tradition were trained to speak extemporaneously, and as a result few of their speech manuscripts have survived. Fortunately, the most representative selections of their persuasion are among the remnants.

The first selection is by Theodore Weld and consists of excerpts from his famous course of lectures on *The Bible Against Slavery*.[1] When Weld lost his voice and joined the main headquarters of the Anti-Slavery Society in New York, one of his first tasks was to write up his lectures as an Anti-Slavery Tract. Although Weld thought of himself as primarily a speaker, he soon learned to be an excellent argumentative writer. Among other things, he discovered that the verbatim transcript of his lectures was unduly repetitive and redundant for the written medium, and he proceeded to pare them down. Through subsequent editions, he cut the lectures which took him as many as seven or eight evenings to deliver into a tract of less than one hundred pages. Nonetheless, the main themes of his argument and the basic style remain in the selections that are presented here.

Finally, the persuasion tract was perhaps as important as Weld's lectures themselves, since the 1830's saw the rise of newspapers and tracts as important rhetorical media for persuasion. The Bible argument in regard to civil rights, discrimination, Black Power, and Black Militancy is less important today than it was when Weld developed it. In the 1830's the rise of a school of propagandists in the South who defended and justified slavery on Biblical grounds made it imperative that slavery be attacked in Scriptural terms. Weld provided that argument for the Abolitionists. Although the content of *The Bible Against Slavery* is archaic, the student of Abolitionist rhetoric can get an excellent feel for the form and style of the discourse as exemplified by the greatest of the evangelical speakers for emancipation.

That the second selection survived for posterity is also a fortunate accident of history. While most of the Lane Rebels were itinerating the black country

[1]The selections are from *The Anti-Slavery Examiner*, No. 6, *The Bible Against Slavery: An Inquiry Into the Patriarchal and Mosaic Systems on the Subject of Human Rights*, 3rd ed. (New York: The American Anti-Slavery Society, 1838).

in remote churches and school houses without even an ambitious local news-
paperman to record their speeches, one of the most illustrious of their
number had returned to his native New England as an agent of the Anti-
Slavery Society. When petitions against slavery in the District of Columbia
were considered by a committee of the Massachusetts State Legislature in
1837, Henry B. Stanton was invited to testify before the committee. A shorthand reporter for *The Liberator* took down his testimony, which continued
over three days, and the transcript was published in three issues of Garrison's paper.

Stanton presented a condensed version of the lectures of the Lane Rebels.
The selection presented here is the major portion of his second day of
testimony and reveals the way the Weld men presented the notion of "immediate abolition gradually accomplished" and their analysis of the Constitution as an antislavery document.[2] Thus, both major persuasive campaigns
of the gospel of Abolition as developed by Weld and the Lane Rebels and
promulgated by the bulk of the seventy antislavery agents are represented in
the first two selections.

Beriah Green was a professor at Western Reserve College when Weld
visited on his travels while promoting manual labor. With Green at Western
Reserve were President Storrs and Elizur Wright. The three faculty members
had become converts to immediate abolition partially as a consequence of
reading Garrison's writings on the subject. After his visit, Weld became an
avowed and unequivocal apostle of immediate emancipation. Green remained
a friend of Weld's and a foremost spokesman for the evangelical position
as he moved on to become President of Oneida Institute and minister at
Whitesboro, New York. Green's sermon on slavery at the Presbyterian
Church in Whitesboro is representative of the thousands of antislavery
sermons of the evangelical traditions.[3]

Theodore Dwight Weld

Theodore Weld was the longest-lived of a long-lived group of reformers
and one of the greatest and most effective of all the abolitionists. For years,
scholars were aware of "some man" who moved in and out of the movement,
and they were aware that this one man was undoubtedly the author of many
of the more famous antislavery tracts; but if Weld had not married another

[2]*The Liberator*, March 18, 1837.
[3]*Things for Northern Men to Do: A Discourse Delivered Lord's Day Evening,
July 17, 1836, in the Presbyterian Church, Whitesboro, New York* (New York: no
publisher, 1836).

zealous reformer, Angelina Grimké, who wrote letters which were saved, his effect in the fight for abolition would not have been known. For as many others sought the spotlight (even those who did so in the belief that any notoriety would further their cause), Theodore Weld was almost morbid in his desire to avoid publicity. He would not sign his name to any published tracts. He would not allow his speeches to be published with his name attached to them. He was the Mr. Anonymous of the movement until a trunkful of Grimké-held letters was found by one of their descendants.

Weld was an extraordinary man. The son and grandson of Congregational ministers, whose ancestry included Jonathan Edwards and Timothy Dwight, he threw himself into whatever he did with such supernatural energy that he quite literally wore himself out on more than one occasion. He was an enormously effective speaker until he broke his voice for good at Troy, New York, after years of successful campaigns covering the northeastern states and the Ohio valley.

His enthusiasm and talent for organizing and leading touched the lives of many others, particularly those in the evangelical faction of the abolitionists: James G. Birney, Henry B. Stanton, Beriah Green, the Grimké sisters, and, in his later years, former President John Quincy Adams.

After his voice failed, Weld began writing tracts and supported the behind-the-scenes campaign that finally got anti-slavery issues debated in the halls of Congress; when he retired from public life in 1843, he felt secure in the knowledge that the country could never bury or try to ignore the issue of slavery again, and he felt strongly that the outcome was destined to be abolition. Although he and his wife and sister-in-law spent most of their lives thereafter running a boarding school, Weld continued to be a powerful influence for abolition until the Emancipation Proclamation.

Theodore Weld was the spearhead of the reform abolitionists. It is an irony that after the Civil War and the passing of the Thirteenth Amendment, the man who was probably the single most effective force in abolishing slavery through government channels refused even to appear in public or receive any acknowledgment whatsoever for his contribution.

born November, 1803, Hampton, Conn.
died February, 1895, Hyde Park, Mass.

The Bible
Against Slavery

The spirit of slavery never seeks shelter in the Bible, of its own accord. It grasps the horns of the altar only in desperation—rushing from the terror of the avenger's arm. Like other unclean spirits, it "hateth the light, neither cometh to the light, lest its deeds should be reproved." Goaded to phrenzy in its conflicts with conscience and common sense, denied all quarter, and hunted from every covert, it vaults over the sacred inclosure and courses up and down the Bible, "seeking rest, and finding none." THE LAW OF LOVE, glowing on every page, flashes around it an omnipresent anguish and despair. It shrinks from the hated light, and howls under the consuming touch, as demons quailed before the Son of God, and shrieked, "Torment us not." At last, it slinks away under the types of the Mosaic system, and seeks to burrow out of sight among their shadows. Vain hope! Its asylum is its sepulchre; its city of refuge, the city of destruction. It flies from light into the sun; from heat, into devouring fire; and from the voice of God into the thickest of His thunders.

* * *

We proceed to state affirmatively that, ENSLAVING MEN IS REDUCING THEM TO ARTICLES OF PROPERTY—making free agents, chattels—converting *persons*, into *things*—sinking immortality, into *merchandize*. A *slave* is one held in this condition. In law, "he owns nothing, and can acquire nothing." His right to himself is abrogated. If he say *my* hands, *my* feet, *my* body, *my* mind, MY*self*, they are figures of speech. To *use himself* for his own good, is a CRIME. To keep what he *earns*, is stealing. To take his body into his own keeping, is *insurrection*. In a word, the *profit* of his master is made the END of his being, and he, a *mere means* to that end—a *mere means* to an end into which his interests do not enter, of which they constitute no portion. MAN, sunk to a *thing!* the intrinsic element, the *principle* of slavery; MEN, bartered, leased, mortgaged, bequeathed, invoiced, shipped in cargoes, stored as goods, taken on executions, and knocked off at public outcry! Their *rights*, another's conveniences; their interests, wares on sale; their happiness, a household utensil; their personal inalienable ownership, a serviceable article, or a plaything, as best suits the humor of the hour; their deathless nature, conscience, social affections, sympathies, hopes—marketable commodities! We repeat it, *the reduction of persons to things*; not robbing a man of privileges, but of *himself*; not loading with burdens, but making him a *beast of burden*; not *restraining* liberty, but subverting it; not curtailing rights, but abolishing them; not inflicting personal cruelty, but annihilating *personality*; not exacting involuntary labor, but sinking him into an *implement* of labor; not abridging human comforts, but abrogating human nature; not depriving an animal of immunities, but despoiling a rational being of attributes—uncreating a MAN, to make room for a *thing!*

That this is American slavery, is shown by the laws of slave states. Judge Stroud, in his "Sketch of the Laws relating to Slavery," says, "The cardinal principle of slavery, that the slave is not to be ranked among sentient beings, but among *things*—obtains as undoubted law in all of these [the slave] states." The law of South Carolina thus lays down the principle, "Slaves shall be deemed, held, taken, reputed, and adjudged in law to be chattels personal in the hands of their owners and possessors, and their executors, administrators, and assigns, to ALL INTENTS, CONSTRUCTIONS, AND PURPOSES WHATSOEVER."—Brevard's Digest, 229. In Louisiana, "A slave is one who is in the power of a master to whom he belongs; the master may sell him, dispose of his person, his industry, and his labor; he can do nothing, possess nothing, nor acquire any thing, but what must belong to his master."—Civ. Code of Louisiana, Art. 35.

This is American slavery. The eternal distinction between a person and a thing, trampled under foot—the crowning distinction of all others—alike the source, the test, and the measure of their value—the rational, immortal principle, consecrated by God to universal homage, in a baptism of glory and honor by the gift of His Son, His Spirit, His word, His presence, providence, and power; His shield, and staff, and sheltering wing; His opening heavens, and angels ministering, and chariots of fire, and songs of morning stars, and a great voice in heaven, proclaiming eternal sanctions, and confirming the word with signs following.

Having stated the *principle* of American slavery, we ask, DOES THE BIBLE SANCTION SUCH A PRINCIPLE? "To the *law* and the *testimony?*" First, the moral law. Just after the Israelites were emancipated from their bondage in Egypt, while they stood before Sinai to receive the law, as the trumpet waxed louder, and the mount quaked and blazed, God spake the ten commandments from the midst of clouds and thunderings. *Two* of those commandments deal death to slavery. "THOU SHALT NOT STEAL," or, "thou shalt not take from another what belongs to him." All man's powers are God's gift to *him*. That they are *his own*, is proved from the fact that God has given them to *him alone*,—that each of them is a part of himself, and all of them together constitute himself. All else that belongs to man, is acquired by the *use* of these powers. The interest belongs to him, because the principal does; the product is his, because he is the producer. Ownership of any thing, is ownership of its *use*. The right to use according to will, is *itself* ownership. The eighth commandment presupposes and assumes the right of every man to his powers, and their product. Slavery robs of both. A man's right to himself, is the only right absolutely original and intrinsic—his right to whatever else that belongs to him is merely *relative* to this, is derived from it, and held only by virtue of it. SELF-RIGHT is the *foundation right*—the *post in the middle*, to which all other rights are fastened. Slaveholders, when talking about their RIGHT to their slaves, always assume their own right to themselves. What slaveholder ever undertook to prove his right to himself? He knows it to be a self-evident proposition, that *a man belongs to himself*—that the right is intrinsic and absolute. In making out his own title, he makes out the title of every human being. As the fact of being *a man* is itself the title, the whole human family have one common title deed. If one man's title is valid, all are valid. If one is worthless, all are. To deny the validity of the *slave's* title is to deny the validity of *his own*; and yet in the act of making a man a slave, the slaveholder *asserts* the validity of his own title, while he seizes him as his property who has the *same* title. Further, in making him a slave, he does not merely disfranchise the humanity of *one* individual, but of UNIVERSAL MAN. He destroys the foundations. He annihilates *all rights*. He attacks not only the human race, but *universal being*, and rushes upon JEHOVAH. For rights are *rights*; God's are no more—man's are no less.

The eighth commandment forbids the taking of *any part* of that which belongs to another. Slavery takes the *whole*. Does the same Bible which prohibits the taking of *any* thing from him, sanction the taking of *every* thing? Does it thunder wrath against him who robs his neighbor of a *cent*, yet bid God speed to him who robs his neighbor of *himself*? Slaveholding is the highest possible violation of the eighth commandment. To take from a man his earnings, is theft. But to take the *earner*, is a compound, life-long theft— supreme robbery, that vaults up the climax at a leap—the dread, terrific, giant robbery, that towers among other robberies a solitary horror, monarch of the realm. The eighth commandment forbids the taking away, and the *tenth* adds, "THOU SHALT NOT COVET ANY THING THAT IS THY NEIGHBOR'S;" thus guarding every man's right to himself and his property, by making not only the actual taking away a sin, but even that state of mind which would *tempt* to it. Who ever made human beings slaves, without *coveting* them? Why take from them their time, labor, liberty, right of self-preservation and improvement, their right to acquire property, to worship according to conscience, to search the Scriptures, to live with their families, and their right to their own bodies, if they do not *desire* them? They COVET them for purposes of gain, convenience, lust of dominion, of sensual gratification, of pride and ostentation. THEY BREAK THE TENTH COMMANDMENT, and pluck down upon their heads the plagues that are written in the book.—*Ten* commandments constitute the brief compend of human duty.—*Two* of these brand slavery as sin.

The giving of the law at Sinai, immediately preceded the promulgation of that body of laws called the "Mosaic system." Over the gateway of that system, fearful words were written by the finger of God—"HE THAT STEALETH A MAN AND SELLETH HIM, OR IF HE BE FOUND IN HIS HAND, HE SHALL SURELY BE PUT TO DEATH." Ex. xxi. 16.

The oppression of the Israelites in Egypt, and the wonders wrought for their deliverance, proclaim the reason for *such* a law at *such* a time—when the body politic became a theocracy, and reverently waited for the will of God. They had just been emancipated. The tragedies of their house of bondage were the realities of yesterday, and peopled their memories with thronging horrors. They had just witnessed God's testimony against oppression in the plagues of Egypt—the burning blains on man and beast—the dust quickened into loathsome life, and swarming upon every living thing—the streets, the palaces, the temples, and every house heaped up with the carcases of things abhorred—the kneading troughs and ovens, the secret chambers and the couches, reeking and dissolving with the putrid death—the pestilence walking in darkness at noonday, the devouring locusts, and hail mingled with fire, the first-born death-struck, and the waters blood, and last of all, that dread high hand and stretched-out arm, that whelmed the monarch and his hosts, and strewed their corpses on the sea. All this their eyes had looked upon,—earth's proudest city, wasted and thunder-scarred, lying in desolation, and the doom of oppressors traced on her ruins in the hand writing of God, glaring in letters of fire mingled with blood—a blackened monument of wrath to the uttermost against the stealers of men. No wonder that God, in a code of laws prepared for such a people at such a time, should light up on its threshold a blazing beacon to flash terror on slaveholders. "*He that stealeth a man and selleth him, or if he be found in his hand, he shall surely be put to death.*" Ex. xxi. 16. Deut. xxiv. 7. God's cherubim and flaming sword guarding the entrance to the Mosaic system!

The word *Ganabh* here rendered *stealeth*, means the taking what *belongs* to another, whether by violence or fraud; the same word is used in the eighth commandment, and prohibits both *robbery* and theft.

The crime specified, is that of depriving SOMEBODY of the ownership of a man. Is this somebody a master? and is the crime that of depriving a master of his servant? Then it would have been "he that stealeth" a *servant, not* "he that stealeth a *man.*" If the crime had been the taking an individual from *another*, then the *term* used would have been expressive of that relation, and most especially if it was the relation of property and *proprietor!*

The crime is stated in a three-fold form—man *stealing, selling,* and *holding.* All are put on a level, and whelmed under one penalty—DEATH.

This *somebody* deprived of the ownership of a man, is the *man himself,* robbed of personal ownership. Joseph said, "Indeed I was *stolen* away out of the land of the Hebrews." Gen. xl. 15. How *stolen?* His brethren sold him as an article of merchandize. Contrast this penalty for *man*-stealing with that for *property*-stealing, Ex. xxii. If a man had stolen an *ox* and killed or sold it, he was to restore five oxen; if he had neither sold nor killed it, two oxen. But in the case of stealing a *man*, the *first* act drew down the utmost power of punishment; however often repeated, or aggravated the crime, human penalty could do no more. The fact that the penalty for *man*-stealing was death, and the penalty for *property*-stealing, the mere restoration of double, shows that the two cases were adjudicated on totally different principles. The man stolen might be past labor, and his support a burden, yet death was the penalty, though not a cent's worth of *property value* was taken. The penalty for stealing property was a mere property penalty. However large the theft, the payment of double wiped out the score. It might have a greater *money* value than a thousand men, yet death was not the penalty, nor maiming, nor branding, nor even *stripes*, but double of *the same kind.* Why was not the rule uniform? When a *man* was stolen why was not the thief required to restore double of the same kind—two men, or if he had sold him, five men? Do you say that the man-thief might not *have* them? So the ox-thief might not have two oxen, or if he had killed it, five. But if God permitted men to hold *men* as property, equally with *oxen*, the man-thief could get men with whom to pay the penalty, as well as the ox-thief, oxen. Further, when *property* was stolen, the legal penalty was a compensation to the person injured. But when a *man* was stolen, no property compensation was offered. To tender money as an equivalent, would have been to repeat the outrage with intolerable aggravations. Compute the value of a MAN in *money!* Throw dust into the scale against immortality! The law recoiled from such supreme insult and impiety. To have permitted the man-thief to expiate his crime by restoring double, would have been making the repetition of crime its atonement. But the infliction of death for *man-stealing* exacted the utmost possibility of reparation. It wrung from the guilty wretch as he gave up the ghost, a testimony in blood, and death-groans, to the infinite dignity and worth of man,—a proclamation to the universe, voiced in mortal agony, "MAN IS INVIOLABLE."—a confession shrieked in phrenzy at the grave's mouth—"I die accursed, and God is just."

If God permitted man to hold man as property, why did he punish for stealing that kind of property infinitely more than for stealing any other kind of property? Why did he punish with death for stealing a very little of *that* sort of property, and make a mere fine, the penalty for stealing a thousand times as much, of any other sort of property—especially if God did by his own act annihilate the difference between man and *property*, by putting him on a level with it?

The atrociousness of a crime, depends much upon the nature, character, and condition of the victim. To steal is a crime, whoever the thief, or whatever the plunder. To steal bread from a full man, is theft; to steal it from a starving man, is both theft and murder. If I steal my neighbor's property, the crime consists not in altering the *nature* of the article but in shifting its relation from him to me. But when I take my neighbor himself, and first make him *property*, and then *my* property, the latter act, which was the sole crime in the former case, dwindles to nothing. The sin in stealing a man, is not the transfer from its owner to another of that which is *already property*, but the turning of *personality* into *property*. True, the attributes of man remain, but the rights and immunities which grow out of them are annihilated. It is the first law both of reason and revelation to regard things and beings as they are; and the sum of religion, to feel and act toward them according to their value. Knowingly to treat them otherwise is sin; and the degree of violence done to their nature, relations, and value, measures its guilt. When things are sundered which God has indissolubly joined, or confounded in one, which he has separated by infinite extremes; when sacred and eternal distinctions, which he has garnished with glory, are derided and set at nought, then, if ever, sin reddens to its "scarlet dye." the sin specified in the passage, is that of doing violence to the *nature* of a *man*—to his intrinsic value as a rational being, and blotting out the exalted distinction stamped upon him by his Maker. In the verse preceding, and in that which follows, the same principle is laid down. Verse 15, "He that smiteth his father or his mother shall surely be put to death." V. 17, "He that curseth his father or his mother, shall surely be put to death." If a Jew smote his neighbor, the law merely smote him in return; but if the blow was given to a *parent*, it struck the smiter dead. The parental relation is the *centre* of human society. God guards it with peculiar care. To violate that, is to violate all. Whoever trampled on that, showed that *no* relation had any sacredness in his eyes—that he was unfit to move among human relations who had violated one so sacred and tender. Therefore, the Mosaic law uplifted his bleeding corpse, and brandished the ghastly terror around the parental relation to guard it from impious inroads.

Why such a difference in penalties, for the same act? Answer. (1.) The relation violated was obvious—the distinction between parents and others manifest, dictated by natural affection—a law of the constitution. (2.) The act was violence to nature—a suicide on constitutional susceptibilities. (3.) The parental relation then, as now, was the focal point of the social system, and required powerful safeguards. *"Honor thy father and thy mother,"* stands at the head of those commands which prescribe the duties of man to man; and, throughout the Bible, the parental state is God's favorite illustration of his own relations to the whole human family. In this case death was to be inflicted not for smiting a *man*, but a *parent*—a *distinction* cherished by God, and around which, He threw up a bulwark of defence. In the next verse, "He that stealeth a man," &c., the SAME PRINCIPLE is wrought out in still a stronger relief. The crime to be punished with death was not the taking of property from its owner, but the doing violence to an *immortal nature*, blotting out a sacred *distinction*, making MEN "chattels." The incessant pains taken in the Old Testament to separate human beings from brutes and things, shows God's regard for his own distinction.

"In the beginning" it was uttered in heaven, and proclaimed to the universe as it rose into being. Creation was arrayed at the instant of its birth, to do it homage. It paused in adoration while God ushered forth its crowning work. Why that dread pause and that creating arm held back in mid career and that high conference in the godhead? "Let us make man in OUR IMAGE after OUR LIKENESS, AND LET HIM HAVE DOMINION over the fish of the sea, and over the fowl of the air, and over the cattle, and over all the earth." Then while every living thing, with land, and sea, and firmament, and marshalled worlds, waited to swell the shout of morning stars—then "GOD CREATED MAN IN HIS OWN IMAGE; IN THE IMAGE OF GOD CREATED HE HIM." This solves the problem, IN THE IMAGE OF GOD, CREATED HE HIM. Well might the sons of God shout, "Amen, alleluia"—"For thou hast made him a little lower than the angels, and hast crowned him with glory and honor. Thou madest him to have dominion over the works of thy hands; thou hast put all things under his feet." Ps. viii. 5, 6. The repetition of this distinction is frequent and solemn. In Gen. i. 26–28, it is repeated in various forms. In Gen. v. 1, we find it again, "IN THE LIKENESS OF GOD MADE HE MAN." In Gen. ix. 6, again. After giving license to shed the blood of "every moving thing that liveth," it is added, *"Whoso sheddeth man's blood, by man shall his blood be shed, for* IN THE IMAGE OF GOD MADE HE MAN." As though it had been said, "All these creatures are your property, designed for your use —they have the likeness of earth, they perish with the using, and their spirits go downward; but this other being, MAN, has my own likeness: "IN THE IMAGE OF GOD made I man;" "an intelligent, moral, immortal agent, invited to all that I can give and he can be." So in Lev. xxiv. 17, 18, 21, "He that killeth any MAN shall surely be put to death; and he that killeth a beast shall make it good, beast for beast; and he that killeth a man shall be put to death." So in Ps. viii. 5, 6, what an enumeration of particulars, each separating infinitely MEN from brutes and things! (1.) *"Thou hast made him a little lower than the angels."* Slavery drags him down among *brutes.* (2.) *"And hast crowned him with glory and honor."* Slavery tears off his crown, and puts on a *yoke.* (3.) *"Thou madest him to have dominion* OVER *the works of thy hands."* Slavery breaks the sceptre, and casts him down *among* those works—yea, *beneath them.* (4.) *"Thou hast put all things under his feet."* Slavery puts HIM under the feet of an "owner." Who, but an impious scorner, dares thus strive with his Maker, and mutilate HIS IMAGE, and blaspheme the Holy One, who saith, *"Inasmuch as ye did it unto one of the least of these, ye did it unto* ME."

In further prosecuting this inquiry, the Patriarchal and Mosaic systems will be considered together, as each reflects light upon the other, and as many regulations of the latter are mere *legal* forms of Divine institutions previously existing. As a *system,* the latter alone is of Divine authority. Whatever were the usages of the patriarchs, God has not made them our exemplars.

Before entering upon an analysis of the condition of servants under these two states of society, we will consider the import of certain terms which describe the mode of procuring them.

As the Israelites were commanded to "buy" their servants, and as Abraham had servants "bought with money," it is argued that servants were articles of *property.* The sole ground for this belief is the terms themselves. How much might be saved, if in discussion, the thing to be proved were always *assumed.* To beg the question in debate, would be vast economy of midnight oil! and a great forestaller of wrinkles and grey hairs! Instead of protracted investigation into Scripture usage, with painful collating of passages, to find the meaning of terms, let every man interpret the oldest book in the world by the usages of his own time and place, and the work is done. And then instead of one revelation, they might be multiplied as the drops of the morning, and every man have an infallible clue to the mind of the Spirit, if he only understood the dialect of his own neighborhood! What a Babel-jargon it would make of the Bible to take it for granted that the sense in which words are *now* used is the *inspired* sense, David says, "I prevented the dawning of the morning, and cried." What, stop the earth in its revolution! Two hundred years ago, *prevent* was used in its strict Latin sense to *come before,* or *anticipate.* It is always used in this sense in the Old and New Testaments.

David's expression, in the English of the nineteenth century, would be "Before the dawning of the morning I cried." In almost every chapter of the Bible, words are used in a sense now nearly or quite obsolete, and sometimes in a sense totally *opposite* to their present meaning. A few examples follow: "I purposed to come to you, but was *let* (hindered) hitherto." "And the four *beasts* (living ones) fell down and worshipped God,"—"Whosoever shall *offend* (cause to sin) one of these little ones,"—"Go out into the highways and *compel* (urge) them to come in,"—"Only let your *conversation* (habitual conduct) be as becometh the Gospel,"—"They that seek me *early* (earnestly) shall find me,"—"So when tribulation or persecution ariseth *by-and-by* (immediately) they are offended." Nothing is more mutable than language. Words, like bodies, are always throwing off some particles and absorbing others. So long as they are mere *representatives*, elected by the whims of universal suffrage, their meaning will be a perfect volatile, and to cork it up for the next century is an employment sufficiently silly (to speak within bounds) for a modern Bible Dictionary maker. There never was a shallower conceit than that of establishing the sense attached to a word centuries ago, by showing what it means *now*. Pity that fashionable mantuamakers were not a little quicker at taking hints from some Doctors of Divinity. How easily they might save their pious customers all qualms of conscience about the weekly shiftings of fashion, by proving that the last importation of Parisian indecency now flaunting on promenade, was the very style of dress in which the pious Sarah kneaded cakes for the angels, and the modest Rebecca drew water for the camels of Abraham's servants. Since such fashions are rife in Broadway *now*, they *must* have been in Canaan and Padanaram four thousand years ago!

The inference that the word buy, used to describe the procuring of servants, means procuring them as *chattels*, seems based upon the fallacy, that whatever *costs* money *is* money; that whatever or whoever you pay money *for*, is an article of property, and the fact of your paying for it *proves* it property. The children of Israel were required to purchase their first-born from under the obligations of the priesthood, Num. xviii. 15, 16; Ex. xiii. 13; xxxiv. 20. This custom still exists among the Jews, and the word *buy* is still used to describe the transaction. Does this prove that their first-born were, or are, held as property? They were *bought* as really as were *servants*. (2.) The Israelites were required to pay money for their own souls. This is called sometimes a ransom, sometimes an atonement. Were their souls therefore marketable commodities? (3.) Bible saints *bought* their wives. Boaz bought Ruth. "So Ruth the Moabitess, the wife of Mahlon, have I *purchased* to be my wife." Ruth iv. 10. Hosea bought his wife. "So I *bought* her to me for fifteen pieces of silver, and for an homer of barley, and an half homer of barley." Hosea iii. 6. Jacob bought his wives Rachael and Leah, and not having money, paid for them in labor—seven years a piece. Gen. xxix. 15–29. Moses probably bought his wife in the same way, and paid for her by his labor, as the servant of her father. Exod. ii. 21. Shechem, when negotiating with Jacob and his sons for Dinah, says, "Ask me never so much dowry and gift, and I will give according as ye shall say unto me." Gen. xxxiv. 11, 12. David purchased Michal, and Othniel, Achsah, by performing perilous services for their fathers. 1 Sam. xviii. 25–27; Judg. i. 12, 13. That the purchase of wives, either with money or by service, was the general practice, is plain from such passages as Ex. xxii. 17, and 1 Sam. xviii. 25. Among the modern Jews this usage exists, though now a mere form, there being no *real* purchase. Yet among their marriage ceremonies, is one called "marrying by the penny." The coincidences in the methods of procuring wives and servants, in the terms employed in describing the transactions, and in the prices paid for each, are worthy of notice. The highest price of wives (virgins) and servants was the same. Comp. Deut. xxii. 28, 29, and Ex. xxii. 17, with Lev. xxvii. 2–8. The *medium* price of wives and servants was the same. Comp. Hos. iii. 2, with Ex. xxi. 32. Hosea seems to have paid one half in money and the other half in grain. Further, the Israelitish female bought servants were *wives*, their husbands and masters being the same persons. Ex. xxi. 8, Judg. xix. 3, 27. If *buying* servants proves them property, buying wives proves them property. Why not contend that the *wives* of the ancient fathers of the faithful were their "chattels," and used as ready change at a pinch; and thence deduce the rights of modern husbands? Alas! Patriarchs and prophets are followed afar off! When will pious husbands live up to their Bible privileges, and become partakers with Old Testament worthies in the blessedness of a husband's rightful immunities! Refusing so to do, is questioning the morality of those "good old patriarchs and slaveholders, Abraham, Isaac, and Jacob."

... Alas! for our leading politicians if "buying" men makes them "chattels." The Whigs say that Benton and Rives are "bought" by the administration; and the other party, that Clay and Webster are "bought" by the Bank. The histories of the revolution tell us that Benedict Arnold was "bought" by British gold. When a northern clergyman marries a rich southern widow, country gossip thus hits off the indecency, "The cotton bags *bought* him," Sir Robert Walpole said, "Every man has his price, and whoever will pay it, can *buy* him," and John Randolph said, "The northern delegation is in the market; give me money enough, and I can *buy* them;" both meant just what they said. The temperance publications tell us that candidates for office *buy* men with whiskey; and the oracles of street tattle, that the court, district attorney, and jury, in the late trial of Robinson were *bought*, yet we have no floating visions of "chattels personal," man auctions, or coffles.

...We argue the voluntariness of servants from their peculiar opportunities and facilities for escape. Three times every year, all the males over twelve years, were required to attend the national feasts. They were thus absent from their homes not less than three weeks at each time, making nine weeks annually. As these caravans moved over the country, were there military scouts lining the way, to intercept deserters?—a corporal's guard at each pass of the mountains, sentinels pacing the hill-tops, and light horse scouring the defiles? The Israelites must have had some safe contrivance for taking their "*slaves*" three times in a year to Jerusalem and back. When a body of slaves is moved any distance in our *republic*, they are hand-cuffed and chained together, to keep them from running away, or beating their drivers' brains out. Was this the *Mosaic* plan, or an improvement introduced by Samuel, or was it left for the wisdom of Solomon? The usage, doubtless, claims a paternity not less venerable and biblical! Perhaps they were lashed upon camels, and transported in bundles, or caged up, and trundled on wheels to and fro, and while at the Holy City, "lodged in jail for safe keeping," the Sanhedrim appointing special religious services for their benefit, and their "drivers" officiating at "ORAL instruction." Mean while, what became of the sturdy *handmaids* left at home? What hindered them from marching off in a body? Perhaps the Israelitish matrons stood sentry in rotation round the kitchens, while the young ladies scoured the country, as mounted rangers, picking up stragglers by day, and patrolled the streets, keeping a sharp look-out at night.

...Abraham's servants are an illustration. At one time he had three hundred and eighteen *young men* "born in his house," and many more *not* born in his house. His servants of all ages, were probably MANY THOUSANDS. How Abraham and Sarah contrived to hold fast so many thousand servants against their wills, we are left quite in the dark. The most natural supposition is that the Patriarch and his wife *took turns* in surrounding them! The neighboring tribes, instead of constituting a picket guard to hem in his servants, would have been far more likely to sweep them and him into captivity, as they did Lot and his household. Besides, there was neither "Constitution" nor "compact," to send back Abrahams's fugitives, nor a truckling police to pounce upon them, nor gentleman-kidnappers, suing for his patronage, volunteering to howl on their track, boasting their blood-hound scent, and pledging their "honor" to hunt down and "deliver up," *provided* they had a description of the "flesh-marks," and were suitably stimulated by *pieces of silver*. Abraham seems also to have been sadly deficient in all the auxiliaries of family government, such as stocks, hand-cuffs, foot-chains, yokes, gags, and thumb-screws. His destitution of these patriarchal indispensables is the more afflicting, since he faithfully trained "his household to do justice and judgment," though so deplorably destitute of the needful aids. Contrast this bondage of Egypt with American slavery. Have our slaves "very much cattle," and "a mixed multitude of flocks and herds?" Do they live in commodious houses of their own, "sit by the flesh-pots," "eat fish freely," and "eat bread to the full?" Do they live in a separate community, in their distinct tribes, under their own rulers, in the exclusive occupation of an extensive tract of country for the culture of their crops, and for rearing immense herds of their own cattle—and all these held inviolable by their masters? Are our female slaves free from exactions of labor and liabilities of outrage? or when employed, are they paid wages, as was the Israelitish woman by the king's daughter? Have they the disposal of their own time, and the means for cultivating social refinements, for practising the fine arts, and for personal improvement? THE ISRAELITES UNDER THE BONDAGE OF EGYPT, ENJOYED ALL THESE RIGHTS AND PRIVILEGES. True, "all the service wherein they made them serve was with rigor." But what was this when compared with the incessant toil of American slaves, the robbery of all their time and earnings, and even the power to own any thing, or acquire any thing?" a "quart of corn a-day," the legal allowance of food! their *only* clothing for one half the year, *"one* shirt and *one* pair of pantaloons!" *two hours and a half* only, for rest and refreshment in the twenty-four!—their dwellings, *hovels*, unfit for human residence, with but one apartment, where both sexes and all ages herd promiscuously at night, like the beasts of the field. Add to this, the ignorance, and degradation; the daily sunderings of kindred, the revelries of lust, the lacerations and baptisms of blood, sanctioned by law, and patronized by public sentiment. What was the bondage of Egypt when compared with this? And yet for her oppression of the poor, God smote her with plagues, and trampled her as the mire, till she passed away in his wrath, and the place that knew her in her pride, knew her no more. Ah! "I have seen the afflictions of my people, and I have heard their groanings, and am come down to deliver them." HE DID COME, and Egypt sank a ruinous heap, and her blood closed over her. If such was God's retribution for the oppression of heathen Egypt, of how much sorer punishment shall a Christian people be thought worthy, who cloak with religion a system, in comparison with which the bondage of Egypt dwindles to nothing? Let those believe who can that God commissioned his people to rob others of *all* their rights, while he denounced against them wrath to the uttermost, if they practised the *far lighter* oppression of Egypt— which robbed its victims of only the least and cheapest of their rights, and left the females unplundered even of these. What! Is God divided against himself? When He had just turned Egypt into a funeral pile; while his curse yet blazed upon her unburied dead, and his bolts still hissed amidst her slaughter, and the smoke of her torment went upwards because she had "ROBBED THE POOR," did He license the VICTIMS of robbery to rob the poor of ALL? As *Lawgiver*, did he *create* a system tenfold more grinding than that for which he had just hurled Pharaoh headlong, and overwhelmed his princes, and his hosts, till "hell was moved to meet them at their coming?"

We now proceed to examine various objections which will doubtless be set in array against all the foregoing conclusions.

*   *   *

The advocates of slavery find themselves at their wits end in pressing the Bible into their service. Every movement shows them hard-pushed. Their ever-varying shifts, their forced constructions, and blind guesswork, proclaim both their *cause* desperate, and themselves. The Bible defences thrown around slavery by professed ministers of the Gospel, do so torture common sense, Scripture, and historical facts it were hard to tell whether absurdity, fatuity, ignorance, or blasphemy, predominates, in the compound; each strives so lustily for the mastery, it may be set down a drawn battle. How often has it been bruited that the color of the negro is the *Cain-mark*, propagated downward. Cain's posterity started an opposition to the ark, forsooth, and rode out the flood with flying streamers! Why should not a miracle be wrought to point such an argument, and fill out for slaveholders a Divine title-deed, vindicating the ways of God to man?

OBJECTION I. "Cursed be Canaan, a servant of servants shall he be unto his brethren." Gen. ix. 25.

This prophecy of Noah is the *vade mecum* of slaveholders, and they never venture abroad without it; it is a pocket-piece for sudden occasion, a keepsake to dote over, a charm to spell-bind opposition, and a magnet to draw around their standard "whatsoever worketh abomination or maketh a lie." But "cursed be Canaan" is a poor drug to ease a throbbing conscience —a mocking lullaby, to unquiet tossings, and vainly crying "Peace be still," where God wakes war, and breaks his thunders. Those who justify negro slavery by the curse on Canaan, *assume* all the points in debate. (1.) That *slavery* was prophesied rather than mere *service* to others, and *individual* bondage rather than *national* subjection and tribute. (2.) That the *prediction* of crime *justifies* it; at least absolving those whose crimes fulfill it, if not transforming the crimes into *virtues*. How piously the Pharaohs might have quoted the prophecy *"Thy seed shall be a stranger in a land that is not theirs, and they shall afflict them four hundred years."* And then, what *saints* were those that crucified the Lord of glory! (3.) That the Africans are descended from Canaan. Whereas Africa was peopled from Egypt and Ethiopia, and they were settled by Mizraim and Cush. For the location and boundaries of Canaan's posterity, see Gen. x. 15–19. So a prophecy of evil to one people, is quoted to justify its infliction upon another. Perhaps it may be argued that Canaan includes all Ham's posterity. If so, the prophecy is yet unfulfilled. The other sons of Ham settled Egypt and Assyria, and, conjointly with Shem, Persia, and afterward, to some extent, the Grecian and Roman empires. The history of these nations gives no verification of the phophecy. Whereas, the history of Canaan's descendants for more than three thousand years, records its fulfilment. First, they were put to tribute by the Israelites; then by the Medes and Persians; then by the Macedonians, Grecians and Romans, successively; and finally, were subjected by the Ottoman dynasty, where they yet remain. Thus Canaan has been for ages the servant mainly of Shem and Japhet, and secondarily of the other sons of Ham. It may still be objected, that though Canaan alone is *named* in the curse, yet the 22d and 24th verses show the posterity of Ham in general to be meant. "And Ham, the father of Canaan, saw the nakedness of his father, and told his two brethren without." "And Noah awoke from his wine, and knew what his YOUNGER son had done unto him, and said," &c. It is argued that this *"younger"* son" can not be *Canaan*, as he was the *grandson* of Noah, and therefore it must be *Ham*. We answer, whoever that *"younger son"* was, *Canaan* alone was named in the curse. Besides, the Hebrew word *Ben*, signifies son, grandson, or *any* of *one* the posterity of an individual. *"Know ye Laban the* SON *of Nahor?"* Laban was the *grandson* of Nahor. Gen. xxix. 5. *"Mephibosheth the* SON *of Saul."* 2 Sam. xix. 24. Mephibosheth was the *grandson* of Saul. 2 Sam. ix. 6. *"There is a* SON *born to Naomi."* Ruth iv. 17. This was the son of Ruth, the daughter-in-law of Naomi. *"Let seven men of his (Saul's)* SONS *be delivered unto us.* 2 Sam. xxi. 6. Seven of Saul's *grandsons* were delivered up. *Laban rose up and kissed his* SONS." Gen. xxi. 55. These were his *grandsons.* *"The driving of Jehu the* SON *of Nimshi."* 2 Kings ix. 20. Jehu was the *grandson* of Nimshi. Shall we forbid the inspired writer to use the *same* word when speaking of *Noah's* grandson? Further, Ham was not the *"younger"* son. The order of enumeration makes him the *second* son. If it be said that Bible usage varies, the order of birth not always being observed in enumerations, the reply is, that, enumeration in that order, is the *rule*, in any other order the *exception*. Besides, if a younger member of a family, takes precedence of older ones in the family record, it is a mark of pre-eminence, either in endowments, or providential instrumentality. Abraham, though sixty years younger than his eldest brother, stands first in the family genealogy. Nothing in Ham's history shows him pre-eminent; besides, the Hebrew word *Hăkkātăn* rendered "the *younger*," means the *little, small*. The same word is used in Isa. xl. 22. "A LITTLE ONE *shall become a thousand.*" Isa. xxii. 24. "*All vessels of* SMALL *quantity.*" Ps. cxv. 13. "*He will bless them that fear the Lord both* SMALL *and great.*" Ex. xviii 22. "*But every* SMALL *matter they shall judge.*" It would be a literal rendering of Gen. ix. 24, if it were translated thus, "when Noah knew what his little son, or grandson *(Beno hakkatan)* had done unto him, he said cursed be Canaan," &c. Further, even if the Africans were the descendants of Canaan, the assumption that their enslavement fulfils this prophecy, lacks even plausibility, for, only a *fraction* of the Africans have at any time been the slaves of other nations. If the objector say in reply, that a large majority of the Africans have always been slaves *at home*, we answer: *It is false in point of fact*, though zealously bruited often to serve a turn; and *if it were true*, how does it help the argument? The prophecy was, "Cursed be Canaan, a servant of servants shall he be *unto his* BRETHREN," not unto *himself!*

OBJECTION II.—"If a man smite his servant or his maid with a rod, and he die under his hand, he shall surely be punished. Notwithstanding, if he continue a day or two, he shall not be punished, for he is his money." Ex. xxi. 20, 21. What was the design of this regulation? Was it to grant masters an indulgence to beat servants with impunity, and an assurance, that if they beat them to death, the offence should not be *capital?* This is substantially what commentators tell us. What Deity do such men worship? Some blood-gorged Moloch, enthroned on human hecatombs, and snuffing carnage for incense? Did He who thundered from Sinai's flames, "THOU SHALT NOT KILL," offer a bounty on *murder?*

Henry Brewster Stanton

Henry B. Stanton grew up in Connecticut, attended the academy in Jewett City, and began his career as a journalist on the Rochester, N.Y., *Monroe*

Telegraph. He was then twenty-one. At twenty-four, he became deputy clerk of the county and began studying law on the side. Influenced by Charles G. Finney and Theodore Weld, he decided to study for the ministry and went to Lane Theological Seminary in Cincinnati. While there, he became increasingly interested in the cause of the abolitionists, and he helped Weld organize an Anti-Slavery Society at the seminary; they began taking their good works out into the community and caused such ripples that the trustees demanded that the society disband, so Stanton, with Weld and many others, left. Stanton decided to become a full-time reformer, and he started then as an agent for the American Anti-Slavery Society in New England.

For many years he combined his talents as a journalist with his intense support of abolition, writing for *The Liberator* and Washington and New York political papers. He began speaking as well; some thought him to be the best of the antislavery orators. He was a good-looking man, charming and eloquent. His passion and purpose were softened somewhat by a keen wit, and it was said that he was a most disarming and compelling speaker. He too was often attacked by mobs, however. His was not a popular topic for the times, charming though he was.

When Stanton was thirty-five, he married another extremely able reformer, Elizabeth Cady. Her principal reform effort was in the area of women's suffrage, but husband and wife supported one another totally and became, like the Welds, one of the effective reform couples of the time.

Elizabeth's father was an attorney, and Stanton returned to the study of law, eventually starting a practice in Boston. His reformer reputation was a handicap when he tried to build a law practice, however, so the Stantons moved to outstate New York, where Henry later became a state senator. He continued to serve in official and unofficial capacities in both political parties and wrote for the New York *Tribune* and *Sun* until he died at the age of eighty-two.

born, Connecticut, 1805
died, New York City, 1887

Remarks Before the Committee of the House of Representatives of Massachusetts

I am aware, Mr. Chairman, that it is customary on occasions like this, to commence by descanting upon the importance of the subject under discussion. This is common place. I dislike to stoop to it on the present occasion, lest my reason for so doing should be regarded as trivial. Yet, I will run the hazard. In courts of justice, the advocate often trembles, as he rises to address the jury, when the pecuniary interests of his client are at stake; then what should be my feelings, when I rise to address you, not in behalf of the pecuniary interests of one client, but in behalf of the liberties and the lives, the interests, temporal and eternal, of thousands? Ay more;–the questions here discussed are not confined in their bearings to the slaves in the District of Columbia; nor in this nation. The cause of freedom throughout the world; the honor of God's law, will be deeply affected by your deliberations. The interests here involved are co-extensive with human hopes and human happiness; wide as the universe, lasting as eternity, high as Heaven. Then, sir, the slave, the master, this Commonwealth, the nation, the world, Jehovah himself, demand that we deliberate patiently, cautiously, impartially. And, gentlemen, your constituents will pardon you for so doing. No subject is more discussed by them, than that now before you; and the intensity of their feelings, not less than their immediate concernment, requires this deliberation at your hands. The Committees of the honorable body, whom you represent, spend many weeks in their investigation of Banks, Rail-Roads, and kindred subjects, and shall you not devote a few brief hours to a matter, whose importance as immeasurably overshadows all pecuniary and fiscal interests, as liberty is worth more than money?

And I ask the indulgent attention of the Committee, because I believe, that as you shall decide, so the Legislature will act. Your number is unusually large; you justly have the confidence of the House, and to you they look to mature this subject for their action. Upon you, therefore, rests the responsibility of a decision. Hear me then for my cause, and bear with me, because I plead not only for the suffering, but the dumb.

The question which will now occupy our attention, is the second one proposed yesterday, viz:—*Ought Congress immediately to abolish slavery, and the slave trade, in the District of Columbia?* The power of Congress to do this, was discussed yesterday. Our present business is with the expediency of exercising that power.

1. I contend that Congress should immediately abolish slavery and the slave trade in that District, because slavery is a system at war with natural justice and moral equity:—is a political and a moral wrong:—a sin against man and God. Hence, no political or moral considerations can justify its continuance for a moment. "Justice," says Gov. McDuffie, "is the highest expediency—and I am sure South Carolina is the last state in the Union,

that would knowingly violate the sacred canon of political morality." Shall Massachusetts be behind South Carolina in political morality? Before I entered the House this afternoon, a friend remarked to me, that it would be of no use to urge the odious character of slavery to satisfy this Committee of the expediency of its immediate abolition. Sir, I will not believe it. Is it true, that the detestable and impious nature of slavery is not, to the head and heart of a Massachusetts legislator, the highest reason for its immediate and total annihilation? Is the old Pilgrim spirit quenched within the legislative halls of this Commonwealth? God forbid..

What then is slavery? It is the worst of all oppressions. It robs men of their instinctive characteristics as rational and immortal beings, and makes them things. In the language of the slaveholding code, (and slavery is the creature of the law,) "Slaves are deemed, sold, taken, reputed and adjudged to be chattels personal, in the hands of their owners and possessors, their administrators and assigns, to all intents, constructions and purposes whatsoever." Thus, the master has as absolute ownership over his slave, as over any other property. The statute uncreates the slave as a man, and re-creates him as a chattel. It annihilates all his rights by annihilating his manhood, by virtue of which alone, he is an owner of rights. His Creator endowed him with sacred rights, pre-eminent among which was the right of personal ownership. Having robbed him of his pre-eminent right, the law is consistent, when it says, "a slave can do nothing, possess nothing, acquire nothing"; for, in the language of the same code, he "is not to be ranked among sentient, rational beings, but among things, as an article of property." To rob men of *property* is manifestly unjust, and your Legislature would not hesitate a moment to declare it expedient to stop such robbery instantly;—but, to *rob men of themselves:*—ah, that is indeed a "delicate question!" Slavery thrusts its robber-arm too far to excite the abhorrence of political morality. If it stopped at the pocket, the civilized world would cry out against it;—but, when it goes through the pocket to the man himself, and by force takes him, body and soul, and converts him into merchandise, and herds him with his four-footed beasts and creeping things, then its abolition is a question of doubtful expediency! To steal your purse, Mr. Chairman, would be palpable injustice;—but to take yourself, and thus annihilate the sun in the solar system of your rights, around which all your rights revolve, and upon which they depend, and without which they are not, is but a venial offence; and to rebuke it, much more to prevent it, is of questionable expediency! Sir, slavery is the acme of injustice and impiety. God gave to man his faculties to be employed in the promotion of his own happiness. But slavery regards the slave not as a being possessing rights and susceptibilities of happiness, but as a mere means of happiness to his master. The object of the system is not to promote the good of the slave, but to use him to promote the good of another. He is a mere tool in the hands of his owner. He is not permitted to use his powers of body, of mind, of soul, to advance his own happiness, or to advance the happiness of others, or to obey his God. Yes, the profit and the pleasure of the owner are the end for which the slave is permitted to exist! He only lives that he may be profitable to his master! In the District of Columbia, there are seven thousand Americans, bearing Jehovah's image, and touched with His immortal fire; who are, by statutory enactments, absolutely annihilated as beings possessing rights and susceptibilities of happiness, and are permitted to live only as appendages to the existence of others; as mere articles of convenience to be used for the pleasure of others; and, so far as it is in the power of human legislation to do it, are divested of every right, natural, social, intellectual, political and moral, and are crowded out of God's creation into the chaos of an anomalous existence, where they are regarded and treated neither as men, nor yet as things;—neither as rational beings, nor yet as brutes;—but as SLAVES.

For this daring,—this impious crusade against Jehovah and His works, somebody is responsible. Who is it? I answer. THE CONGRESS OF THE UNITED STATES. This system is its handy work. It lives, and moves, and has its being in that District, by the express permission of Congress. Then let that body, let those who elect that body, and those who have influence with that body, take the responsibility of continuing this system of "complicated villany"; but let them answer it to that Being, who has said, "Vengeance is mine, I will repay."

The right of absolute ownership over the slave as a chattel, is the fountain head, from which all the cruelties of the system flow. The innumerable inflictions, exactions and privations, such as stripes, toil, denial of wages, with all the other positive evils of the system, flow spontaneously from this fountain head. Having robbed the slave of himself, and thus made him a thing, Congress is consistent in denying to him all protection of law as a man. His labor is coerced from him, by laws passed by Congress;—no bargain is made, no wages given. His provender and covering are at the will of his owner. His domestic and social rights are as entirely disregarded, in the eye of the law, as if Deity had never instituted the endearing relations of husband and wife, parent and child, brother and sister. THERE IS NOT THE SHADOW OF LEGAL PROTECTION FOR THE FAMILY STATE AMONG THE SLAVES OF THE DISTRICT OF COLUMBIA. What think you of this, Sir, as a husband and a father? Neither is there any real protection in law, for the limbs and the lives of slaves of that District. The shadow of legal protection for life and limb, is indeed extended to them, but the substance is not there. No slave can be a party before a judicial tribunal, in the capital of this Republic, in any species of action against any person, no matter how atrocious may have been the injury received. He is not known to the law as a person;—much less, a person having civil rights. Says Stroud, in his admirable "Sketch of the laws relating to slavery," "it is an inflexible and universal rule of slave law, that the testimony of a colored person, whether bond or free, cannot be received against a white person!" Slavery thus puts the *life* of its victims into the power of the master. The master may murder by system, with complete legal impunity, if he perpetrates his deeds only in the presence of colored persons! What think you as a Legislator, sir, of such a system in the Capital of a land of light and law,—which boasts of equal rights, of trials by jury, of courts of justice, and whose Constitution says, "no person shall be deprived of life, liberty, or property, without due process of law." Is it expedient to abolish it? And this system, in that District, is hereditary and perpetual. Thus Congress, in regard to one-fifth of those over whom it exercises exclusive legislation, has perverted civil law from a blessing into a curse; and, to its victims, has made our free institutions an engine of the most odious tyranny. It is the constitutional guardian of the rights, and the sworn protector of the interests, of all the people in that District. It has offered the rights of seven thousand citizens, a bleeding sacrifice on the altar of cupidity, passion and power. IT IS RECREANT TO ITS HIGH TRUSTS.

But, sir, the slave trade in that District demands our attention. How humiliating, that the Capital of our nation should be one of the foulest slave markets in the world!

* * *

The following advertisement is cut from a recent Washington paper.

CASH FOR 400 NEGROES

Including both sexes, from 12 to 25 years of age. Persons having likely servants to dispose of, will find it to their interest to give us a call, as we will give higher prices in cash than any other purchaser who is now, or may hereafter come into this market.

Franklin & Armfield.

Franklin & Armfield are extensive dealers in human flesh, at the Capital. They have a regular line of "Packets," running from Alexandria to New Orleans, whose chief business is the transportation of slaves. I present their case only as a specimen of the trade in the District. Ay, sir, there is a keen competition in this brokerage in human blood. Franklin & Armfield are but one of the many firms, who drive this trade at the seat of the Federal Government. See the audacity with which they offer "higher prices" than any other purchaser in "THIS MARKET!" Where do we witness this? On the coast of Africa? No! For there, if caught, Franklin & Armfield would be hung as pirates. But, in the Capital of "the freest nation on earth." And who are these "negroes?" Are they of the Caffres in Africa? No! For then, Franklin & Armfield would die as pirates. But, they are American born citizens!—and, if it would add to their claims for mercy, I might say, many of them are as white as your distinguished Senator in Congress!

*   *   *

This traffic is not confined to the legal slave:—it clutches the rights of the free. Says Mr. Miner, in the preamble to his resolution,

> Free persons of color coming into the District, are liable to arrest, imprisonment, and to be sold into slavery for life, for jail fees, if unable from ignorance, or misfortune, or fraud, to prove their freedom.

By a law of the District, authorized of course by Congress, all negroes found residing in the city of Washington, who shall not be able to establish their title to freedom, are committed to jail as *absconded slaves!* Most wicked and unconstitutional law! It is the common law, even of Monarchies, that men are to be presumed innocent, and consequently free, till they are proved guilty. But by this law, *color* is made a crime, which first robs citizens of their constitutional rights, and is then taken as evidence that they are slaves: —and to crown all, a large posse of constables and other officers, some of them in the pay of the Government, are, by their oaths, obliged to execute these laws. The result is, that citizens, as free as your committee, are often arrested, imprisoned, and then sold for their jail fees as slaves for life! See the following record of our baseness. A Washington paper has the following

NOTICE

Was committed to the prison of Washington Co. D.C., on the 19th day of May, 1834, as a run-away, a Negro man who calls himself David Peck. He is 5 feet 8 inches high. Had on, when committed, a check shirt, linen pantaloons, and straw hat. He says he is free, and belongs to Baltimore. The owner or owners are hereby requested to come forward, prove him, and take him away, or ["or" what? said Mr. Stanton; he will be set free? We should naturally think so; remembering that he was an American citizen, in the Capital of "the freest Government on earth." But NO! Listen.] or he will be sold for his prison and other expenses as the Law Directs.

James Williams,
Keeper of the Prison of Washington County, District of Columbia.
For *Alexander Hunter, M.D.C.*

The above is but a specimen. Four other persons, at least, who said they were free, have been advertised in a similar way within the last year. I will not comment on such facts. It would be insulting to the patriotism and humanity of the Committee. Shall the voice of this ancient Commonwealth be dumb, when slavery plays such tragedies of cruelty on the theatre of our Capital? If so,

> Then, by our Fathers' ashes, has the spirit
> Of the true hearted and the unshackled gone.

* * *

In the City Laws, sanctioned by Congress, I find an "Act to provide a revenue for the Canal Fund," which lays an impost as follows: "For a License to trade or traffic in Slaves for profit, whether as Agent or otherwise, Four Hundred Dollars." Thus, what is piracy on the coast of Africa, is licensed in the City of Washington. Says Dr. Samuel Johnson, "the loudest yelps for liberty are among the drivers of Slaves." Dr. Johnson was an eminent lexicographer, and gave admirable definitions to terms.

And now, Mr. Chairman, what do the petitioners ask you to request Congress to do? I answer;—merely to repeal these odious statutes immediately, and to enact others, if necessary, in their stead. By immediate abolition, they do not intend that the Slaves of the District should be "turned loose";—nor, that they should be, as a *sine qua non* to abolition, immediately invested with all political rights, such as the elective franchise. But, simply, that Congress should immediately restore to every Slave, the ownership of his own body, mind and soul. That they should no longer permit them to be "deemed, held, and sold, as chattels personal, to all intents, constructions and purposes whatsoever"; but should give the slaves a fee simple in their own blood, bones, and brains. That they should no longer be regarded as things without rights, but as men with rights. In a word, that the right of property, on the part of the master over the slave, should instantly cease. This being done, of course the slave should be legally protected in life and limb,—in his earnings, his family and social relations, and his conscience. We only ask, that the master should stop taking from the slave those things which of right belong to him:—and that Congress should give equal and exact justice to all concerned. Sir, is this just? Is it expedient? To give impartial legal protection in that District, to all its inhabitants, would annihilate slavery. And is not innocence entitled to the protection of law? The people wait to hear your answer to this question! Slavery and the slave-trade could not survive the introduction, into that District, of this plain principle, viz, *that innocence is entitled to the protection of law*; a principle so self-evidently just, so necessary to the existence of human society in its most degraded forms, that even semi-barbarians acknowledge and act upon it. Give the slave, then, equal legal protection with his master, and, at its first approach, slavery and the slave-trade flee in panic, as does darkness before the full orbed sun. I still press the point; is it expedient for all the inhabitants in our Capital, to have the protection of law? or shall the rights of the weaker be made common plunder of the stronger?

As to the immediate investment of the slaves with the elective franchise, and other mere conventional rights, we leave that to the wisdom of Congress. We only say, let there be no tests on account of color. Strike a dead level, and whose head soever reaches above it, let him enjoy the advantage, whatever may be his phrenological conformation. Let the quality of the brains, and the color of the heart, be the standard, rather than the color of the skin, and the texture of the hair.

I am asked, if the slaves would not become paupers,—or might not kill their masters? I answer; that same power which repealed the slave code, would make all necessary provisions to prevent pauperism, and to secure the general welfare. The entire resources of the country would be at the disposal of Congress; and, at any moment, it could bury the emancipated negroes of the District, under an avalanche of cannon balls.

A member of your Committee, Mr. Chairman, has asked me to answer the inquiry, whether the negroes of the District would be as well off when free, as they now are while slaves.

Mark, sir, the kind of abolition for which I contend: to wit, the restoration to the slave of personal ownership, and the protection of law. Then the inquiry resolves itself into this,—whether the slaves would be as well off to be men, as God made them, as to be things, as He did not make them. In a word, whether it will conduce to the happiness of the world, to regard things and beings just as they are, or just as they are not. Men better off without compensation for their labor than with? Then repeal your laws for the protection of private property, and the collection of debts. Men better off without legal protection than with? Then burn your statute books, abolish your judiciary, and raze your legislative halls to their foundation, and cry havoc, and let slip theft and robbery, assault and murder. Men happier without the ownership of their own minds than with? Happier that their wills should be under the absolute control of another, than that they should control them themselves? Impossible: for it is equivalent to saying, that a man is better pleased to do as another pleases, than to do as he himself pleases.

But, sir, with all respect for the honorable member, his inquiry assumes what I totally deny:—to wit, that a Slave can be well off. He may be fed well, may be clothed well, not severely whipped, not over worked. But this is regarding man as a mere *animal*. *Horses* may be fed well, covered well, not over whipped, nor worked; and may be *held and used as chattels*; and not contravene any law of their nature. But man has a nobler nature. His spirit soars upward. He was created "a little lower than the angels, and crowned with glory and honor, and *set over the works of God's hands.*" Is it treating such a being well, to take him from this high station, in close fellowship with angels, and tarnish his glory and his honor, by transforming him into merchandise, and driving him or leading him like a brute, and selling him in the shambles to the highest bidder? Said the immortal Henry, "Give me liberty, or give me death!" and this nation responds to the sentiment a loud Amen! Is it good treatment to inflict on men that which is worse than murder? There is more in slavery than the deprivation of bread, and the infliction of stripes. Its plough-share of ruin goes over the soul. Hence, slavery is the mother of degradation. Said an emancipated slave to me in the city of Cincinnati, Ohio, "I had rather be a freeman, and live under the cruel laws of Ohio, and beg my bread from door to door, and go down to the Ohio river to drink, than to be a slave in Virginia, where I could not own myself, and where I heard the cries of my poor perishing brethren." As you love freedom, listen to a slave! Show me the man who now eats plain and scanty food, wears coarse clothing, and works hard and long, who would exchange such a life, for one of luxury, splendid dress, and fashionable ease, on the condition that he was to be the absolute and perpetual property of another, to all intents, constructions and purposes whatsoever. I would like to look that man in the face! Better off in slavery? We ask Congress to give them impartial justice. This, Congress can do, and is bound to do. And this, I am sure, would be better than abject slavery.

I have no time to glance at facts. Read the entire history of emancipation; and this fact challenges contradiction, viz. that the condition of the emancipated negro, physically, pecuniarily, socially, intellectually, morally, is decidedly superior to his condition while a slave. St. Domingo and the British West Indies, settle this beyond dispute.

2. I assert that Congress ought immediately to abolish slavery in the District of Columbia, because it is the Capital of this Republic; is the seat of our National Legislature, and of the Supreme Court: the public offices, the public records, and the public archives are there; and [*now sir, for the inference,*] the existence of slavery there, is totally incompatible with that freedom of locomotion, of speech, of the press, and of debate, which are

necessary to transact the public business of the nation. It is needless to say, that every citizen should be able in safety to visit the Capital of the Republic, whatever may be his opinion on any subject. But, while slavery exists there, this is impossible.

*   *   *

Sir, it is a delusion to think that "abolitionists" only are excluded from the Capital of your Nation. It is doctrines which are outlawed there. And such doctrines! You, sir, could not visit the seat of our Federal Government in safety, if you dared to utter the noble sentiments in your Bill of Rights. The eloquent Channing has been denounced on the floor of Congress, this winter, as the vilest of incendiaries, and I would not insure his life there a day. The Genius of Slavery will not tolerate the sentiment, that "man should not be held as property." It presides at the Capital. Its altars are there. Its bloody decree has gone forth, "WORSHIP OR DIE"! Hundreds of thousands in this Nation, are outlawed at its own Capital, for holding and uttering the self-evident principles, on which its Constitution is founded, and in defence of which, Bunker's mount smoked with blood.

In our National Legislature, freedom of speech is struck dumb, by the omnipotence of slavery; and its members are overawed in debate, and cannot give utterance to their thoughts without hazarding their lives. The Genius of Despotism presides over the public councils. Witness the threat to assassinate JOHN QUINCY ADAMS last winter, because he dared to vindicate the right of petition. Slavery is indeed an inexorable Moloch, when it will not spare the venerable sage of Quincy. Read the following audacious threat, by Waddy Thompson, of South Carolina, uttered on the floor of the House, during the present month. Mr. Adams had presented petitions, relating to slavery, and had propounded a question to the Speaker, about a certain petition. Concerning him, Mr. Thompson says,

"Does that gentleman know that there are laws in all the slave States, and here, for the punishment of those who excite insurrection? I can tell him that there are such things as grand juries; and if, sir, the juries of this District have, as I doubt not they have, proper intelligence and spirit, he may yet be made amenable to another tribunal, and we may yet see an incendiary brought to condign punishment."

The French Convention, during the reign of Terror, when the streets of Paris ran with blood, legislated at the point of the assassin's steel. Said a member, as he arose to address the President, "the eyes of assassins flash upon us from those windows, and the gleam of their daggers is seen within these walls." At this period, France was in name a Republic, in reality a

Despotism. The American Congress is now the theatre, on which is re-acted the tragic scenes of the French Convention. I will read an extract of a private letter from Hon. John Quincy Adams, to a friend in this State, dated Washington, 26th January, 1837. Says Mr. Adams, "My effort here has been, to sustain the right of petition in the citizen, and the freedom of speech in this House, and the freedom of the press, and of thought, out of it. My freedom of speech in the House has been, and is, suppressed. The vindication of the rights of the people must ultimately rest upon themselves." And, sir, to the vindication they will generously and promptly come; and their rulers must yield to the pressure of the public tide, or be overwhelmed.

The war has but just begun. Of these trials, sir, we have yet scarcely touched the border ground. Abolitionists may yet be Members of Congress. And, an unparalleled change of the public sentiment in their favor, shows that they soon will be. For THE PEOPLE will be abolitionists; and that they will elect men, who will faithfully represent them in Congress, I cannot doubt. Such Members will be among the proscribed; and will be Lynched, as was Dresser, or be arrested as was Crandall, for opinion's sake. And is Washington the spot for the Supreme Legislature of a free people? Shall our Representatives deliberate with threats of indictment in their ears, and gags in their mouths, and cords around their necks, and the assassin's steel at their backs? Slavery must fall there, or to this complexion it will come at last.

Judges of the Supreme Court, in expounding the rights of man, may yet be arraigned as incendiaries: or, perhaps, in their turn, stand as criminals at the bar of Judge Lynch's Court. The Charge of His Honor Judge Story, to the Grand Jury of Portsmouth, N.H., in 1820, in which he denounced slavery and the slave trade, has been indicted in this modern Court for the Correction of Errors. Lawyers, suspected of aversion to the "Patriarchal Institution," in their attendance upon the Supreme Court, may be put to death, without benefit of clergy. Daniel Webster with his Plymouth Speech in his pocket "may yet see an incendiary brought to condign punishment." You, yourself, sir, if you shall dare to report on our petitions, in accordance with the cherished principles and policy of Massachusetts will be outlawed at our Capital. How humiliating are such disclosures to an American heart. I again press the point; is this city of charters and chains, of gags and grand juries, of constitutions and kidnappers, the spot where the national business should be transacted, and the national honor dwell?

The remedy for these evils is obvious. *Abolish Slavery in the District.* Remove the cause, and the effect ceases. A wise Providence has so ordered, that perfect freedom and absolute slavery cannot, for a long time, co-exist on the same soil. The mighty throes, which now toss the body politic of this nation, are the strugglings of these opposite principles for the mastery. Freedom and Slavery! Sir, they are eternal antagonisms. They have no affinities, and will not be at peace with each other. Rather let us attempt to mingle light and shade, heat and cold, sickness and health, right and wrong, heaven and hell, than hope that freedom of speech, of debate, and the press, can dwell in the District of Columbia, or in this nation, while slavery is tolerated. Slavery is darkness, and free discussion is light. They cannot commingle. Freedom of speech and of the press are now pouring a blaze of light from every part of the civilized world, upon the darkness of slavery. They are disclosing to view its haggard deformity; and smiting with fear and trembling the consciences of its abettors. Sir, its throne would stand more securely on the heaving crater of a volcano, than on the waves of free discussion. To perpetuate slavery, the conscience of the master must be buried. Free discussion sounds the blast of resurrection over its grave, and with the authority of God, bids it "come forth!" Freedom of debate, on the floor of Congress, and a free press in the District, would win over the conscientious slaveholder, and thus, the ranks being broken, an invincible array of truth would march into the very centre of the enemy's camp. Every converted slaveholder is a deserter, carrying strength and invaluable knowledge, over to the cause of freedom. His defection destroys the union of the opposing forces, and dispels the charm of invincibility, which hovers around their standard. Says Gen. Duff Green, (an acute observer,) "We have most to fear from the effect of organized action upon the consciences and fears of the slaveholders themselves; from the insinuation of these dangerous heresies [the equality of man, and the inalienability of human rights], into our schools, our pulpits, and our domestic circles." Precious confession! And so, lest the truth should reach the consciences of slaveholders, at the Capital, and rouse their fears, they have offered up freedom of thought, of speech, and of the press, in Congress and out of Congress, on the altar of slavery. Says Mr. Pinckney in his celebrated Report, the District was ceded to the United States, "that there might be a seat for the Federal Government, where the power of self-protection would be ample and complete." Is the self-protection of Congress ample and complete, while its Members are compelled to say, "my freedom of speech in the House has been, and is, suppressed"? So too, of all other departments of the Federal Government. Then, let slavery there be abolished. And can it be that Congress has no right to do so, and thus render its own self-protection, and that of the other branches of the Government, ample and complete, when that, according to Mr. Pinckney, was the very object of the cession?

3. Slavery should be immediately abolished at the seat of Federal Government, because it is dangerous to the security of the national property,—the public buildings, stores and archives,—and also, to the lives of the Members of Congress, to the liberties of the nation, and the perpetuity of our free institutions.

The slaves of that District have every natural inducement to be the deadly foes of this government. Holy writ informs us, that "oppression maketh man mad";—and the history of revolutions, written in blood, confirms its truth. On the annual return of our "nation's jubilee," the entire American people, in solemn assembly, declare that "all men are created equal," and pointing to the graves of their fathers, swear by their ashes, that "resistance to tyrants is obedience to God." Our forts and our navies echo it back in articulate thunder. We laud the valor of the men of the Revolution, because for a trivial tax on tea and paper, unjustly imposed, they bared their bosoms to the shafts of battle, choosing rather to die instantly as freemen, than to live as slaves. But, is a tax on tea to be compared in atrocity with a tax on heart and sinew, body and soul;—an impost, which clutches the man himself, and drowns his entire being in the vortex of its rapacity? If you will not hear me, listen to Thomas Jefferson.

> What an incomprehensible machine is man! who can endure toil, famine, stripes, imprisonment, and death itself, in vindication of his own liberty, and the next moment be deaf to all those motives, whose power supported him through his trial, and inflict on his fellow-man a bondage, one hour of which is fraught with more misery than ages of that which he rose in rebellion to oppose.

And who whelms the slaves at our Capital in this tide of "misery"? THE NATIONAL LEGISLATURE. Its laws forge the chains, and rivet the manacles. And can the slave love such institutions, and such a country. Listen again to Jefferson.

"With what execration should the statesman be loaded, who, permitting one half of the citizens to trample on the rights of the other, transforms those into despots, and these into enemies; destroys the morals of one part, and the *amor patriae* of the other."

Ay, sir, slavery destroys the *"amor patriae"* of its victims. Who will rebuke the slave of the District, if he reason thus: "What is this Capitol to me? There the scourges are twisted that lacerate my back. There the laws are framed which make me a brute. What are these records and documents to me? They are the sources, whence my oppressor derives his arbitrary power. What to me are these arsenals and navies? Not for the protection of my wife and children, my property and life;—but to intimidate me to submission. I'll plot (not *treason*, for I have no country) but rapine and flames, and thus glut my vengeance." And, to the members of Congress he might say, "'On me you inflict a bondage, one hour of which is fraught with more misery than ages of that, which you rose in rebellion to oppose.' 'Resistance to tyrants is obedience to God.' 'Give me liberty, or give me death.' 'I'll perish in the last ditch in defence of my rights.' Then to the onslaught!" Remember, sir, that I, in common with all abolitionists, counsel the slave to peace and to submission. We deny his right to fight even for liberty, and nothing would grieve us more, than to see a drop of the slaveholders' blood shed. *We* are not the incendiaries. But your revolutionary monuments, your fourth of July orations, your patriotic odes, your military parades; *they* are incentives to insurrection. Southern members of Congress say, they dread insurrection because of the agitation of this question. If sincere, *they* certainly have need to dread it in the District of Columbia.

* * *

The continuance of slavery there and elsewhere, endangers the perpetuity of our Republic, because it provokes the judgments of God. Certainly, Mr. Chairman, this consideration will not be lost upon the Legislators of a professedly Christian State. Domestic tyranny is the fatal shoal upon which many a proud State of antiquity has laid its bones. The fragments of Greece and Rome, magnificent in their ruins, should warn us from following in their fatal track. The American nation is intoxicated with the delusion, that her liberties are impregnable. That there is, in the structure of her government, some perennial conservative, by which she will rise elastic and invigorated from assaults without and commotions within. An inflated patriotism utters the delusive words, *Esto perpetua!* An indomitable ambition echoes them back, *Esto perpetua!* An ineffable self-complacency, which has dethroned reason, mistakes the echo for the voice of God. And, like the victim of consumption, hope is strongest in the hour of dissolution! Fatal charm! True, the voice of God is heard: but it is startling denunciation. Look over our country, and see it tossing on the wild waves of civil commotion. Look into our national counsels, and see them rent by civil feuds. The humble Christian, who reads his Bible, and communes with his God, knows the cause. For it, he looks beyond Tariffs, and Banks, and the rivalry of parties. He sees that this nation has forgotten God. That she has grown rich upon His mercies, and then, in her pride, has trodden the Indian and the Negro, whose condition entitled them to her generous protection, under the hoof of her ambition. During her mad career of folly and crime, God's eye has been upon her, and His ear open to the cry of the perishing. The alternative of Jefferson is now presented to her. Let her choose. Says the sage of Monticello, speaking of the slaves.

> When the measure of their tears shall be full,—when their groans shall have involved heaven itself in darkness,—doubtless a God of justice will awaken in their distress, and by diffusing light and liberality among their oppressors, or at length, by his exterminating thunder, manifest his attention to the things of this world, and that they are not left to the guidance of a blind fatality.

But a greater than Jefferson has left us the record of nations overthrown by the "exterminating thunder" of Jehovah, for the sin of oppression. Where now is Tyre—the city of the sea—which *traded the persons of men,* and vessels of brass in her market"?—Desolate,—destroyed!—the ploughshare of ruin, driven to the beam amidst her foundations, by the hand of God! What was the fate of slaveholding Egypt?—God visited her in judgment. Her first-born perished at a blow. Death was in all the dwellings of her princes. But the Hebrews sprinkled the blood of a slaughtered beast upon their doorposts, and the Angel of the Pestilence passed over them, and they escaped. Let, then, the free states of this Union, if they would escape the coming storm of Divine displeasure, sprinkle the blood of slavery on the door posts of our Capitol. So shall the Avenger pass over them and spare them, when He comes with His "exterminating thunder!"

Listen again to the author of the Declaration of Independence.

> And can the liberties of the nation be thought secure, when we have refused the only firm basis, a conviction in the minds of the people that these liberties are the gift of God? That they are not to be violated but with his wrath. Indeed, I tremble for my country, when I reflect that God is just; that his justice cannot sleep forever; that a revolution in the wheel of fortune, an exchange of situation is among possible events; and that it may become probable by a supernatural interference. The Almighty has no attribute which can take sides with us in such a contest.

Will not political men listen to prophecies like these? It is not necessary that heaven should empty the reservoir of its wrath upon this nation, as it did upon Egypt. The materials of our ruin are ample within us, and around us. The Indian, the Negro, the Mexican, the Haitian, all have a fearful account to adjust with us. And, if our internal commotions increase in ferocity for a few coming years in the ratio of the past, we are a people dissevered, with no bond of union, and our fall will add another to the list of nations, ruined by their abuse of the mercies, and their contempt of the precepts of Jehovah.

4. It is expedient that slavery at the Capital should be abolished, because its toleration brings into contempt our nation's boasted love of equal rights, justly exposes us to the charge of hypocrisy, paralyzes the power of our free principles, and cripples our moral efforts for the overthrow of oppression throughout the world.

The citizens of this nation have deep responsibilities, as republicans, as Christians, as citizens of the world. Our character and reputation are moral capital, loaned us by God, to be invested for the political and moral renovation of the human race. The Reformers of South America and Europe, have anxiously looked to us as the pioneer nation in the cause of human liberty, and hoped that our experiment would demonstrate even to tyrants, that man is capable of self-government. But, by cherishing in the heart of the republic such a system of cool-blooded oppression, as the sun has rarely seen, we have rolled back the tide of reform in other nations, and cut the sinews of struggling humanity. The enemies of free principles in England point to our slavery, to our Lynch code, and our mob conservation, to prove, that Republics are the worst of Despotisms. Sir Robert Peel, the leader of the Conservatives in Great Britain, laughs us to scorn at the public dinners of the aristocracy, and cheered on by our hypocrisy, rides rough shod over the plebian reformers.

* * *

But upon us, as *northern men*, this point bears with peculiar pressure. The free States have the power to abolish slavery in the District. So long as we refuse to do it, with what face can we declare to our southern fellow-citizens, that we are opposed to slavery? Go there, sir, and reprove the slave-holder, and urge upon his the duty of emancipation. He will meet you with the scorching rebuke, "Go back to your free States, and abolish your own slavery in the District of Columbia. Look to your own State Legislature at home, which dares not declare, that Congress ought to abolish the slavery in which your own Commonwealth is implicated. You opposed to slavery? Then pluck the beam from your own eye." Sir, would not your tongue cleave to the roof of your mouth? Would you tell him, you were a member of the very Legislature, which denied the prayer of these memorialists? Ay, more! Should he know from your lips, that you were the chairman of the very committee, who reported against the prayer? Would fire burn this disclosure out of you? Excuse these personalities sir, for I plead for those who cannot plead for themselves;—for those who have, by the highest legislative body in the Union, been denied the poor privilege of petitioning for mercy.

The north must abolish slavery in the District, or her moral power for the removal of slavery in the nation, is at an end.

5. This object should be accomplished without delay, so that Congress may speedily and effectually undo the wretched work of the last session. The report of the Hon. Mr. Pinckney, adopted last May, attempts to prove, that Congress ought not to *interfere, in any way,* with slavery in the District, because, it would be unwise, impolitic, a violation of the public faith, (tantamount to a violation of the Constitution,) and dangerous to the Union; and, in addition to this, *it contains a thorough defence of slavery on principle, as a wise and benevolent institution!* These doctrines were sanctioned by a body, a large majority of whose members are from the free States, and by it, were sent out to the world, as the voice of America. As a citizen of the free States, as an American, as a man, I repudiate, I abjure, I abhor them. They are not the sentiments of the free States, but a foul libel upon our freedom and our religion. The memorialists demand, that the Representatives from the free States wipe out this blot; and atone for the outrage, by destroying the system, thus made the occasion of libelling both man and God. Where is the voice of this Commonwealth, when such doctrines are promulgated to the world, by the suffrages of New England? Is this the padlock on our lips?

6. Slavery in the District should be destroyed, because it is made the occasion of denying the sacred right of petition. The gentleman, who preceded me, has dwelt at large on this point. But, I cannot pass it over in silence. The right of petition is the last, which a people, determined to be free, should ever surrender, or permit to be abridged. It is the barrier against the aggressions of the governors upon the governed;—the shield, by which the minority ward off the assaults of the majority. This government was established to protect the minority. The unabridged right of petition is the corner stone of the edifice. The resolution passed by the House of Representatives on the 18th ultimo, is a fearful abridgment of this right. It is the *precedent* established by that resolution, which I most dread. We are a precedent-loving, a precedent-fearing nation. Our Courts of Justice, and our Legislative Halls, are the slaves of precedent. They worship their own folly, merely because it is their own folly. The people bow to the same inexorable deity. *Precedent,*—precedent, is the order of the day; the divinity of the hour. Congress has, for certain causes, denied to the people the right of petition, in regard to slavery. The precedent is established. Tomorrow, for certain causes, she denies it in regard to the currency. The precedent is strengthened. The next day, for the same cause, she refuses to receive petitions concerning the Tariff. The precedent, gathering courage, demands fresh

victims. Petitions concerning Commerce, Intemperance, Indian treaties, Secret societies and Mobs, are next offered on the altar. The Idol becomes more rapacious. He demands that all petitions should be thrown back into the faces of the petitioners. The people, tamed into subserviency by yielding, without resistance, to reiterated aggressions, meekly bow the neck, and kiss the yoke. Mr. Chairman, the present crisis thunders in our ears, *Obsta Principiis!* Oppose Beginnings! To launch forth in this stream of precedent, is ruin. The cataract is just below us. Let us stand on terra firma. Slight aggressions by Buonaparte, unresisted by the French people, encouraged to mightier strides in the road to arbitrary power. Step by step, he reached the summit of despotism, with willing slaves shouting their approving hosannahs at his heels.—*Obsta Principiis!* At the last session, the House of Representatives took the first step. It cautiously surveyed the whole ground, before it set down its foot. The present session, the precedent having been established, it took the second step with alarming promptitude. Let us prevent the third. How? By abolishing slavery in the District, now made the pretext for trifling with, trampling upon, the inestimable right of petition.

Beriah Green

Beriah Green, who spent most of his days as an active abolitionist in Whitesboro, New York, was born in Connecticut and raised in Vermont. He was the oldest of six children, and he developed both a keen mind and a genuine respect for physical labor. His life was a deliberate combination of the twin uses of mind and body, for while he became an intellectual, a teacher, scholar, minister, orator, and writer, he continued to use his hands for menial work, and he always had a strong feeling for the practical implementation of his convictions.

Green was valedictorian at Middlebury College when he was twenty-four. He went on to Andover Seminary to prepare for the ministry, but his poor eyesight and poor health forced him to finish his studies pretty much on his own. Later, however, he was ordained a Congregational minister. His ill health seemed to vanish through the years; he survived a first wife, married another, begat ten children, and died in his eightieth year (after twenty-five years of retirement) while speaking in Whitesboro's Town Hall against the local liquor traffic—a reformer to the end.

For about six years after he was ordained, Green preached in Long Island and Vermont, and then he was invited to take over the Chair of

Sacred Literature at Western Reserve College in Hudson, Ohio. Green had brooded for years about the un-Christian aspects of slavery. Further reading of Garrison's tracts and discussions with other faculty members, Elizur Wright and President Storrs, had solidified his thoughts and rekindled his interest in abolition. At this same time, Theodore Weld visited Western Reserve as an agent for the manual labor schools. Who influenced whom is debatable, but the results are history; from late 1832, both Green and Weld became staunch antislavery proponents. On four consecutive Sundays in the latter part of 1832, Beriah Green delivered sermons in the chapel that were clearly abolitionist. He began to attract attention not only in Ohio but in the East, so much so that in 1833 he was made president of the convention in Philadelphia which created the American Anti-Slavery Society.

In 1833 Green left Ohio and became preseident of the Oneida Institute in Whitesboro; the school was run on the principle of both intellectual and manual training. Green's interest in Oneida was no doubt influenced by the fact that Theodore Weld had attended Oneida. Also, Oneida Institute welcomed students of all races and nationalities. Beriah Green meant to convert all mankind to Christianity. He believed, further, that Christian scholars should learn to get their hands dirty alongside those whom they must labor to convert. He believed firmly that clean, pudgy scholars were repugnant to the great mass of fine, ordinary mankind. Green was a doer.

Unfortunately, financial problems forced the closing of the Oneida Institute in 1843. Fortunately for Green, the Whitesboro Presbyterian church had split on the question of slavery, and in 1847 he became the minister of the abolitionist "wing," which called itself the Congregational Church. He remained there until his retirement in 1867.

Throughout his various careers, Beriah Green was intensely upset by any injustices in any society brought about by prejudice, selfishness, and ignorance. He spoke of the American Indians in much the same terms he did the Afro-Americans; in one of his own books he noted and deplored two incidents where qualified and able black students were denied the right to study at two colleges of their choice.

At the same time that Green lauded the judgment and power of those who were benevolent of heart, he berated selfishness and the lack of true judgment of those who judged another on false grounds. In his words,

The arrangements of human society are artificial. Birth, complexion, place, a thousand things which have nothing to do with constitutional character or moral worth, have had a controlling influence on public sentiment. Prejudices as rank as dung hill weeds have been allowed to spring up and grow. Men have been courted or shunned, loved or hated, caressed or scorned, irrespective of their good or ill desert.

born March, 1795, Preston, Conn.
died May, 1874, Whitesboro, N. Y.

Things
for Northern Men
to Do

> Thus saith the Lord of Hosts, the God of Israel; Amend your ways and your doings, and I will cause you to dwell in this place. Trust ye not in lying words, saying, The temple of the Lord, the temple of the Lord, the temple of the Lord are these. For if ye thoroughly amend your ways and your doings, if you thoroughly execute judgment between a man and his neighbor; if ye oppress not the stranger, the fatherless, and the widow, and shed not innocent blood in this place, neither walk after other gods to your hurt; then will I cause you to dwell in this place, in the land that I gave to your fathers, for ever and ever. *Jeremiah* vii, 3–7.

The general sentiment among the Hebrews, with which Jeremiah had almost alone to contend, is clearly indicated by a shocking assertion, which they were wont to throw into the face of Jehovah. Crimes of all sorts and sizes they were in the habit of committing; and then, reeking with corruption and red with blood, of coming and standing before God in his temple, to insult Him with the declaration, that they *"were delivered to do all such abominations."* Things had taken such a shape and posture, that they could do no better than to violate the most sacred relations, and break the strongest ties which bound them to heaven and earth. They were connected with a system of abominations which they could not dissolve, and from which they could not break away. With the different parts of this system, the fibres of society had been intertwisted. It was supported by confirmed usages and venerated institutions. What hazards must they not encounter, what risks must they not run, in opposing the sentiment which generally prevailed around them! They thought it better to go with the multitude *to do evil,* than incur popular odium in resisting it. They could not keep their character and retain their influence, without taking a share in popular iniquity. Their wickedness was a matter of necessity. Still they could not refuse to see that it was driving their country to fearful extremities. Ruin stared them in the face. What could they do? On the one hand, driven by such strong necessities to sin; and on the other, exposed to such exterminating judgments for their iniquities!

Just here the prophet met them. The difficulties in which they were involved, and the dangers to which they were exposed, they owed to themselves. And if they stoutly persevered in the crooked ways they had so rashly trodden, they were undone. Nothing would then save them from the dishonored graves, which their own hands had been so long employed in digging. Yet they need not perish. If they would avoid presumption, they might escape despair. They might not charge the blame of their iniquities on God. They might not allege, that "they were delivered to do the abominations" they were guilty of. So long as they did so, their repentance and salvation were impossible. The work, which demanded their attention, lay directly before them. This done, and all their perplexities, and difficulties, and embarrassments would instantly vanish. This done, destruction, with its open jaws now ready to devour them, would at once flee away. This done, and benignant heaven would pour upon them the choicest, most enduring benefits.

How often, when the sin of slavery has been urged on the consciences of our fellow-citizens, have our ears been pained with inquiries such as these;—Why trouble us with your impertinence? what is American slavery to us? we will do nothing to give it countenance—we can do nothing to hasten its abolition. In all its bearings, it is a matter belonging wholly to the South. Let southern wisdom and benevolence dispose of it. Why should *we* interfere? Have we not enough of business, appropriately our own, to engross our thoughts and occupy our powers? And if we should attempt something, what could we do to relieve our country of this heavy burden? It has so incorporated itself with all our institutions, that its removal must break up the very foundations of our republic. Things have grown into such a state, that slavery, whatever it may be, and whatever it may do, must, so far as our exertions are concerned, be let alone.

But is it so? Has the North nothing to do with a system of oppression, under which more than two millions of our countrymen are crushed? What! has the North done nothing for the establishment;—is the North now doing nothing for the protection and support of this horrid system? Nothing, in the civil compact she was so active in forming—which she is so anxious to maintain? Nothing, in lending her assistance to protect the traffic in human souls and bodies in the District of Columbia? Nothing, in those arrangements, by which she throws back the fugitive to the whip of his tormentor? Nothing, in consenting to the multiplied wrongs which are heaped upon colored freemen? Nothing, in cherishing against them a most insane and malignant prejudice? Nothing, in so closing her eyes, and ears, and lips to the claims of her helpless, outraged brethren? Nothing, in trying in such various ways to discourage the friends of human nature among us from opening their lips for the dumb? In silently permitting or loudly encouraging the rabble, made up of ignorant, thoughtless, wretched creatures, who know not, and care not, what they do, to wage open war upon them? Nothing, in giving up her own children to the mad-dog violence of southern tyranny, to be insulted, scourged, murdered? Has the North nothing to do with a system of oppression, which is corrupting the morals, and wasting the strength, and blasting the character, of the nation? Nothing to do with a system which is poisoning the heart of the church, and eating up the vitals of the republic? Yes, verily. The North has much to do with American slavery. It has deeply involved her in guilt. It is exposing her, every day, and at a thousand points, to the most mortifying insults, and to the deadliest injuries. In what dreams do we indulge? Can the South be rent with earthquakes, scathed with thunderbolts for crimes, *clearly national*, while the North looks on with the airs of an unconcerned spectator? No, no. If the ship, to change the figure, strikes on the rocks, which "dead ahead" lift up their horrid forms, must we not go down together—swallowed up by the same waves?

But what can *we do?* exclaim a thousand northern voices. I answer, you can,

I. *Thoroughly examine and freely discuss the whole subject of American slavery.* That the subject is one of the first *importance*, every one is ready to admit. Its bearings on the interests of both bond and free are direct and vital. It deeply affects the character, condition, and prospects of the *master*. It exposes him to reproach and infamy. It frets away the ties of domestic life. It subjects his children to temptations, greatly hazardous to their virtue, usefulness, and peace. It is a moth, silently eating up his worldly substance. It involves him in guilt. It opens the way to his inmost spirit for keen remorse and killing fears. It feeds his lusts and inflames his passions. It nourishes within him a spiteful opposition to inquiry, admonition, faithful warning. It works him into a fiery, petty despot. It arms his will against his reason. It exposes him to the withering displeasure of righteous heaven. To the slave, it is the scythe of death; to his head, heart, estate, it is destruction. It sternly and stoutly refuses to *let him be a man*. No other race of beings in heaven, or on earth, can be found with which he may be classed. Of course, it virtually drives him headlong from the universe. Without an inch of ground where he may place his feet, he finds himself friendless and desolate—an outcast amidst his father's family. What dreadful thoughts, then, may not slavery be expected to nourish in his bosom! What desperate deeds may it not nerve his hands to work! This is slavery in its influence upon the growing population of this republic. This is the malignant fiend, which is continually stalking through our land, "breathing out threatenings and slaughter," and "scattering" everywhere and every day "firebrands, arrows, and death." If it is not driven back to hell, it will at no distant day turn this garden of the world into a "place of skulls!"

Can any thing, then, exceed the *importance* of the subject of slavery? It is important, vitally so, to every man, woman, and child in our republic. No matter what may be his color, character, or standing, to him it is important. As it has a powerful bearing on every department of life, to every department of life it is important.

American slavery is, moreover, admitted to be a subject difficult to dispose of. This is the testimony of grave divines and profound statesmen; of shrewd politicians and acute philosophers. It is the complaint of the inexperienced and unlettered. Go where you will, and urge on whom you may the evils of slavery, and how generally will you not be reminded, that you have touched upon a delicate and difficult subject! Slavery is almost universally admitted to be wrong and hurtful; but the wisest heads and the best hearts among us, we are told, are sadly puzzled with the problem, how can we get rid of what has well nigh identified itself with our very existence. Will not the nation bleed "to death," if the cancer is extracted?

Here, then, we have a matter to dispose of as difficult as it is important. The monster, fattening on the blood of our countrymen, has already acquired the size and strength of a giant. Every hour adds something to its ferocity and greediness. If let alone, it will swallow up the nation. Something must be done. But what? That is the question. How shall we obtain the right answer? By shutting up our eyes? and closing our ears? and holding our tongues? By refusing to read? to reflect? to inquire? to discuss? Is this the way to escape from such perplexities and embarrassments? No. If we sit still, we must die. Where great difficulties are to be encountered, and formidable obstacles to be removed, it is our wisdom and our duty to summon and employ the collected powers of the nation. Every body should be encouraged to read, and think, and inquire, and discuss; and all in good earnest. The whole mass of mind among us should be aroused. Let all who will, present their expedients, propose their plans, bring forward their methods. Every thing should be thoroughly scrutinized, with the fixed determination of making "full proof" of the best methods. Thus, in any other case where we had so much at stake, we should be sure to conduct. Is this the course, my brethren, which you have recommended and pursued? Have you opened your eyes on the various bearings and tendencies of American slavery? Have you diligently collected facts, and thoroughly examined them, and done your best, with skill and judgment, to arrange them, and made them the occasion of laying hold on great elemental principles, in the light of which you might shape your plans and expend your powers? Have you studied the recorded experience of philanthropists abroad, especially in Great Britain? And have you made yourselves familiar with the history of emancipation, wherever the enslaved have been enfranchised? And have you done all this in good faith and sober earnest? resolved to turn every thing to the highest practical account? If not, is it well for you to ask, what can the North attempt for the abolition of American slavery? And so to put this question, as if nothing could be done?

II. *You can regard the enslaved as the children of our common Father, Saviour, and Sanctifier.* Thus regarding them, you cannot help presenting them at the throne of His grace. With what unwearied importunity will you not pour out prayers, that the Former of their bodies and the Father of their spirits would graciously look upon the wrongs, which they can neither endure nor escape. As their wise and merciful Creator, you will entreat Him to open His eyes upon His own image, on His handiwork, now marred, broken, trampled in the dust. As their Redeemer, you will beseech Him to behold the purchase of His blood, thrown away as mere refuse amidst worthless rubbish. As their Sanctifier, you will entreat Him to pity those, who are entitled to His heavenly gifts, who are driven as if they were cattle from His gracious presence....

We are able to act worthy of the bonds which tie us to the slave, and identify our interests with his. He is our brother by nature. "God hath made of one blood" the bond and the free. We may own, and cherish, and honor, the dear and strong links which bind us indissolubly together. If we will open our eyes, we cannot help seeing, that *as citizens of this republic,* our interests are identified with the interests of the enslaved. We may refuse to study their condition and relations. The laws, "written in blood," which protect, not *their* persons and interests, but their *heartless tyrants* in insulting and destroying them, we may refuse to read. We may close our eyes to the history of their wrongs, of their unrequited labors, and unavenged injuries. From a pretended regard to the union, which binds us to their oppressors, we may thus stand aloof from our bleeding brothers; may give them up without remonstrance or inquiry to the "tender mercies of the cruel." But we ought to know what we may easily and certainly perceive, that the interests of the slave are identified with ours. To leave him to perish is to cut our own throats! American slavery makes the creatures who support it, more and more eager, insolent, and outrageous in their claims on all around them for homage and subserviency. These petty tyrants are by no means satisfied with domineering over the helpless slave. Their despotic spirit overleaps the limits of their plantations. It lifts its head among the freemen of the North, threatening to strangle in its snaky folds every one who may dare to resist its claims or oppose its progress. Can we stand by in safety and see it crush and swallow our enslaved brethren? Surely not. The fangs which are now dripping in their blood, must ere long be fastened in our shrinking flesh. Have not slaveholders at the South clearly betrayed a disposition to invade the rights and trample on the interests of the freemen of the North? Have they not insulted us and threatened us? Have they not swung their fists in our faces, and brandished their daggers above our heads? Have they not goaded on their miserable creatures among us to acts of lawless violence;—acts, in which our persons have been rudely attacked, our reputation spitefully assailed— all our privileges as American citizens vilely set at nought? Have they not treated us as outlaws in our own country? And with more than savage fierceness—with the open-mouthed eagerness of insatiate blood-hounds—sought to imbrue their hands in the blood of "law-abiding," unoffending freemen? And can we mistake their spirit and designs? Why, they already treat us, as if we had sold our birth-right; as if we had been reduced to brute beasts; as if like goods and chattels we were good for nothing but to gratify the passions and subserve the interests of a bloated aristocracy! If we permit the spirit of tyranny among us to feed and fatten—to grow and thrive upon the blood of the slave, we are undone! I repeat it; nothing but the most wilful blindness can prevent every man of you from seeing that his interests are identified with those of the enslaved.

* * *

III. *The people of the North can avail themselves of the light, which the history of emancipation sheds upon the claims of the enslaved.* How many among us speak as if the subject of abolition had never been discussed and disposed of! They tremble at the thought of making what they regard as an untried experiment. As an abstract matter, they find no difficulty in seeing and saying, that the slave is robbed of inalienable rights; and that he is fairly entitled to the immediate enjoyment of those privileges, which have been wrested from him by remorseless tyranny. But they are afraid to act on abstract principles, though legibly written on the very foundations of their nature! Those first truths which are wrought into the very texture of their hearts; which they cannot deny without stifling the voice of reason, they dare not reduce to practice! Convictions inherent in the simplest elements of humanity, they hesitate to embody in their conduct! They loudly call for *facts*; as if it were possible, that these, whenever and wherever found, could be at variance with the principles of their own nature! And these, they imagine, have not yet occurred!

If such facts have occurred, why have they not been urged on the attention of the American community? Why have we, to so wide an extent, been left in ignorance of some of the most interesting and important events in the history of man? Let the conductors of our periodical presses give an answer. What defence can they set up of the mean and treacherous silence they have selfishly maintained, when they ought to have spoken in tones of thunder? Why have they not kept their readers familiar with the history of emancipation; especially as given in the records of the British Legislature? Were they afraid to let the light of truth shine upon us? Afraid of what? To see us give up our foolish prejudices and groundless fears? Afraid to assist us in escaping from the scorn and abhorrence of the civilized world, by ceasing to utter in defence of slavery, such silly words as would disgrace the lips of an idiot? No. These mercenary creatures were afraid that their subscription list would be reduced, if they should give offence to the chivalry of the South! Let them take home to their hearts the solemn warning, that the chivalry of the South will fail to protect them from the frown of insulted humanity! The hour of retribution is coming on apace. They have no time to lose. Let them make haste and repent.

But apologies for ignorance of the history of emancipation, we can no longer make. Light now shines around us. The stale and malignant slanders, by which the reputation of the enfranchised slaves of *St. Domingo* was long ago so eagerly assailed, we can no longer repeat with impunity. Nothing but stupid negligence or wilful blindness can now prevent our seeing that the sudden and universal abolition of slavery in that island involved in all its bearings the most substantial benefits. When the rubbish of ages had been removed, crushed humanity by its own inherent elasticity, assumed at once under God the erect posture and dignified port, which are everywhere its natural guise. Here are facts enough to encourage the most timid friend of man, to maintain in behalf of the enslaved the claims of naked rectitude. And these facts lie within your reach. Have you laid your hands upon them, and turned them to the highest practical account?

With the history of the exertions, which have opened the way for the abolition of slavery in the British West Indies, we ought to make ourselves familiar. And here, we cannot fail to see, *that the motives to philanthropic*

effort in England were far less powerful than among ourselves. The evils to
be removed and the dangers to be encountered were far less formidable. The
existence of Great Britain was not identified with the existence of the West
Indies. The latter might have sunk under the weight of crime to the bottom
of the ocean, without touching the vitals of the former. The dreadful tendencies of slavery were, moreover, developed at a great distance from the eyes
of the British public. The ocean lay between them and the monuments of
oppression. Their ears were not wounded by the clanking of chains. Their
eyes were not pained by the sight of fresh wounds. The groans, and tears,
and blood, which servitude wrung from its victims, they were not constrained
to witness. All, all its naked abominations, so well adapted to rouse and fire
the soul of the philanthropist, lay beyond the proper limits of their country.
The influence of the West India party in England was powerful. A vast
amount of capital was enlisted in support of slavery. Whatever intrigue,
sophistry, and bribery could effect, was attempted. Formidable obstacles were
thrown in the way of the friends of emancipation at every step of their
progress. Great expenses, moreover, were to be incurred by the nation in
carrying out their designs. The slave could not be enfranchised unless millions
of dollars were thrown away upon his oppressor. And this money was to be
drawn from a treasury already laden with debt!

And to whom, in such circumstances, was the cause of the enslaved
committed? To the rich, the great, the powerful? To those who stood at the
head of the nation, whose names, and places, and connexions would give to
their opinions the power of argument and the authority of law? Nay, to
whom was committed the law-making power; whose will could wither, and
blast, and destroy for ever the demon of oppression? Far otherwise. *Granville
Sharpe*, a private gentleman, without patronage and power, had the honor of
correcting and instructing the English courts where the claims of the slave
were to be disposed of. It was for *Thomas Clarkson* to inform the minds
of the first statesmen of his country respecting the deadly tendencies of the
slave-trade, and with "his excellent confederates, the Quakers," to rouse the
spirit of the nation to its enormities. It was for unpatronized citizens, and
unbeneficed clergymen to plead the cause of bleeding humanity; to bring
every feeling heart to sympathize with the "suffering and the dumb," and
every generous arm to exert itself for the outraged and down-trodden. Under
the impulse of disinterested compassion and unwearied love, thousands, men,
women, and children, standing midway between the top and the bottom of
society, strove in innumerable ways to break the yoke of servitude. They
tried every method, which approved wisdom and fervent benevolence could

devise. They made "full proof" of the power of moral suasion. They exhibited pictures, stated facts, urged arguments. They entreated, warned, rebuked. They summoned poetry, eloquence, philosophy; and these powerful allies came to their assistance. Petition after petition—earnest, decisive, pointed—they poured upon the ears and pressed upon the hearts of their rulers. They "held on their way," till a public sentiment was formed, which swept away the monuments of slavery.

The history of emancipation teaches us to ply the South with strong argumentation, earnest entreaty, pointed rebuke. The pretended friends and apologists of the South, have at different times and on various occasions, tried to dissuade us from attempting anything to convince the slave-holder of his guilt and danger, on the ground, that his known character must render all such attempts for ever fruitless. He has been likened to a "mad bull," who, if you should attempt to reason with him, would be sure to bellow and toss his horns! If we would escape being gored to death, we have been warned to keep our distance and hold our tongues! Before we had time to dispose of such owl-like warnings, we have been required to admire the republican spirit and generous chivalry of these citizen "mad bulls." Now it cannot be denied, that the South has given too much occasion for a description of character, so repulsive, disgusting, execrable. The facts, and arguments, and entreaties of the friends of human nature, her citizens have met with furious threatenings, bloody whips, and murderous halters! If they had been able to defend their peculiar institutions in a more manly way, doubtless they would have done so. But this frantic violence, which has turned the whole South in a stupendous bedlam, cannot last long. After a few spasmodic efforts to break the force of truth, milder moods will be assumed. She could do no less than second the kind efforts of her apologists at the North, who, with unparalleled meanness and savage atrocity undertook, as a "business transaction," or an electioneering trick, to put down the abolitionists. She has, therefore, lashed herself into fury, which must soon "burn out" by its own violence.

The slaveholder, while he retains a particle of human nature, must be accessible to moral suasion. If the system of oppression which he is so anxious to sustain, has placed him beyond the reach of this, it is murderous beyond the strongest charges of its most determined foes. But we have abundant evidence that he retains enough of the elements of humanity to feel the force of truth. He is not entirely dead to the light of reason, or the impulses of compassion, or the dictates of self-love. He cannot refuse to be wrought upon by the power of moral suasion. So far from this, that a glimpse of his own features, even when obscurely reflected on his eye, tor-

tures him. Listen to the confession of a distinguished Southern divine, recently made in the presence of a multitude of hearers; the confession, that
a piece of handkerchiefs, found in a box of goods from New York, threw
a whole community in the land of chivalry and of slaves, into rage and
trepidation! What ailed the handkerchiefs? Were they charged with the
infection of some deadly distemper? No such thing. They were marked by
pictures of Southern life!—pictures faintly exhibiting the condition of the
slaves! That was all! And yet our grave divine declared with apparent sympathy in the spirit he described, that if the man who had thus dared to
expose the South to the South, could have been caught by the South, he
would doubtless have been put to death! Can a people be regarded as dead
to moral suasion, who can thus be reached, and wrung, and convulsed by the
pictures printed on a sixpenny handkerchief! What might thus be inferred
from this and kindred facts, has been once and again acknowledged by supporters of American slavery, of high standing and great authority. These
men assure us that they have no fears of our exciting among them a servile
insurrection. Such a fear, they cannot but see and own, must be absurd and
ridiculous. They have other fears. If the friends of Human Freedom should
find access to the ears and hearts of those who live amidst the monuments
of slavery, they might even there raise up friends and coadjutors. Even there
the standard of immediate and universal emancipation might be erected, and
thousands eagerly flock around it. Thus Southern tyranny would be exposed
and denounced by Southern philanthropy! The oppressor cannot bear the
thought of having his own neighbors—his intimate acquaintances point at
him, as feasting on the unrequited labor of the helpless poor.

From how many statesmen at the South has not the confession been extorted—extorted by the remorse and fear which they could neither dissipate nor
conceal—that the infamy with which they were already branded by all the
philanthropists of Christendom, was fast becoming insupportable! The
plunder of our goods we do not dread, they exclaim; but what is more to
be deprecated, *the loss of character*. What can our goods be worth, while we
are constrained to bear the scorn and execration of the civilized world, as
a nest of pirates? So sensitive, and irritable, and apprehensive has the South
become, that she fears to admit a newspaper, pamphlet, nay, a page of fiction
into her presence, till assured they contain no exposure or reproof of her
favorite sin! She is trying to establish a censorship of the press so rigid and
extensive, as to exclude every ray of light from the knot of snakes she is
nestling in her bosom! Is this the people whom you say we cannot reach by
moral suasion? Who cannot be wrought upon by warning, expostulations,

and appeals? Who cannot be moved by admonition, or rebuke, or entreaty? How shallow and superficial must that thinker be, who, for a moment can admit such a supposition! And so we must not expect to awaken in the slaveholder a sense of his guilt and danger, because a single word of expostulation so annoys and distresses him! And because his inward pains make him rave and foam, we are to run away, disheartened and affrighted! How silly and how wicked that would be! Let him writhe and rave. Let him flout and foam; kick, and strike, and bite. He cannot escape from the fires which surround him. The sooner he spits out his venom and exhausts his fury the better. He must not be permitted to escape. He must not have a moment's respite. Wherever he may turn, truth's searching rays must be kept upon him. After rending and tearing him a little longer, the demon, which has so long had possession of him will retire, and leave him in his right mind to appropriate wholesome instruction. Every one of you, my hearers, might contribute something to hasten this result. What have you done?

Your hold, as an American citizen, upon the District of Columbia, you may turn to high account in the cause of human freedom.—Along with myriads of the friends of man, you can put your name to a petition to the national legislature for the abolition of slavery at the centre of the republic. Less than this you cannot do, without involving yourself, personally, in the guilt of slavery. Harbor not the thought for a moment, that such efforts must be useless. Useless they cannot be. Their various bearings cannot but be powerful and happy. It will *do you* good, good unspeakable, thus to "remember those who are in bonds." It will keep you alive to their condition, claims, and prospects. It will give you a deeper interest and greater power, at the throne of mercy. Never fear, moreover, that you will pour your petitions on deaf ears and palsied arms. Tyrants there may have "bound themselves by a great curse," that your voice shall not be heard. But these poor creatures are as weak as they are insolent. They cannot dispose of your petitions without attending directly or indirectly to your claims. Your petitions must be read. The facts you state; the arguments you employ; your earnest remonstrances, your strong appeals, your loud warnings, your fervent entreaties, will force their way into ears, which a thousand artifices may have been employed in vain to stop. And those ears will tingle. Tongues, which a thousand artifices had been employed in vain to tie, will be set in motion. Tyrants may roar, and stamp, and curse. But what then? Surely, the noise and tumult in which they may give vent to their windy rage, will but ill promote the cause of *silence*. By the very act of swearing that a word shall not be spoken, their own oath they violate! Their hot blood and rash tongues will drive them headlong into fiery debate. The discussion of the matter may be furious; but discussion will arise. The agitation of the subject may be fierce; but agitation cannot be avoided. Come it will, whoever may object. *Nay, nothing can more certainly and effectually introduce it than objections!* Urge your petitions, then. Let them fly by thousands on the wings of every breeze. Laden with the names of all who love their country, let them speak "the words of truth and soberness" to every trembling Felix who has a place in the national legislature.

And let me remind you, that every ray of light which is emitted from the *centre of the nation, will reach every point of the circumference.* Whatever facts are there presented, whatever discussions are there had, whatever doctrines are there maintained, will arrest the attention of the whole republic. Influences there exerted, cannot fail to affect the public sentiment on the broadest scale. Impulses there given, will move every limb of the "body politic." The hand, that grapples with the monster, slavery, there has access to his very vitals. It was long ago maintained by the advocates of immediate emancipation; it is, I believe, now generally admitted, that the abolition of slavery in the District of Columbia must open the way for universal freedom. The efforts there made in behalf of the oppressed cannot be confined there. Who could hope to keep the chain of servitude strong and bright in Maryland, in Virginia—*any where* in the republic, after the fetter-links had there been dissolved? On that elevated spot, the battles of universal freedom may be fought and her most splendid victories achieved. And it is the birth-right of *every American* to mingle in this conflict. How, then, can you say, whoever you may be, that you can do nothing to hasten the redemption of the captive? Up, and gird on your armor. The foe is directly before you; ravaging the inheritance left you by your fathers! Up, and give him battle! Never let your sword find its sheath, till he spreads his dragon wings, and hides himself among less malignant fiends in hell. Let those, whom you employ to promote the public welfare, know that you *are bent* on the abolition of slavery; that you will never cease to shout in their ears the demands of truth and freedom. Let them see that you are in earnest; and they will not venture to disregard your will. When you say THEY MUST, they will make haste to break every yoke, and give deliverance to the victims of oppression. In the name of God, then, and for the sake of bleeding humanity, *speak the word!*

Our ecclesiastical connexions with churches which tolerate in their members the sin of slaveholding, we ought at once to dissolve. Till we do this, we can never reach the vitals of the evil, with which we are bound to contend. Could either of the principal religious denominations at the South be brought in the spirit of true repentance to renounce the crime of oppressing the poor, the monster, which is now fattening on the blood of innocence, must fall beneath the fatal blow. The enormous guilt of stealing men could not fail to attract universal attention. Every man's mind and mouth would be full of the matter. A new channel would at once be opened for public sentiment. Myriads would rush to the work of demolishing the old Bastile. The rusty key of this dreadful prison is even now in the hands of the church. But instead of using it to "open the doors" to those who are pining in its damp dark dungeons, she is lending her influence to multiply the victims of despair. She is not only the unblushing, heartless, flippant advocate of slavery; but she is not afraid or ashamed to be seen riveting the chain, swinging the whip, wielding the branding iron! She even blesses herself for her pious liberality in putting "the price of blood" into the "treasury of the Lord!" She sells the Saviour's poor to build up the Saviour's kingdom! To obtain the means of sending the Gospel to the heathen, she drives her own children to the market! And worse than all, she blasphemously pretends, that she doth all this in the name and by the authority of the God of truth and mercy! She tortures the sacred volume, to force it to justify the crime of robbing the poor even to the stealing of their babes! Thus, slavery has come to be the pet-sin of a large portion of the American church!

The church must be aroused to her guilt in this matter, or she is undone. The blighting curse of God will waste and wither her. Nothing but repentance can hold her back from the grave of infamy, which is even now yawning, impatient to swallow its prey! Nor can she perish alone. The republic must rot with her in the same dishonored tomb!

Let all professed Christians, who enslave their brethren, know that no honest man can "give them the hand of fellowship," as the disciples of the Saviour. Let them be debarred from the table of the Lord. Let them, if religious teachers they can claim to be, be excluded from the pulpit. Let them see that their sin is no longer to be "winked at;" that if they continue deaf to the voice of Christian reproof, they must be to the whole company of their disgraced and offended brethren, as a "heathen man and publican." They will doubtless be greatly vexed and shocked. They will doubtless remonstrate and complain. They will affirm, and deny, and threaten. But no shift, no turn, no expedient can save them from torturing convictions and stinging remorse. They will find "burning coals" in their bosoms. And the "accursed thing" they will put away.

Look at the present attitude of our brethren in Great Britain. So ill have they been requited, so shamefully have they been abused, for their efforts to reclaim and save us, that they begin to feel the necessity of renouncing all fellowship with the slaveholding churches of America. And can these churches endure the thought of being thus held up to the abhorrence and execration of mankind, as plunderers and pirates? So disgraced and abhorred, can they help loosening their hands from their brother's throat? This problem, each of you, my brethren, can assist in solving. Stand aloof, then, from what may wear the face of Christian intercourse with the oppressors of the poor.

But your regard for the "peace of the church," you allege, forbids your assuming such an attitude! What; so superior to your Saviour in your love of peace! What; sacrifice truth, and righteousness, and humanity to peace! Thus did not your Lord. Instead of whispering peace in the ears of hypocrites and infidels, He presented a sword to their naked breasts. Upon the heads of those, who "devoured widows' houses and for a pretence made long prayers," He scattered coals of fire. What; do you expect peace as the fruit of a compromise with wickedness! What *sort of peace* can you procure on such conditions? I will take the liberty to tell you. That false peace, which, like the dead calm at sea, foretokens a storm! A peace, which cannot but open the way for war! Peace on such terms, all the righteous on earth and in heaven must pronounce accursed! Alas, alas! We have had enough of that kind of peace! Cursed be the hour, when cunning and malignant fiends persuaded us to "sell our brother into Egypt;" "when he besought us and we would not hear!" Sold our brother for rice and cotton; for sugar and tobacco! Parted with our birth-right for a mess of pottage! Gave him up into the hands of robbers and assassins! And by a most bloody bargain, agreed to help them, if need be, to bind him and lay him upon the altar, a sacrifice to devils! And pocketed the money! And blessed the contract! And praised the enterprise and cunning which filled our greedy mouths with the "wages of iniquity!" And set us to defend our plunder with tiger-like ferocity! Yes, cursed be that hour; the darkest in our country's annals! Then did a pitiful, shortsighted policy triumph over us! Stifling every dictate of justice; every impulse of compassion; every sentiment of humanity! Infecting us with guilt! Luring us on to ruin! *Cursed be that hour!* And yet a little while, "all the people," amidst tears of repentance or the pangs of retribution, will shout, "AMEN!"

"The whoredoms of our mother Jezebel and her witchcrafts are too many" to admit the hope of peace! "Who ever hardened himself against the Lord and prospered!" Have we not made merchandise of the souls of men—souls purchased by the pure and precious blood of the Christ of God! And this to gratify lust, and pride, and selfishness, too gross and monstrous to be endured by the rudest savages! And do we not insist upon maintaining the habit of robbing the poor—of wresting away his hard-earned wages—nay, of stealing his babes, with a stoutness of heart, a stiffness of neck, an impudence of face, which are seldom found in any, who have not "sold themselves to work iniquity!" And yet talk of peace! So much in love with peace, as "to suffer sin upon our brother!" And leave the wicked without warning! With his prey in his teeth! And the avenger at his heels! Out upon such peace! We have had too much of it already! Such peace a little longer, and we are all dead men!

If we would have peace, let us listen to the voice which calls us to duty and to glory. Let us, with sackcloth upon our loins and dust upon our heads, kneeling with broken hearts at the foot of the Cross, call the nation to repentance. With many tears—*for we have all sinned*—let us lift up a great and lamentable cry. And let us "spare not," till "every yoke is broken!"

Peace on cheaper terms we cannot have. If we let our iniquities alone, they will not let us alone! If we sleep, our damnation will not slumber! Our compromise with slavery is full of ruin. Our "convenant with death shall be disannulled, and our agreement with hell shall not stand." "The overflowing scourge shall pass through, and shall we not be trodden down by it?" Awake, then, awake, my brethren! "Consider the poor;" and ye shall be "blessed!" Cease "to accept the persons of the wicked; do justice to the afflicted and needy; rid them out of the hand of the wicked." "Then thou shalt raise up the foundation of many generations; and thou shalt be called the repairer of the breach, the restorer of paths to dwell in."

The Quadroon Girl
Henry Wadsworth Longfellow*

The Slaver in the broad lagoon
 ' Lay moored with idle sail;
He waited for the rising moon,
    And for the evening gale.

Under the shore his boat was tied,
    And all her listless crew
Watched the gray alligator slide
    Into the still bayou.

Odors of orange-flowers and spice
    Reach them from time to time,
Like airs that breathe from Paradise
    Upon a world of crime.

The Planter, under his roof of thatch,
    Smoked thoughtfully and slow;
The Slaver's thumb was on the latch;
    He seemed in haste to go.

He said, "My ship at anchor rides
    In yonder broad lagoon;
I only wait the evening tides,
    And the rising of the moon."

Before them, with her face upraised,
    In timid attitude,
Like one half curious, half amazed,
    A Quadroon maiden stood.

Her eyes were, like a falcon's, gray;
    Her arms and neck were bare;
No garment she wore save a kirtle gay,
    And her own long, raven hair.

And on her lips there played a smile
    As holy, meek, and faint,
As lights in some cathedral aisle
    The features of a saint.

"The soil is barren, the farm is old,"
    The thoughtful Planter said;
Then looked upon the Slaver's gold,
    And then upon the maid.

*From Tract No. 1, New England Anti-Slavery Tract Association (Boston: J. W. Alden Publishing Agent, n.d.).

His heart within him was at strife
  With such accursed gains;
For he knew whose passions gave her life,
  Whose blood ran in her veins.

But the voice of nature was too weak;
  He took the glittering gold!
Then pale as death grew the maiden's cheek,
  Her hands as icy cold.

The Slaver led her from the door;
  He led her by the hand,
To be his slave and paramour
  In a strange and distant land!

SOUTHEASTERN COMMUNITY COLLEGE LIBRARY

Part II
Agitators
for Radical Abolition

Texts for speeches by the radical abolitionists are more available than for the evangelicals, because the Garrisonians' base of operation was the intellectual center of Boston and their leading spokesman was Wendell Phillips, whose speeches were widely published. Garrison, as editor of *The Liberator*, often published his own speeches. The practice of the time was to have the speech taken down in shorthand, transcribed into longhand, set in type, and then submitted to the speaker in galley proof for editing. The result is that the edited speech resembled the original but was not a close recording of the speech as delivered. William Lloyd Garrison, for example, in a letter in the Garrison papers at the Boston Public Library, wrote Oliver Johnson as follows:

> You will see in the Liberator, this week, the speech of Mr. Phillips, delivered at New York, as revised and corrected by himself. And such revision, correction, alteration, and addition you never saw, in the way of emendation! More than two columns of the Tribune's report were in type before P. came into our office; and the manipulations these required was a caution to all reporters and type-setters! I proposed to P. to send his altered "slips" to Barnum as a remarkable curiosity, and Winchell suggested having them photographed! But P. decided to make his speech as complete and full as he could, and I am glad you are to receive it without being put to any trouble about it. Doubtless you will be requested to make some new alterations; for he is continually criticizing what he has spoken, and pays no regard to literal accuracy.

What we reproduce here, then, are excerpts from the speeches as edited and printed. The printed version often reached as wide, if not a wider, audience than the speech itself and thus was a more important persuasive message than the original.

William Lloyd Garrison's address delivered on the Fourth of July, 1838, at the request of the Board of Managers of the Massachusetts Anti-Slavery Society reveals Garrison at his prime as an agitator and proponent of im-

93

mediate emancipation.[1] The speech is long, repetitive, and rambling. What we present here are representative excerpts that reveal one of the basic rhetorical strategies and tactics of the master agitator of abolition.

Stephen S. Foster was not as able a stylist as was Garrison, but he was representative of the rhetoric of agitation. Foster's *The Brotherhood of Thieves: A True Picture of the American Church and Clergy* is in the form of a letter to Nathanial Barney of Nantucket.[2] The letter is an argumentative piece although designed for publication rather than for delivery as a lecture. The style of the letter is oral in the sense that it is filled with rhetorical questions, personal pronouns, and apostrophes and exclamations, revealing the fact that the source of much of the material was the antislavery lecture, which, as was so often the case, was then adapted to the written polemic.

When Wendell Phillips spoke to the Massachusetts Anti-Slavery Society at the Melodeon in January, 1853, he presented one of the few detailed discussions of the rhetorical strategy of the agitators.[3] Phillips essentially analyzed and defended the rhetoric of agitation. Note that his defense was largely on the grounds of effect. Note also that he claims all antislavery speakers for his side, including Weld and the evangelicals. The speech is typical of Wendell Phillips' erudition, wide-ranging copiousness, and stylistic brilliance. He indulges in less attack upon the cherished common values than he sometimes did, but because the theme of the speech is central to the focus of the book, we have included it here. The Garrison and Foster selections provide a good sample of agitation.

William Lloyd Garrison

Had the abolitionists kept books, William Lloyd Garrison would doubtless have had a goodly number of debit entries as well as a long column under assets. The man was a paradox in many ways: a brilliant, zealous, stubborn crusader, an agitator to the core, he was not only an inept politician, but he believed so fervently that the Truth would mow down all opposition that he opposed any political organization among the abolitionists almost to the end, even after it was obvious that the organizations were growing more effective all along. He was an imaginative, tireless worker who had

[1]*The Liberator*, July 13, 1838.
[2](Concord, N. H.: Parker Pillsbury, 1884).
[3]*Speeches, Lectures and Letters by Wendell Phillips* (Boston: Lee and Shepard, Publishers, 1863), pp. 98–153.

chronic health problems, probably bronchial in nature, though he may have been something of a hypochondriac also; he was a sucker for all the patent medicines and quack cures that came along. Though he was a gracious and generous host in his own home, in public he was often a humorless, disagreeably opinionated man. Even his friends had trouble liking him at times. He was tenacious and hard-working but at the same time hopelessly disorganized.

Most reports say that Garrison's speaking delivery was dull, almost monotonous, yet the overall effect of his speaking was compelling. His conviction and graphic style were so thorough that he got through to his listeners in spite of the fact that he lacked the physical presence or fine voice of many other speakers. People were undoubtedly interested in hearing him speak partly to see what he would say next. He certainly "told it like it was," at least from his own point of view. As one of his own supporters said, he was "irrepressible, uncompromising, . . . inflammatory," and had to admit to "excessive harshness of language." In today's parlance, we would have to say he probably turned off as many as he turned on.

Garrison took on slavery after attacking drunkenness, and along with slavery he added campaigns against the orthodox churches ("cages of unclean birds, Augean stables of pollution") and government, the Constitution ("a convenant with death and an agreement with hell"), theatres ("deep and powerful sources of evil"), the use of tobacco, capital punishment, imprisonment for debt, and all other abolitionists who did not see things his way. He was a lifelong champion of equal rights for women. He was, to those who differed with him, a real troublemaker. Even to those who agreed with this or that reform he was undertaking, he was a difficult, admirable, incurably optimistic, often illogical, extraordinarily persistent extremist. He lacked perspective and any sense of proportion.

Garrison's drunkard father deserted the family when the boy was three; he was brought up as a ward of a local family and apprenticed at a Newburyport, Massachusetts, paper at fifteen. At twenty-one he edited the local *Free Press* and joined the *National Philanthropist* staff in Boston when he was twenty-three. He became a friend of Benjamin Lundy, a Quaker already much concerned with antislavery, and by the age of twenty-four Garrison had found his real, lifelong cause: abolition. His speeches on the subject were heard by thousands and read by thousands more as published in his own paper, *The Liberator,* as well as in others. He published *The Liberator,* the greatest abolition newspaper, for thirty-five years, from January, 1831, until December, 1865, finally figuring the job was done.

Garrison married Helen Benson when he was thirty-one, and apparently she kept the house going with her talent for organization. She was as systematic as he was not, and she acted as a tactful buffer on the many occasions when her husband had gone too far, irritating and angering the very people he wanted to go along with him.

Garrison was nearly six feet tall; his face was stern, but he wore glasses that seemed to soften his expression. Philosophically he was a believer in nonresistance, the nonviolence position of his day, but he was, in this as in almost all else, paradoxical; in his pacifism he was downright militant. Hoping to have Truth slay his opposition, he got himself dragged through the streets of Boston once with a rope tied around his neck. He spent the night in jail (for his own safety) and left town for a few weeks afterwards until things cooled down.

Some called Garrison an idealist, the chief impetus in the abolition fight; others say he was a fanatic, impractical and disorganized, an irritant who accomplished some good but in about the most obnoxious way possible. He distrusted Abraham Lincoln, and only after the Emancipation Proclamation was he ready to give Washington's Congressmen any credit for furthering his cause. After the Civil War, however, he was more than ready to share the glory. He joined the peace ceremonies at Fort Sumter, saying among other things, "I hate slavery as I hate nothing else in this world. It is not a crime, but the sum of all criminality." And, standing over Calhoun's grave, he added, "Down into a deeper grave than this slavery has gone, and for it there is no resurrection."

born December, 1805, Newburyport, Mass.

died May, 1879, New York City

July 4th Address,
1838

Fellow Citizens: What a glorious day is this! what a glorious people are we! This is the time-honored, wine-honored, toast-drinking, powder-wasting, tyrant-killing fourth of July—consecrated, for the last sixty years, to bombast, to falsehood, to impudence, to hypocrisy. It is the great carnival of republican despotism, and of christian impiety, famous the world over! Since we held it last year, we have kept securely in their chains, the stock of two millions, three hundred thousand slaves we then had on hand, in spite of every effort of fanaticism to emancipate them; and, through the goodness of God, to whom we are infinitely indebted for the divine institution of negro slavery, have been graciously enabled to steal some seventy thousand babes, the increase of that stock, and expect to steal a still greater number before another "glorious" anniversary shall come round! We have again struck down the freedom of speech in Congress, and utterly banished it from one half of the Union, by the aid of pistols, bowie-knives, and lynch law. We have also renewedly decided, in both houses of Congress, that the right of petition is not to be allowed to those who are the advocates of immediate and universal emancipation. As to the Indian tribes, we have done the best we could to expel and exterminate them; and the blood upon our hands, and the gore upon our garments, show that our success has almost equalled our wishes. We have driven the Cherokees, at the point of the bayonet, into a distant wilderness, from their abodes of civilization—violated the most solemn treaties ever entered into between man and man—and committed nameless and numberless outrages upon the domestic security and personal rights of these hapless victims—all for the laudable purpose of getting their lands, that the "divine institution" of slavery may be extended, and perpetuated to the latest generation, as the cornerstone of our republican edifice! We have trampled all law and order under foot, resolved society into jacobinical clubs, and filled the land with mobs and riots which have ended in arson and murder, in order to show our abhorrence of those who "plead for justice in the name of humanity, and according to the law of the living God." Hail, Columbia! happy land! Hail, the return of the fourth of July, that we may perjure ourselves afresh, in solemnly invoking heaven and earth to witness, that "we hold these truths to be self-evident— that all men are created equal; that they are endowed by their Creator with certain inalienable rights; that among these are life, LIBERTY, and the pursuit of happiness!" "Sound the trumpet—beat the drum!" Let the bells give their merriest peals to the breeze—unfurl every star-spangled banner— thunder mightily, ye cannon, from every hill-top—and let shouts arise from every plain and valley; for tyrants and their minions shall find no quarter at our hands this day!

Disgusting spectacle! The climax of brutality, and the lowest descent of national degradation!

I use strong language, and will make no apology for it, on this occasion. In contemplating this subject, no man, who is true to his nature, can speak but in the language of hot displeasure, and caustic irony, and righteous denunciation. Every word will burn like molten lead, and every sentence glow like flaming fire. What are they but a nation of dastards, who, making high pretensions to honesty and a sacred regard for the rights of man, are seen, year after year, openly and shamelessly reducing one-sixth of the population to chains and slavery, herding the sexes together like beasts, robbing them of the fruits of a toil extorted by a cart-whip, and shutting out from their minds, as far as practicable, all knowledge, both human and divine? The catalogue of our crimes and abominations is without end; and there is nothing that can be tortured into an excuse or apology for their perpetration. Will any man call this declamation? Granted! The day is consecrated to declamation, such as bursts from the lips of James Otis, and Joseph Warren, and Patrick Henry, in the days when a three-penny tax upon tea was not to be endured, and when taxation without representation was deemed an outrage worth periling the lives of the colonists to redress!—Declamation? Who will venture to utter that taunt? Is the picture I have sketched overdrawn? Can the most lynx-eyed lawyer detect a single flaw in the indictment? The facts being admitted, metaphysics are rendered needless. As a freeman, I require no argument to convince me, that to enslave or oppress one of my race, is to lift the battle-axe of sedition against the throne of God. Honest, righteous, soul-stirring declamation against tyranny, is music to my ears. But what harmony is there between the clanking of chains, and the shouts of the forgers of those chains? between the shrieks of lacerated and bleeding humanity, and the vauntings of those who wield the lash? between the groans of toil-worn slaves, and the exaltations of hypocritical freemen?

I present myself as the advocate of my enslaved countrymen, at a time when their claims cannot be shuffled out of sight, and on an occasion which entitles me to a respectful hearing in their behalf. If I am asked to prove their title to liberty, my answer is, that the fourth of July is not a day to be wasted in establishing "self-evident truths." In the name of the God, who has made us of one blood, and in whose image we are created; in the name of the Messiah, who came to bind up the broken-hearted, to proclaim liberty to the captives, and the opening of the prison to them that are bound; in the name of the Holy Ghost, whom to despise is to perish; I demand the immediate emancipation of all who are pining in slavery on the American soil, whether they are fattening for the shambles in Maryland and Virginia, or are wasting, as with a pestilent disease, on the cotton and sugar plantations of Alabama and Louisiana; whether they are males or females, young or old, vigorous or infirm. I make this demand, not for the children merely, but the parents also; not for one, but for all; not with restrictions and limitations, but unconditionally. I assert their perfect equality with ourselves, as a part of the human race, and their inalienable right to liberty and the pursuit of happiness. That this demand is founded in justice, and is therefore irresistible, the whole nation is this day acknowledging, as upon oath at the bar of the world. And not until, by a formal vote, the people repudiate the Declaration of Independence as a rotten and dangerous instrument, and cease to keep this festival in honor and liberty, as unworthy of note or remembrance; not until they spike every cannon, and muffle every bell, and disband every procession, and quench every bonfire, and gag every orator; not until they brand Washington, and Adams, and Jefferson, and Hancock, as fanatics and madmen; not until they place themselves again in the condition of colonial subserviency to Great Britain or transform this republic into an imperial government; not until they cease to point exultingly toward Bunker Hill, and the plains of Concord and Lexington; not, in fine, until they deny the authority of God, and proclaim themselves to be destitute of principle and humanity; will I argue the question, as one of doubtful disputation, on an occasion like this, whether our slaves are entitled to the rights and privileges of freemen. There is no man to be found, unless he has a brow of brass and a heart of stone, who will dare to contest it on a day like this. A state of vassalage is pronounced, by universal acclamation, to be such as no man, or body of men, ought to submit to for one moment. I therefore tell the American slaves, that the time for their emancipation is come; that, their own task-masters being witnesses, they are created equal to the rest of mankind, and possess an inalienable right to liberty; and that no man has a right to hold them in bondage. I warn them not to fight for their freedom, both on account of the hopelessness of the effort, and because it is contrary to the will of God; but I tell them, not less emphatically, it is not wrong in them to refuse to wear the yoke of slavery any longer. Let them shed no blood—enter into no conspiracies—raise no murderous revolts; but, whenever and wherever they can break their fetters, God give them the courage to do so! And should they attempt to elope from their house of bondage, and come to the North, may each of them find a convert from the search of the spoiler, and an invincible public sentiment to shield them from the grasp of the kidnapper! Success attend them in their flight to Canada, to touch whose monarchical soil insures freedom to every republican slave! . . .

Oppression and insurrection go hand in hand, as cause and effect are allied together. In what age of the world have tyrants reigned with impunity, or the victims of tyranny not resisted unto blood? Besides our own grand insurrection against the authority of the mother country, there have been many insurrections, during the last two hundred years, in various sections of the land, on the part of the victims of our tyranny, but without the success that attended our own struggle. The last was the memorable one in Southampton, Virginia, headed by a black patriot, nicknamed, in the contemptuous nomenclature of slavery, Nat Turner. The name does not strike the ear so harmoniously as that of Washington, or Lafayette, or Hancock, or Warren; but the name is nothing. It is not in the power of all the slaveholders upon earth, to render odious the memory of that sable chieftan. "Resistance to tyrants is obedience to God," was our revolutionary motto. We acted upon that motto—what more did Nat Turner? Says George McDuffie, "A people who deliberately submit to oppression, with a full knowledge that they are oppressed, are fit only to be slaves. No tyrant ever made a slave—no community, however small, having the spirit of freemen, ever yet had a master. It does not belong to men to count the costs, and calculate the hazards of vindicating their rights, and defending their liberties!"—So reasoned Nat Turner, and acted accordingly. Was he a patriot, or a monster? Do we mean to say to the oppressed of all nations, in the 62d year of our independence, and on the 4th of July, that our example in 1775 was a bad one, and ought not to be followed? As a christian abolitionist, I for one, am prepared to say so—but are the people ready to say, that no chains ought to be broken by the hand of violence, and no blood spilt in defence of inalienable human rights, in any quarter of the globe? If not, then our slaves will peradventure take us at our word, and there will be given unto us blood to drink, for we are worthy. Why accuse abolitionists of stirring them up to insurrection? The charge is false—but what if it were true? If any man has a right to fight for liberty, this right equally extends to all men subjected to bondage. In claiming this right for themselves, the American people necessarily concede it to all mankind. If, therefore, they are found tyrannizing over any part of the human race, they voluntarily seal their own death-warrant, and confess that they deserve to perish. . . .

Fellow-citizens! at this hour—O, blush for shame!—on this advent of Liberty, there are millions of our countrymen in chains, not in Turkey or Algiers, but in our very midst! And such a fate, and such woes, and such deprivations, and such liabilities, and such torments, as are theirs!—and such owners, and such overseers, and such drivers, as are theirs!—and such breaking of heart-strings, and such darkening of intellects, and such ruin of souls, as are theirs!—"without God, and without hope," without the bible, without marriage, without the slightest personal protection, and without any prospect of escape!—ranked and herded with brute beasts, and treated accordingly!—their bodies branded with red hot irons, or scarred by the flesh-devouring lash, or galled by the iron chain! and their spirits "which are God's," trodden upon at every stride of despotism, till they are crushed to the earth—or if, by the power of the Holy Ghost, any of them chance to be "born again," this fact is duly announced by the auctioneer whenever they are brought under his hammer for sale; for it is notorious, that christians bring higher prices as working-cattle in the United States, than unbelievers—a "Christ within" being considered as enhancing the value of every chattel!—These things are trite, because they are true; but are they less dreadful on that account? . . .

I am still resolved to link my destiny with that of the slave, to plead his cause, to rebuke his oppressor, and to AGITATE THE LAND, whether there be over my head a serene or a troubled sky—whether round about me are the elements of peace or of strife—whether men will hear or forbear. The object I have in view is godlike—the principles I enunciate are just, immutable, eternal—the result of the contest must be the downfall of slavery, either with or without the consent of the planters, either by the power of moral suasion or by physical force, either by a peaceful or a bloody process. Die it must, and die soon—but whether a peaceful or a violent death, it is for us to determine.

It is useless, it is dreadful, it is impious for this nation longer to contend with the Almighty. All his attributes are against us, and on the side of the oppressed. Is it not a fearful thing to fall into the hands of the living God? Who may abide the day of his coming, and who shall stand when he appeareth as "a swift witness against the adulterers, and against false-swearers, and against those that oppress the hireling in his wages, the widow, and the fatherless, and that turn aside the stranger from his right?" Woe to this bloody land! it is all full of lies and robbery—the prey departeth not, and the sound of a whip is heard continually....

One thing I know full well. Calumniated, abhorred, persecuted as the abolitionists have been, they constitute the body guard of the slaveholders, not to strengthen their oppression, but to shield them from the vengeance of their slaves. Instead of seeking their destruction, abolitionists are endeavoring to save them from midnight conflagration and sudden death, by beseeching them to remove the cause of insurrection; and by holding out to their slaves the hope of a peaceful deliverance. We do not desire that any should perish. Having a conscience void of offence in this matter, and cherishing a love for our race which is "without partiality and without hypocrisy," no impeachment of our motives, or assault upon our character, can disturb the serenity of our minds; nor can any threats of violence, or prospect of suffering, deter us from our purpose. That we manifest a bad spirit, is not to be decided on the testimony of the southern slave-driver, or his northern apologist. That our philanthropy is exclusive, in favor of but one party, is not proved by our denouncing the oppressor, and sympathizing with his victim. That we are seeking popularity, is not apparent from our advocating an odious and unpopular cause, and vindicating, at the loss of our reputation, the rights of a people who are reckoned among the offscouring of all things. That our motives are not disinterested, they who swim with the popular current, and partake of the gains of unrighteousness, and plunder the laborers of their wages, are not competent to determine. That our language is harsh, uncharitable, unchristian, they who revile us as madmen, fanatics, incendiaries, enemies of the Union, traitors, cut-throats, etc., etc., cannot be allowed to testify. That our measures are violent, is not demonstrated by the fact, that we wield no physical weapons, pledge ourselves not to countenance insurrection, and present the peaceful front of non-resistance to those who put our very lives in peril. That our object is chimerical, or unrighteous, is not substantiated by the fact of its being commended by Almighty God, and supported by his omnipotence, as well as approved by the wise and good in every age and in all countries. If the charge, so often brought against us, be true, that our temper is rancorous and our spirit turbulent, how has it happened, that, during so long a conflict with slavery, not a single instance can be found in which an abolitionist has committed a breach of the peace, or violated any law of his country? If it be true, that we are not actuated by the best feelings of humanity, nor sustained by the highest principles of rectitude, nor governed by the spirit of forbearance, I ask, once more, how it has come to pass, that when our meetings have been repeatedly broken up by lawless men, our property burnt in the streets, our dwellings sacked, our persons brutally assailed, and our lives put in imminent peril, we have refused to lift a finger in self-defence, or to maintain our rights in the spirit of worldly patriotism?

Will it be retorted, that we dare not resist—that we are cowards? Cowards! No man believes it. They are the dastards, who maintain that might makes right—whose arguments are brickbats and rotten-eggs, whose weapons are dirks and bowie-knives, and whose code of justice is lynch law. A love of liberty, instead of unnerving men, makes them intrepid, heroic, invincible. It was so at Thermopylae—it was so on Bunker Hill. Who so tranquil, who so little agitated, in storm or sunshine, as the abolitionists?

But what consternation, what running to and fro like men at their very wit's end, what trepidation, what anguish of spirit, on the part of their enemies? How southern slavemongers quake and tremble at the faintest whisperings of an abolitionist! . . .

The charge, then, that we are beside ourselves, that we are both violent and cowardly, is demonstrated to be false, in a signal manner. I thank God, that "the weapons of our warfare are not carnal, but spiritual." I thank him, that, by his grace, and by our deep concern for the oppressed, we have been enabled, in christian magnanimity, to pity and pray for our enemies, and to overcome their evil with good. Overcome, I say: not merely suffered unresistingly, but conquered gloriously.

Now are our brows bound with victorious wreaths!

God grant that we may go on to the end, as we have begun! If it must be so, let the defenders of slavery still have all the brickbats, bowie-knives and pistols, which the land can furnish; but let us still possess all the arguments, facts, warnings and promises, which insure the final triumph of our holy cause. Let us take unto ourselves the whole armor of God, that we may be able to withstand in the evil day, and having done all, to stand—having our loins girt about with truth, and having on the breast-plate of righteousness, and our feet shod with the preparation of the gospel of peace; above all, taking the shield of faith, wherewith we shall be able to quench all the fiery darts of the wicked; and taking the helmet of salvation, and the sword of the Spirit, which is the word of God.

Stephen Symonds Foster

The "other" Stephen Foster of the Civil War era, not the composer, was a New Englander. Brought up as a farmer, later in life he returned very successfully to farming, but the interim years were exciting ones for the young minister who became an agitator, called by some second in effect only to Garrison in the early years of the agitation for the abolition movement.

Foster rose to prominence as a radical reformer, an abolitionist, champion of women's suffrage (his wife, Abby Kelley, was one of the most important women in this early suffrage reform), temperance worker, and friend of labor. He spent many lean years between his student days at Dartmouth and his later years on his farm near Worcester stumping about the countryside (sometimes with Garrison, a close friend) speaking in a beautiful voice, in an uncompromising attack upon the evils of slavery.

Foster apparently had a tenacity for logical reasoning that allowed him no compromises. He was so impressed by the Sermon on the Mount that he developed from this his own humanitarian creed, and he tried to make his life fit this creed at all cost. He decided to become a minister, but while at Dartmouth, if any of the established or accepted doctrines butted up against any of his own interpretations, he balked. He refused to serve in the state militia while at college and ended up in jail for a while. The rural jails in New England were so bad at that time that Foster agitated for reforms which eventually led to sweeping reforms in the state penal system.

Foster started at Union Theological Seminary after Dartmouth but was soon at odds with seminary policies, and he left and began making anti-slavery speeches anywhere he could. His main theme was that slavery was an American institution, not just a Southern one. He believed that the churches themselves as well as business and politics were all still committed to things as they were (the actual or implied consent to slavery for economic reasons) and he soon began stopping by during church services, politely disrupting to ask if he could speak to the congregation about the slavery problem. He was told to leave, thrown out many times, even prosecuted by some—but he did manage to publicize his cause this way.

Apparently, Stephen Foster thrived on a steady diet of speaking, being jeered at, pelted with things, threatened, hardly making enough to live on, for he continued this stump reform campaigning for half a dozen years, not staying anywhere for long. Not until he married Abigail Kelley and they settled on a farm did he even think about anything but his exhausting speaking campaign.

After their marriage, though they built one of the most prosperous farms in the community, both Fosters continued speaking, he for abolition and she for equal rights for women. Contemporaries said that Stephen Foster had a fine voice, that he was rather ungainly looking, with hands showing the toil of his earlier years. He was a vehement and vitriolic denouncer on the platform, without humor, though he is said to have been a kind and gentle man in private life. Though few know the name these days, Stephen Foster, the agitator, ranked close behind William Lloyd Garrison and Wendell Phillips in getting the antislavery movement going in New England, and his importance to the abolition movement should be noted.

born November, 1809, Canterbury, New Hampshire
died September, 1881, Worcester, Mass.

The Brotherhood
of Thieves

Esteemed Friend:

In the early part of last autumn, I received a letter from you, requesting me to prepare an article for the press, in vindication of the strong language of denunciation of the American church and clergy, which I employed at the late Anti-Slavery Convention on your island, and which was the occasion of the disgraceful mob, which disturbed and broke up that meeting. In my answer, I gave you assurance of prompt compliance with your request; but, for reasons satisfactory to myself, I have failed to fulfill my promise up to the present time. The novelty of the occasion has now passed away; the deep and malignant passions which were stirred in the bosoms of no inconsiderable portion of your people, have, doubtless, subsided; but the important *facts* connected with it are yet fresh in the memories of all; and, as the occasion was one of general, not local, interest, and the spirit which was there exhibited was a fair specimen of the general temper and feeling of our country towards the advocates of equal rights and impartial justice. I trust it will not be deemed amiss in me to make it a subject of public notice, even at this late period.

But in the remarks which I propose to make, it will be no part of my object to vindicate myself in the opinion of the public, against the foul aspersions of those whose guilty quiet my preaching may have disturbed. Indeed, to tell the truth, I place a very low estimate on the good opinions of my countrymen—quite as low, I think, as they do on mine, if I may judge from their very great anxiety to have me speak well of them, which I *positively* never can, so long as their national capital is a human flesh-mart, and their chief magistrate is a slave-breeder. The most that I can do is to pledge myself never to mob them, nay, that I will not even be *displeased* with them, for speaking ill of me, while their character remains what it now is. My opponents, among whom rank most of the church and clergy of the country, have disturbed a majority of the meetings which I have attended, within the last nine months, by drunken, murderous mobs, and in several instances, they have inflicted severe injury upon my person; but I value this violence and outrage as proof of their deep conviction of the truth and power of what I say. I deem the *reproach* of such men sufficient praise. And I here tender them my thanks for the high compliment they have so often paid to my opinions, in the extreme measures to which they have resorted to *compel* me to speak in their praise. But so long as their character remains such that I can bestow no commendations, I shall ask none in return.

Nor is it my intention in this letter, to weaken, by explanations, the force of my testimony against the popular religion of our country, for the purpose of allaying the bloody spirit of persecution which has of late characterized the opposition to my course. True, my life is in danger, especially whenever I attempt to utter my sentiments in houses dedicated to what is called the worship of God; but He who has opened to my view other worlds, in which to reap the rewards and honors of a life of toil and suffering in the cause of truth and human freedom in this has taught me to "be not afraid of them that kill the body, and after that have no more that they can do." Hence I have no pacificatory explanations to offer, no coward disclaimers to make. But I shall aim to present to the comprehension of the humblest individual, into whose hands this letter may chance to fall, a clear and comprehensive view of the intrinsic moral character of that class of our countrymen who claim our respect and veneration, as ministers and followers of the Prince of Peace. I am charged with having done them great injustice in my public lectures, on that and various other occasions. Many of those, who make this charge, doubtless, honestly think so. To correct their error—to reflect on their minds the light which God has kindly shed on mine—to break the spell in which they are now held by the sorcery of a designing priesthood, and prove that priesthood to be a "Brotherhood of Thieves" and the "Bulwark of American Slavery"—is all that I shall aim to do.

But I ought, perhaps, in justice to those who know nothing of my religious sentiments, except from the misrepresentations of my enemies, to say, that I have no feelings of personal hostility towards any portion of the church or clergy of our country. As children of the same Father, they are endeared to me by the holiest of all ties; and I am as ready to suffer, if need be, in defence of their rights, as in defence of the rights of the Southern slave. My objections to them are purely conscientious. I am a firm believer in the Christian religion, and in Jesus, as a divine being, who is to be our final Judge. I was born and nurtured in the bosom of the church, and for twelve years was among its most active members. At the age of twenty-two, I left the allurements of an active business life, on which I had just entered with fair prospects, and, for seven successive years, cloistered myself within the walls of our literary institutions, in "a course of study preparatory to the ministry." The only object I had in view in changing my pursuits, at this advanced period of life, was to render myself more useful to the world, by extending the principles of Christianity, as taught and lived out by their great Author. In renouncing the priesthood and an organized church, and laboring for their overthrow, my object is still the same. I entered them on the supposition that they were, what from a child I had been taught to regard them, the enclosures of Christ's ministers and flock, and his chosen instrumentalities for extending his kingdom on the earth. I have left them from an unresistible conviction, in spite of my early prejudices, that they are a "hold of every foul spirit," and the devices of men to gain influence and power. And, in rebuking their adherents as I do, my only object is to awaken them, if possible, to a sense of their guilt and moral degradation, and bring them to repentance, and a knowledge of the true God, of whom most of them are now lamentably ignorant, as their lives clearly prove.

The remarks which I made at your Convention were of a most grave and startling character. They strike at the very foundation of all our popular ecclesiastical institutions, and exhibit them to the world as the apologists and supporters of the most atrocious system of oppression and wrong, beneath which humanity has ever groaned. They reflect on the church the deepest possible odium, by disclosing to public view the chains and handcuffs, the whips and branding-irons, the rifles and bloodhounds, with which her ministers and deacons bind the limbs and lacerate the flesh of innocent men and defenceless women. They cast upon the clergy the same dark shade which Jesus threw over the ministers of his day, when he tore away the veil beneath which they had successfully concealed their diabolical schemes of personal aggrandizement and power, and denounced them before all the people, as a "den of thieves," as "fools and blind," "whited sepulchres," "blind guides, which strain at a gnat, and swallow a camel," "hypocrites, who devour widows' houses, and for a pretence make long prayers," "liars," "adulterers," "serpents," "a generation of vipers," who could not "escape the damnation of hell." But, appalling and ominous as they were, I am not aware that I gave the parties accused, or their mobocratic friends, any just cause of complaint. They were all spoken in public, in a free meeting, where all who dissented from me were not only invited, but warmly urged, to reply. I was an entire stranger among you, with nothing but the naked truth and a few sympathizing friends to sustain me, while the whole weight of popular sentiment was in their favor. Was the controversy unequal on their part? Were they afraid to meet me with the same honorable weapons which I had chosen? Conscious innocence seldom consents to tarnish its character by a dishonorable defence. Had my charges been unfounded, a refutation of them, under the circumstances, would have been most easy and triumphant. My opponents, had they been innocent, could have acquitted themselves honorably, and overwhelmed their accuser in deep disgrace, without the necessity of resorting to those arguments which appeal only to one's fears of personal harm, and which are certain to react upon their authors, when the threatening danger subsides.

But if all that I have alleged against them be true, it was obviously my right, nay, my imperative duty, to make the disclosures which I did, even though it might be, as you well know it was, at the peril of my life, and the lives of my associates.

In exposing the deep and fathomless abominations of those *pious* thieves, who gain their livelihood by preaching sermons and stealing babies, I am not at liberty to yield to any intimidations, however imposing the source from whence they come. The right of speech—the liberty to utter our own convictions *freely*, at all times and in all places, at discretion, unawed by fear, unembarrassed by force—is the gift of God to every member of the family of man, and should be preserved inviolate; and for one, I can consent to surrender it to no power on earth, but with the loss of life itself. Let not the petty tyrants of our land, in church or state, think to escape the censures which their crimes deserve, by hedging themselves about with the frightful penalties of human law, or the more frightful violence of a drunken and murderous mob. There live the men who are not afraid to die, even though called to meet their fate within the gloomy walls of a dismal prison, with no kind hand to wipe the cold death-sweat from their sinking brow; and they scorn a fetter on *limb* or *spirit*. They know their rights, and know how to defend them, or to obtain more than an equivalent for their loss, in the rewards of a martyr to the right. While life remains, they will speak, and speak *freely*, though it be in "A Voice from the Jail;" nor will they treat the crimes and vices of slave-breeding priests, and their consecrated abettors of the North, with less severity than they do the crimes and vices of other marauders on their neighbors' property and rights. Nor should the friends of freedom be alarmed at the consequences of this faithful dealing with "spiritual wickedness in high places." The mobs which it creates are but the violent contortions of the patient, as the deep gashes of the operator's knife sever the infected limb from his sickly and emaciated body.

The fact that my charges against the religious sects of our country were met with violence and outrage, instead of sound arguments and invalidating testimony, is strong presumptive evidence of their truth. The innocent never find occasion to resort to this disgraceful mode of defence. If our clergy and church were the ministers and church of Christ would their reputation be defended by drunken and murderous mobs? Are brickbats and rotten eggs the weapons of truth and Christianity? Did Jesus says to his disciples, "Blessed are ye when the *mob* shall speak well of you, and shall defend you"?

The church, slavery, and the mob, are a queer trinity! And yet that they are a trinity—that they all "agree in one"—cannot be denied. Every assault which we have made on the bloody slave system, as I shall hereafter show, has been promptly met and repelled by the church, which is herself the claimant of several hundred thousand slaves; and whenever we have attempted to expose the guilt and hypocrisy of the church, the *mob* has uniformly been first and foremost in her defence. But I rest not on presumptive evidence, however strong and conclusive, to sustain my allegations against the American church and clergy. The proof of their identity with slavery, and of their consequent deep and unparalleled criminality, is positive and overwhelming, and is fully adequate to sustain the gravest charges, and to justify the most denunciatory language that has ever fallen from the lips of their most inveterate opponents.

I said at your meeting, among other things, that the American church and clergy, as a body, were thieves, adulterers, man-stealers, pirates, and murderers; that the Methodist Episcopal church was more corrupt and profligate than any house of ill-fame in the city of New York; that the Southern ministers of that body were desirous of perpetuating slavery for the purpose of supplying themselves with concubines from among its hapless victims; and that many of our clergymen were guilty of enormities that would disgrace an Algerine pirate!! These sentiments called forth a burst of holy indignation from the *pious* and *dutiful* advocates of the church and clergy, which overwhelmed the meeting with repeated showers of stones and rotten eggs, and eventually compelled me to leave your island, to prevent the shedding of human blood. But whence this violence and personal abuse, not only of the author of these obnoxious sentiments, but also of your own unoffending wives and daughters, whose faces and dresses, you will recollect, were covered with the most loathsome filth? It is reported of the ancient Pharisees and their adherents, that they stoned Stephen to death for preaching doctrines at war with the popular religion of their times, and charging them with murder of the Son of God; but their successors of the modern church, it would seem, have discovered some new principle in theology, by which it is made their duty not only to stone the heretic himself, but all those also who may at any time be found listening to his discourse without a permit from their priest. Truly, the church is becoming "terrible as an army with banners."

This violence and outrage on the part of the church were, no doubt, committed to the glory of God and the honor of religion, although the connection between rotten eggs and holiness of heart is not very obvious. It is, I suppose, one of the mysteries of religion which laymen cannot understand without the aid of the clergy; and I therefore suggest that the pulpit make it a subject of Sunday discourse. But are not the charges here alleged against the clergy strictly and literally true? I maintain that they are true to the very letter; that the clergy and their adherents are literally, and beyond all controversy, a "brotherhood of thieves;" and, in support of this opinion, I submit the following considerations:—

You will agree with me, I think, that slaveholding involves the commission of all the crimes specified in my first charge, viz., theft, adultery, man-stealing, piracy, and murder. But should you have any doubts on this subject, they will be easily removed by analyzing this atrocious outrage on the laws of God, and the rights and happiness of man, and examining separately the elements of which it is composed. Wesley, the celebrated founder of the Methodists, once denounced it as the "sum of all villanies." Whether it be the sum of *all* villanies, or not, I will not here express an opinion; but that it is the sum of at least *five*, and those by no means the least atrocious in the catalogue of human aberrations, will require but a small tax on your patience to prove.

1. Theft. To steal, is to take that which belongs to another, without his consent. Theft and robbery are, *morally*, the same act, different only in form. Both are included under the command, "Thou shalt not steal;" that is, thou shalt not take thy neighbor's property. Whoever, therefore, either secretly or by force, possesses himself of the property of another, is a thief. Now, no proposition is plainer than that every man owns his own industry. He who tills the soil has a right to its products, and cannot be deprived of them but by an act of felony. This principle furnishes the only solid basis for the right of private or individual property; and he who denies it, either in theory or practice, denies that right, also. But every slaveholder takes the entire industry of his slaves, from infancy to gray hairs; they dig the soil, but he receives its products. No matter how kind or humane the master may be,— he lives by plunder. He is emphatically a freebooter; and, as such, he is as much more despicable a character than the common horse-thief, as his depredations are more extensive.

2. Adultery. This crime is disregard for the requisitions of marriage. The conjugal relation has its foundation deeply laid in man's nature, and its strict observance is essential to his happiness. Hence Jesus Christ has thrown around it the sacred sanction of his written law, and expressly declared that the man who violates it, even by a lustful eye, is an adulterer. But does the slaveholder respect this sacred relation? Is he cautious never to tread upon forbidden ground? No! His very position makes him the minister of un-bridled lust. By converting woman into a commodity to be bought and sold,

and used by her claimant as his avarice or lust may dictate, he totally annihilates the marriage institution, and transforms the wife into what he very
significantly terms a "BREEDER," and her children into "STOCK."

This change in woman's condition, from a free moral agent to a chattel,
places her domestic relations entirely beyond her own control, and makes
her a mere instrument for the gratification of another's desires. The master
claims her body as his property, and, of course, employs it for such purposes
as best suit his inclinations,—demanding free access to her bed; nor can she
resist his demands but at the peril of her life. Thus is her chastity left entirely
unprotected, and she is made the lawful prey of every pale-faced libertine
who may choose to prostitute her! To place woman in this situation, or to
retain her in it when placed there by another, is the highest insult that any
one could possibly offer to the dignity and purity of her nature; and the
wretch who is guilty of it deserves an epithet compared with which adultery
is spotless innocence. *Rape* is his crime! death his desert,—if death be ever
due to criminals! Am I too severe? Let the offence be done to a sister or
daughter of yours; nay, let the Rev. Dr. Witherspoon, or some other *ordained*
miscreant from the South, lay his vile hands on your own bosom companion,
and do to her what he has done to the companion of another,—and what
Prof. Stuart and Dr. Fisk say he may do, "without violating the Christian
faith,"—and I fear not your reply. None but a moral monster ever consented
to the enslavement of his own daughter, and none but fiends incarnate ever
enslave the daughter of another. Indeed, I think the demons in hell would
be ashamed to do to their fellow-demons what many of our clergy do to their
own church members.

3. Man-stealing. What is it to steal a man? Is it not to claim him as your
property?—to call him yours? God has given to every man an inalienable
right to himself,—a right of which no conceivable circumstance of birth,
or forms of law, can divest him; and he who interferes with the free and
unrestricted exercise of that right, who, not content with the proprietorship
of his own body, claims the body of his neighbor, is a man-stealer. This
truth is self-evident. Every man, idiots and the insane only excepted, knows
that he has no possible right to another's body; and he who persists, for a
moment, in claiming it, incurs the guilt of man-stealing. The plea of the
slave-claimant, that he has bought, or inherited, his slaves, is of no avail.
What right had he, I ask, to purchase, or to inherit, his neighbors? The purchase, or inheritance of them as a legacy, was itself a crime of no less
enormity than the original act of kidnapping. But every slave-holder, whatever his profession or standing in society may be, lays his felonious hands

on the body and soul of his equal brother, robs him of himself, converts him into an article of merchandise, and leaves him a mere chattel personal in the hands of his claimants. Hence he is a kidnapper, or man-thief.

4. Piracy. The American people, by an act of solemn legislation, have declared the enslaving of human beings on the coast of Africa to be piracy, and have affixed to this crime the penalty of death. And can the same act be piracy in Africa, and not be piracy in America? Does crime change its character by changing longitude? Is killing with malice aforethought, no murder, where there is no human enactment against it? Or can it be less piratical and Heaven-daring to enslave our own native countrymen, than to enslave the heathen sons of a foreign and barbarous realm? If there be any difference in the two crimes, the odds is in favor of the foreign enslaver. Slaveholding loses none of its enormity by a voyage across the Atlantic, nor by baptism into the Christian name. It is piracy in Africa; it is piracy in America; it is piracy the wide world over; and the American slaveholder, though he possess all the sanctity of the ancient Pharisees, and make prayers as numerous and long, is a *pirate* still; a base, profligate adulterer, and wicked contemner of the holy institution of marriage; identical in moral character with the African slave-trader, and guilty of a crime which, if committed on a foreign coast, he must expiate on the gallows.

5. Murder. Murder is an act of the mind, and not of the hand. "Whosoever hateth his brother is a murderer." A man may kill,—that is his hand may inflict a mortal blow,—without committing murder. On the other hand, he may commit murder without actually taking life. The intention constitutes the crime. He who, with a pistol at my breast, demands my pocket-book or my life, is a murderer, whichever I may choose to part with. And is not he a murderer, who, with the same deadly weapon, demands the surrender of what to me is of infinitely more value than my pocket-book, nay, than life itself—my liberty—myself—my wife and children—all that I possess on earth, or can hope for in heaven? But this is the crime of which every slave-holder is guilty. He maintains his ascendency over his victims, extorting their unrequited labor, and sundering the dearest ties of kindred, only by the threat of extermination. With the slave, as every intelligent person knows, there is no alternative. It is submission or death, or, more frequently, protracted torture more horrible than death. Indeed, the South never sleeps, but on dirks, and pistols, and bowie knives, with a troop of blood-hounds standing sentry at every door! What, I ask, means this splendid enginery of death, which gilds the palace of the tyrant master? It tells the story of his guilt. ⁴ The burnished steel which waits beneath his slumbering pillow, to drink

the lifeblood of outraged innocence, brands him as a murderer. It proves, beyond dispute, that the submission of his victims is the only reason why he has not already shed their blood.

By this brief analysis of slavery, we stamp upon the forehead of the slave-holder, with a brand deeper than that which marks the victim of his wrongs, the infamy of theft, adultery, man-stealing, piracy, and murder. We demonstrate, beyond the possibility of doubt, that he who enslaves another—that is, robs him of his right to himself, to his own hands, and head, and feet, and transforms him from a free moral agent into a mere *brute*, to obey, not the commands of God, but his claimant—is guilty of every one of these atrocious crimes. And in doing this, we have only demonstrated what, to every reflecting mind, is self-evident. Every man, if he would but make the case of the slave his own, would feel in his inmost soul the truth and justice of this charge. But these are the crimes which I have alleged against the American church and clergy....

The guaranty of personal security against their slaves, given by the North to the slave-claimants, is the very lifeblood of the slave system. Divested of the protection of Northern bayonets, the slave power could not sustain itself a single hour, as the South herself is forced to admit. "Suppose the Union to be dissolved, what has the South to depend upon? All the crowned heads are against her. A million of slaves are ready to rise and strike for freedom at the first tap of the drum." And why, I ask, do they not *now* rise? Not, surely, because, in a country like ours, such a step would be deemed morally wrong. The doctrine taught in all our pulpits, and received by the church universally, is, that "resistance to tyrants is obedience to God." Our clergy tell us that self-defence, and the protection of our families, is a duty which we may not innocently neglect, while they denounce nonresistance as the "doctrine of devils." Why, then, do not the slaves assert their freedom, and meet the invaders of their rights in mortal combat, as our fathers did? Why is not Madison Washington George Washington? And why are not Charles Remond and Frederic Douglass and Lundsford Lane, the Henrys and Hancocks and Adamses of a second American Revolution?

But one answer can be given to this question, and that is the one already given by the Maryville *Intelligencer*. The consciousness that, in a controversy with their masters, they must meet the combined forces, military and naval, of the whole country, alone deters them from such a movement. It is not the lily-fingered aristocracy of the South that they fear, as the South herself tells us, but the "white slaves" of the North, who have basely sold themselves for scullions to the slave power, and who are always ready to do the bidding of their haughty proprietors, whatever service they may require at their hands. The slaves know too well, that, should they unfurl the banner of freedom, and demand the recognition of their liberty and rights at the point of the bayonet, the *Northern* pulpit, aghast with holy horror at the incendiary measure, would raise the maddening cry of *insurrection*—the *Northern* church, animated by a kindred spirit, and echoing the infamous libel, would pour forth her sons in countless hordes, and a mighty avalanche of *Northern* soldiery, well disciplined for their work of death by long experience in *Northern* mobs, would rush down upon them from our *Northern* hills in exterminating wrath, and sweep away, in its desolating ruins, the last vestige of their present "forlorn hope!" Do I misrepresent the church and clergy? No! You, at least, know that this would be but to redeem their plighted faith. They stand before the world and before high Heaven sworn to protect every slave-breeder in the land in his *lawful* business of rearing men and women for the market; nor have they, as a body, ever shown any symptoms of intention to violate the requirements of their oath. They preach and practice allegiance to a government which is based upon the bones and sinews, and cemented with the blood, of millions of their countrymen, and hold themselves in readiness to execute its every decree, at the point of the bayonet. Thus emphatically are they the *holders* of the slaves—the bulwarks of the bloody slave system—and as such, at their hands, if there be any truth in Christianity, will God require the blood of every slave in our land. And, for one, so long as they continue in their present position, I deem it the duty of every friend of humanity to brand them as a Brotherhood of thieves, adulterers, man-stealers, pirates, and murderers, and to prove to the world that, in sustaining the slave system, they do actually commit all these atrocious crimes.

The Federal Compact contains another provision, as I have already intimated, which, in its operation, is no less fatal to the liberties of our enslaved countrymen than that which we have just considered; and one which implicates every friend and supporter of the Union in all the guilt and moral turpitude of slaveholding. I refer to that article of the Constitution which requires the surrender of fugitive slaves. If the Northern States were *really* free, the slaves would forthwith escape into them, and slavery would soon become extinct by emigration, as Mr. Underwood has well said. But what is now the fact? Is there liberty for the slave anywhere within the borders of the United States? When he steps upon the soil of Pennsylvania, or New York, or Massachusetts, do his shackles fall? Can he stand erect, and say, "I am free?" No! He is still a crouching slave—still clanks his chains, and starts affrighted at the crack of the driver's whip. Hotly pursued by the human hounds, which, like the fabled vulture of Prometheus, have long gorged themselves upon his vitals, he reaches forth his imploring hands to the professed ministers and followers of the meek and loving Saviour, and, with looks that would draw tears from adamant, beseeches them by all that is endearing in the ties of our common nature, and by all that is horrible in the doom of a recaptured slave, to save him from the fangs of these terrible monsters. But what is their reply? "Go back"—shame, shame on the church!—"Go back, and wear your chains! True, 'all men are created equal, and endowed by their Creator with certain inalienable rights, among which are life, liberty, and the pursuit of happiness;' and God said. 'Thou shalt not deliver to his master the servant which is escaped from his master unto thee'—but—but—but we have covenanted with the wretches who have robbed you of these rights, never to give you shelter, nor protection; but to return you, if found within our borders, again into their power."

This is no picture of the fancy, as thousands of our unhappy countrymen would testify from sad experience, if they could but speak. Indeed, it is the language of every citizen of the North who holds any other relation to the Federal Compact than that which George Washington and the first American Congress held to the colonial edicts of George III; for that instrument, as interpreted by the Supreme Court, pledges all who assent to it to withhold protection from every man who is claimed as a fugitive slave, and allow him to be dragged back into bondage. But have the Northern church and clergy ever refused to fulfil the requisitions of this infamous compact with Southern man-stealers? Have they trampled its provisions under their feet, and indignantly demanded its repeal? Never! On the contrary, with comparatively few exceptions, they have ranged themselves in one of the two great political parties which have long vied with each other in their support of slavery, and at the same time have waged an exterminating warfare against every movement in favor of universal freedom. In connection with these parties, they have kidnapped and returned into slavery vast numbers of those who, at different periods, had been so fortunate as to escape from the power of their masters; and in more instances than one have they indicted and imprisoned abolitionists for giving them succor. Thus have the church and clergy of the North voluntarily consented to become the watch-dogs of the plantation; and from long and intimate acquaintance with their fidelity in this service, I have no hesitation in recommending them to their Southern masters, as worthy candidates for the honors of a *brass collar*. And if I were to specify cases of extraordinary merit in this regard, I should name Chief

Justice Shaw and Judge Story, and the clergy generally of the city of Boston, as especially entitled to remembrance by James B. Gray, for their prompt and cordial acquiescence in his recent claim of George Latimer. It would be but an act of *justice* in Mr. G. to expend a part of the money for which he sold George in collars, inscribed with the initials of his own name, for these distinguished kidnappers. Their conduct on that occasion, as I can testify from personal observation, richly entitles them to some such lasting memento of their loyalty to the slave power.

There is another view of this subject, which presents the guilt of the Northern church and clergy in a still more glaring light. It is this: To legalize crime, and throw around it the sanction of statutory enactments, is, undeniably, an act of much greater wickedness than to perpetrate it after it has been made lawful. Thus the members of a legislative body, which should enact a law authorizing theft or murder, would more deserve the penitentiary, or gallows, than the man who merely steals, or, in a fit of anger, takes his neighbor's life. The former justify crime, and make it honorable, and thus obliterate all distinction between virtue and vice; the latter merely commits it, when legalized, but attempts no justification of his offence. But the religious professions of the country have legalized slavery, and the infernal slave trade, in the District of Columbia, and in the Territory of Florida! They have made their national capital one of the greatest slave marts on the globe; and they now hold in slavery, by direct legislation, more than thirty thousand human beings, whom they have sternly refused to emancipate. No sect can claim exemption from this charge. In whatever else they differ, they have all united, without exception, by the almost unanimous voice of their members, in opposing the abolition of slavery in those places where they have the power to emancipate, and have declared to the world, by their vote the most effective way in which they could speak on the subject), that it was their sovereign will and pleasure that the traffic in human beings, which they have branded as piracy on the coast of Africa, should be lawful and honorable commerce in the United States; and that the capital of this land of boasted freedom should be the Guinea Coast of America. Not a mother has been robbed of her babe within the District of Columbia, not a solitary woman has been sold there, without the legal sanction of more than seven eighths of every religious sect of the North. Even the Free-Will Baptists and the Quakers, with all their professed abhorrence of slavery, and their numerous public testimonies against it, in consideration of the paltry sum of four hundred dollars paid into their national treasury, license the auctioneer in human flesh in the city of Washington. I charge this offence upon these denominations, because the immediate agents in granting these licenses are men of their own choice, and men, too, who were selected with the full knowledge of the fact that they were in favor of legalizing the slave-trade, and, if elected to office, would license it in the District of Columbia. The abolitionists have long and earnestly besought the pretended ministers and followers of Christ, of the different sects, to elect men to office who would abolish all legal enactments in favor of slavery, wherever they had the power to do it; but their entreaties have been totally disregarded, and themselves treated with the most profound contempt.

The nature and enormities of the domestic slave-trade which is now carried on in the District of Columbia, on an extensive scale, under the legal sanction of nearly the entire body of the church and clergy, may be seen in the following eloquent and just description of it from a Southern pen. The language is severe, but it is the severity of truth. The only fault I find with it is, that its heaviest strokes are not aimed at those who have thrown the shield of government around this infernal traffic, and made it lawful and honorable commerce. I copy it:

[*From the Millennial Trumpeter, Tenn.*]

"Droves of negroes, chained together in dozens and scores, and hand-cuffed, have been driven through our country in numbers far surpassing any previous year. And these vile slavedrivers and dealers are swarming like buzzards round a carrion, throughout this country. You cannot pass a few miles in the great roads without having every feeling of humanity insulted and lacerated by this spectacle. Nor can you go into any county, or any neighborhood, scarcely, without seeing or hearing of some of these despicable creatures, called negro-drivers.

"WHO IS A NEGRO-DRIVER? One whose eyes dwell with delight on lacerated bodies of helpless men, women, and children; whose soul feels diabolical raptures at the chains, and hand-cuffs, and cart-whips, for inflicting tortures on weeping mothers torn from helpless babes, and on husbands and wives torn asunder forever. Who is a negro-driver? An execrable demon, who is only prevented by want of power, fellow-citizens, from driving your wives, and sons, and daughters, in chains and hand-cuffs, with the blood-stained cart-whip to market. Yea, his hardened heart would make but little difference, whether he made his ill-gotten gain by selling them to a merciless cotton or sugar grower, or by sending them directly to the flames of hell. Is your insulted humanity, ye sons of Tennessee, your insulted sense of right and wrong, your abused conviction of the rights of man, satisfied by saying the tears, and groans, and blood, of these human droves are not the tears, and groans, and blood, of our wives, children, brothers, and fathers; or these 'blood-snuffing vultures' of hell should not set their polluted tread on our soil with impunity? Their lives should atone for their audacity. And is the fountain of your sympathies dried up for the poor oppressed African, merely because he is helpless and defence-less? Is the hand of efficient aid drawn back, merely because the enchained, bleeding victim cannot help himself? Is not the African thy brother? Is he not a man, with all the sympathies and sensibilities of our nature? Was he not made in the image of God? Did not Christ die to redeem him? And shall we suffer these miscreant fiends to drive our fellow-men in chains before our eyes, as brutes are driven to market?

"The laws, you say, protect these ruffians in their nefarious traffic. Yea, the laws are often made by wretches whose characters are frequently a *fac simile* of these negro-drivers, whose moral picture would darken the black canvass of the pit. There are, at this very time, miscreants engaged in this trade, who once polluted our legislative halls. But suppose villains enough of the right hue let into the legislature, and pass laws that one order of society may violate the honor of your wives and daughters; would such a law on the pages of our statute-book secure the perpetrator from condign punishment? What can the dead letter of a statute-book do, in opposition to the public opinion of an enlightened and virtuous community?"

Dark and revolting as is the picture which I have here drawn, there yet remains to be added another shade of still deeper hue. Through whose agency was it, I ask, that a *thief* now fills the presidential chair? John Tyler, the present head and representative of the federal government, is a veteran slave-breeder—a negro-thief of the old Virginia school, who has long supported his own family in princely luxury by desolating the domestic hearthstones of his defenceless neighbors, and whose crimes in this regard, had they been perpetrated North instead of South, of Mason's and Dixon's line, would have consigned him to the state's prison for at least two centuries, or until released by death from his ignominious confinement. Of Mr. Tyler's cabinet, a majority are negro thieves—five of the judges of the Supreme Court are negro thieves—the president of the United States Senate is a negro thief—the speaker of the House of Representatives is a negro thief—the officer first in command in the U. S. army is a negro thief—a majority of all our ministers to foreign courts are negro thieves. And yet these men were all elected to office by the votes, direct or indirect, of the great body of the Northern church and clergy. But why have the clergy and their adherents shown this preference for thieves to rule the nation, and shape its destinies? Doubtless, because they are a "brotherhood of thieves," as like always seeks its like. Away, then, with all their pretentions to Christianity, or even *common honesty*. The man who votes with either of the great political parties does necessarily and inevitably legalize slavery, both of these parties being pledged not only to execute all the provisions of the Constitution in favor of slavery, but to go even farther, and perpetuate the system, with all its abominations, in the District of Columbia; the man who legalizes slavery, and throws around it the protecting shield of the government, is the most guilty and atrocious of slaveholders; and every slaveholder, as I have already shown, is guilty of the crimes of theft, adultery, man-stealing, piracy, and murder. It follows, then, as a legitimate and certain conclusion, that, as the ministers and members of the Northern church, with comparatively few exceptions, have ranged themselves in the ranks of the Whig or Democratic party, and have thus not only voluntarily formed a political alliance with the slave-claimants, in all the different states of the Union, guaranteeing their personal security, and the return of their fugitive slaves, but have also given their direct sanction to slavery, by legalizing it, and refusing to emancipate those whom they have a constitutional right to set free, they are slaveholders in the most odious sense of this term, and, as such, are guilty of all the crimes alleged against them in my first charge.

From the conclusion to which we have here arrived there is no possible escape. Two and a half millions of our countrymen, now loaded with chains and fetters, demand their liberty at our hands. Shall they be free? What say the Northern church and clergy? By voting for men to rule the country who are known to be the uncompromising opponents of abolition, they answer— No! By refusing to annul that portion of the Federal Compact which requires them to return fugitives from slavery, and put down the slaves, should they attempt to regain their liberty by a resort to arms, they answer—No! By stifling the voice of free discussion, and stirring up mobs against the abolitionists, they answer—No! Whatever influence they possess, as citizens, is all thrown into the scale of slavery. They looked upon John Tyler as he robbed the frantic mother of her babe, and forthwith made him president of the United States! They have seen Henry Clay and John C. Calhoun tear the tender and confiding wife from the fond embrace of her husband, and sell her to a stranger, and they are now eager to confer on them the same splendid honors! And at this very moment, they stand, with sword in hand, ready to thrust it into the heart of the slave, should he assert his freedom, and extend the hand of protection to his insulted and outraged wife and daughters!

Should these charges chance to meet the eye of the guilty authors of this wrong, they will doubtless ask, "Is thy servant a dog that he should do this great thing?" Yes, I answer, emphatically, ye are *dogs*—the *watch-dogs of your Southern masters, whose plantations ye guard*—and as such, ye are more brutal and inhuman than the servant of the Syrian king. Ye daily rob more than three hundred of your own country-women of their new-born babes, and doom those babes to a fate more horrible than *death*, breaking the mother's heart! Ye have recklessly trampled under foot the sacred institution of marriage, consigned every sixth woman in the country to a life of hopeless concubinage and adultery, and turned your famous Ten-Miles-Square into a mart where the rich aristocrat may lawfully sell the poor man's wife for purposes of prostitution, thus legalizing violence on female chastity in its most horrible and disgusting forms. Think, ye fathers and mothers, against whom I bring these tremendous charges; O, think of your own daughters on the block of the auctioneer, to be sold to any vile and loathsome wretch who may choose to purchase them, to pander to his beastly lusts! See your own darling son, in the person of George Latimer, kidnapped in open day, in the heart of New England's metropolis, and under the very eye of her pulpit: behold him manacled in open court, and dragged in chains through the streets of that proud city, not by a drunken mob, but by the police, with the city marshal at their head; and finally immured with felons in a dismal cell, there to wait, for weeks, with trembling anxiety, the horrible doom of a recaptured slave—and tell me if they are not *dogs*, nay, *fiends incarnate,* who perpetrate such outrages! But remember, *"Thou* art the man!"* What I have here supposed to be done to thy son and daughters, *thou* hast done to the son and daughters of another!

*   *   *

I come now to the last charge in the long catalogue of allegations which I have made against the American church and clergy. It is this—"That many of our clergy are guilty of enormities that would disgrace an Algerine pirate." And needs this allegation any further proof, after the appalling developments which I have already made? If so, I challenge a comparison between the conduct of many of the American clergy, and the Algerine pirates. Look on the darkest page of Moorish history, and tell me, has the Algerine ever sold his sister of the same faith for a "BREEDER" to "STOCK" the plantation of her haughty proprietor with human cattle, perchance the offspring of his own body? Has he shipped his brother Algerine to a foreign realm, and sold him for a galley-slave, to one of a religion differing from his own? Has he denied to a portion of his own countrymen the right to read the Koran (his Bible), and sold those countrymen into slavery to raise funds to send that same Koran to those who were ignorant of its contents in other lands? Has he ever claimed the wife and daughters of his Mahometan brothers as his *property?* Has he robbed the frantic mother of her babe, and with the price of that babe's body and soul replenished his communion cup? Nay, has he even compelled the heart-broken mother, if she observe the ordinances of her religion at all, to drink from that cup the wine which was purchased with her own child's blood? Such enormities even the tongue of calumny dares not impute to the Algerine pirate, in a solitary instance. And yet they are the settled policy of no inconsiderable portion of the American clergy!

They stain and darken almost every page of the modern history of the American church; and if generally known, they would render that church a stench in the nostrils of the heathen of every realm on the globe!

My task is done. My pledge is redeemed. I have here drawn a true but painful picture of the American church and clergy. I have proved them to be a BROTHERHOOD OF THIEVES! I have shown that multitudes of them subsist by ROBBERY and make THEFT their trade!—that they plunder the cradle of its precious contents, and rob the youthful lover of his bride!—that they steal "from principle," and teach their people that slavery "is not opposed to the will of God," but "IS A MERCIFUL VISITATION!"—that they excite the mob to deeds of violence, and advocate LYNCH LAW for the suppression of the sacred right of speech!—I have shown that they sell their own sisters in the church for the SERAGLIO, and invest the proceeds of their sales in BIBLES for the heathen!—that they rob the forlorn and despairing mother of her babe, and barter away that babe to the vintner for wine for the Lord's supper! I have shown that nearly all of them *legalize* slavery, with all its barbarous, bitter, burning wrongs, and make PIRACY lawful and honorable commerce; and that they dignify slaveholding, and render it popular, by placing MAN-STEALERS in the Presidential chair! I have shown that those who themselves abstain from these enormities, are in church fellowship with those who perpetrate them; and that, by this connection, they countenance the wrong, and strengthen the hands of the oppressor! I have shown that while with their lips they profess to believe that LIBERTY is God's free and impartial gift to all, and that it is *"inalienable,"* they hold 2,500,000 of their own country-men in the most abject bondage; thus proving to the world, that they are not *Infidels* merely, but blank ATHEISTS—disbelievers in the existence of a God who will hold them accountable for their actions! These allegations are all supported by evidence which none can controvert, and which no impartial mind can doubt. The truth of them is seen on every page of our country's history; and it is deeply *felt* by more than two millions of our enchained countrymen, who now demand their plundered rights at their hands. In making this heart-rending and appalling disclosure of their hypocrisy and crimes, I have spoken with great plainness, and at times with great severity; but it is the severity of truth and love. I have said that *only* which I could not in kindness withhold! and in discharging the painful duty which devolved upon me in this regard, I have had but a single object in view—the redemption of the oppressor from his *guilt*, and the oppressed from his *chains*. To this darling object of my heart, this letter is now dedicated. As it goes out through you, to the public, a voice of terrible warning and admonition to the guilty oppressor, but of consolation, as I trust, to the despairing slave, I only ask for it, that it may be received with the same kindness, and read with the same candor, in which it has been written.

With great respect and affection,
Your sincere friend,
S. S. Foster.

Canterbury, N. H., July, 1843.

Wendell Phillips

Wendell Phillips was a handsome, wealthy young Boston aristocrat, cordial and charming. He was a product of the Boston Latin School, Harvard College, and Harvard Law School. He had been an able debater and had distinguished himself in declamation in school, but he really began his career as a reform orator one day when he was twenty-six years old and got mad.

The attorney general of Massachusetts had spoken at a public meeting in Faneuil Hall, favorably comparing the assassination of Elijah Lovejoy, the abolitionist editor at Alton, Illinois, with the acts of the Revolutionary patriots. Already beginning to join himself in spirit to the abolitionists, Phillips simply could not take this, and other friends of his who were at the meeting encouraged him to stand up and give the other side. Apparently the moment and the man met, and Phillips' speech that day, a stirring indictment of Lovejoy's murderers, turned out to be one of the more famous of many thousands of speeches he made during a lifetime of reform speaking, on abolition and other topics he felt needed reform. He was not fascinated by the law, and the seeds of agitation were within him. He had inherited money, and so had his wife, and she supported him both morally and financially; thereafter he was able to devote most of his energies to reform, spending about thirty years almost totally on the problem of American slavery.

Phillips was an aristocrat in appearance, a gentleman who wore his self-assurance graciously. He had a fine voice and was a very persuasive speaker. While he spoke thousands of times on less controversial reforms as well (he gave one speech, "The Lost Arts," over two thousand times, for example), Phillips become more vehement as he agitated for abolition. He was almost mobbed often, but apparently he was less corrosive than his sometime friend Garrison, and he escaped imprisonment and actual bodily harm.

Phillips' family came to regard him as a fanatic; his wife, shortly after their marriage, became a semi-invalid and spent much of her time in her bedroom; nevertheless, the great encouragement she gave him seemed sufficient, and he never swerved from his course as a tireless crusader against the various evils in America as he saw them. (He was taking on the causes of women's rights, labor, and academic conservatism in his later years).

We are told that Wendell Phillips spoke clearly and effectively, without many excesses and flourishes; he read constantly and remained a scholar throughout his life. Sometimes he went too far, like all extremists, and was sarcastic, bitter, even unfair to those whom he opposed; but he had very high ideals and he continued courageously even in the face of what must have been a great deal of opposition from his former social friends, his own family, and many from whom he chose to be estranged because of his fervent reform principles. Though Wendell Phillips was the aristocratic abolitionist, he was no less sincere or effective than his more humbly born associates.

born November, 1811, Boston, Mass.
died February, 1884, in Boston

The Philosophy
of the Abolition Movement

Mr. Chairman: I have to present, from the business committee, the following resolution: —

> *Resolved*, That the object of this society is now, as it has always been, to convince our countrymen, by arguments addressed to their hearts and consciences, that slaveholding is a heinous crime, and that the duty, safety, and interest of all concerned demand its immediate abolition, without expatriation.

I wish, Mr. Chairman, to notice some objections that have been made to our course ever since Mr. Garrison began his career, and which have been lately urged again, with considerable force and emphasis, in the columns of the London Leader, the able organ of a very respectable and influential class in England. I hope, Sir, you will not think it waste of time to bring such a subject before you. I know these objections have been made a thousand times, that they have been often answered, though we generally submitted to them in silence, willing to let results speak for us. But there are times when justice to the slave will not allow us to be silent. There are many in this country, many in England, who have had their attention turned, recently, to the antislavery cause. They are asking, "Which is the best and most efficient method of helping it?" Engaged ourselves in an effort for the slave, which time has tested and success hitherto approved, we are very properly desirous that they should join us in our labors, and pour into this channel the full tide of their new zeal and great resources. Thoroughly convinced ourselves that our course is wise, we can honestly urge others to adopt it. Long experience gives us a right to advise. The fact that our course, more than all other efforts, has caused that agitation which has awakened these new converts, gives us a right to counsel them. They are our spiritual children: for their sakes, we would free the cause we love and trust from every seeming defect and plausible objection. For the slave's sake, we reiterate our explanations, that he may lose no tittle of help by the mistakes or misconceptions of his friends.

All that I have to say on these points will be to you, Mr. Chairman, very trite and familiar; but the facts may be new to some, and I prefer to state them here, in Boston, where we have lived and worked, because, if our statements are incorrect, if we claim too much, our assertions can be easily answered and disproved.

The charges to which I refer are these: that, in dealing with slaveholders and their apologists, we indulge in fierce denunciations, instead of appealing to their reason and common sense by plain statements and fair argument;— that we might have won the sympathies and support of the nation, if we would have submitted to argue this question with a manly patience; but, instead of this, we have outraged the feelings of the community by attacks, unjust and unnecessarily severe, on its most valued institutions, and gratified our spleen by indiscriminate abuse of leading men, who were often honest in their intentions, however mistaken in their views;—that we have utterly neglected the ample means that lay around us to convert the nation, submitted to no discipline, formed no plan, been guided by no foresight, but hurried on in childish, reckless, blind, and hot-headed zeal,—bigots in the narrowness of our views, and fanatics in our blind fury of invective and malignant judgment of other men's motives.

There are some who come upon our platform, and give us the aid of names and reputations less burdened than ours with popular odium, who are perpetually urging us to exercise charity in our judgments of those about us, and to consent to argue these questions. These men are ever parading their wish to draw a line between themselves and us, because *they must be permitted* to wait,—to trust more to reason than feeling,—to indulge a generous charity,—to rely on the sure influence of simple truth, uttered in love, &c., &c. I reject with scorn all these implications that *our* judgments are uncharitable,—that *we* are lacking in patience,—that *we* have any other dependence than on the simple truth, spoken with Christian frankness, yet with Christian love. These lectures, to which you, Sir, and all of us, have so often listened, would be impertinent, if they were not rather ridiculous for the gross ignorance they betray of the community, of the cause, and of the whole course of its friends.

The article in the Leader to which I refer is signed "Ion," and may be found in the Liberator of December 17, 1852. . . .

"Ion's" charges are the old ones, that we Abolitionists are hurting our own cause,—that, instead of waiting for the community to come up to our views, and endeavoring to remove prejudice and enlighten ignorance by patient explanation and fair argument, we fall at once, like children, to abusing everything and everybody,—that we imagine zeal will supply the place of common sense,—that we have never shown any sagacity in adapting our means to our ends, have never studied the national character, or attempted to make use of the materials which lay all about us to influence public opinion, but by blind, childish, obstinate fury and indiscriminate denunciation, have become "honestly impotent, and conscientious hinderances."

These, Sir, are the charges which have uniformly been brought against all reformers in all ages. "Ion" thinks the same faults are chargeable on the leaders of all the "popular movements" in England, which, he says, "are led by heroes who *fear* nothing and who *win* nothing." If the leaders of popular movements in Great Britain for the last fifty years have been *losers*, I should be curious to know what party, in "Ion's" opinion, have won? My Lord Derby and his friends seem to think Democracy has made, and is making, dangerous headway. If the men who, by popular agitation, outside of Parliament, wrung from a powerful oligarchy Parliamentary Reform, and the Abolition of the Test Acts, of High Post Rates, of Catholic Disability, of Negro Slavery and the Corn Laws, did "not win anything," it would be hard to say what winning is. If the men who, without the ballot, made Peel their tool and conquered the Duke of Wellington, are considered unsuccessful, pray what kind of a thing would success be? Those who now, at the head of that same middle class, demand the separation of Church and State, and the Extension of the Ballot, may well guess, from the fluttering of Whig and Tory dove-cotes, that soon they will "win" that same "nothing." Heaven grant they may enjoy the same *ill success* with their predecessors! On our side of the ocean, too, we ought deeply to sympathize with the leaders of the temperance movement in their entire want of success! If "Ion's" mistakes

about the antislavery cause lay as much on the surface as those I have just
noticed, it would be hardly worth while to reply to him; for as to these,
he certainly exhibits only "the extent and variety of his misinformation."

His remarks upon the antislavery movement are, however, equally inac-
curate. I claim, before you who know the true state of the case,—I claim
for the antislavery movement with which this society is identified, that,
looking back over its whole course, and considering the men connected
with it in the mass, it has been marked by sound judgment, unerring foresight, the most sagacious adaptation of means to ends, the strictest self-
discipline, the most thorough research, and an amount of patient and manly
argument addressed to the conscience and intellect of the nation, such as
no other cause of the kind, in England or this country, has ever offered. I
claim, also, that its course has been marked by a cheerful surrender of all
individual claims to merit or leadership,—the most cordial welcoming of the
slightest effort, of every honest attempt, to lighten or to break the chain of
the slave. I need not waste time by repeating the superfluous confession that
we are men, and therefore do not claim to be perfect. Neither would I be understood as denying that we use denunciation, and ridicule, and every other
weapon that the human mind knows. We must plead guilty, if there be
guilt in not knowing how to separate the sin from the sinner. With all the
fondness for abstractions attributed to us, we are not yet capable of that.
We are fighting a momentous battle at desperate odds,—one against a
thousand. Every weapon that ability or ignorance, wit, wealth, prejudice, or
fashion can command, is pointed against us. The guns are shorted to their
lips. The arrows are poisoned. Fighting against such an array, we cannot
afford to confine ourselves to any one weapon. The cause is not ours, so
that we might, rightfully, postpone or put in peril the victory by moderating
our demands, stifling our convictions, or filing down our rebukes, to gratify
any sickly taste of our own, or to spare the delicate nerves of our neighbor.
Our clients are three millions of Christian slaves, standing dumb suppliants
at the threshold of the Christian world. They have no voice but ours to utter
their complaints, or to demand justice. The press, the pulpit, the wealth, the
literature, the prejudices, the political arrangements, the present self-interest
of the country, are all against us. God has given us no weapon but the
truth, faithfully uttered, and addressed, with the old prophets' directness, to
the conscience of the individual sinner. The elements which control public
opinion and mould the masses are against us. We can but pick off here
and there a man from the triumphant majority. We have facts for those
who think, arguments for those who reason; but he who cannot be reasoned

out of his prejudices must be laughed out of them; he who cannot be argued out of his selfishness must be shamed out of it by the mirror of his hateful self held up relentlessly before his eyes. We live in a land where every man makes broad his phylactery, inscribing thereon, "All men are created equal," —"God hath made of one blood all nations of men." It seems to us that in such a land there must be, on this question of slavery, sluggards to be awakened, as well as doubters to be convinced. Many more, we verily believe, of the first than of the last. There are far more dead hearts to be quickened, than confused intellects to be cleared up,—more dumb dogs to be made to speak, than doubting consciences to be enlightened. [Loud cheers.] We have use, then, sometimes, for something beside argument.

What is the denunciation with which we are charged? It is endeavoring, in our faltering human speech, to declare the enormity of the sin of making merchandise of men,—of separating husband and wife,—taking the infant from its mother, and selling the daughter to prostitution,—of a professedly Christian nation denying, by statute, the Bible to every sixth man and woman of its population, and making it illegal for "two or three" to meet together, except a white man be present! What is this harsh criticism of motives with which we are charged? It is simply holding the intelligent and deliberate actor responsible for the character and consequences of his acts. Is there anything inherently wrong in such denunciation or such criticism? This we may claim,—we have never judged a man but out of his own mouth. We have seldom, if ever, held him to account, except for acts of which he and his own friends were proud. All that we ask the world and thoughtful men to note are the principles and deeds on which the American pulpit and American public men plume themselves. We always allow our opponents to paint their own pictures. Our humble duty is to stand by and assure the spectators that what they would take for a knave or a hypocrite is really, in American estimation, a Doctor of Divinity or Secretary of State.

The South is one great brothel, where half a million of women are flogged to prostitution, or, worse still, are degraded to believe it honorable. The public squares of half our great cities echo to the wail of families torn asunder at the auction-block; no one of our fair rivers that has not closed over the negro seeking in death a refuge from a life too wretched to bear; thousands of fugitives skulk along our highways, afraid to tell their names, and trembling at the sight of a human being; free men are kidnapped in our streets, to be plunged into that hell of slavery; and now and then one, as if by miracle, after long years, returns to make men aghast with his tale. The press says, "It is all right"; and the pulpit cries, "Amen." They print the

Bible in every tongue in which man utters his prayers; and get the money to do so by agreeing never to give the book, in the language our mothers taught us, to any negro, free or bond south of Mason and Dixon's line. The press says, "It is all right"; and the pulpit cries, "Amen." The slave lifts up his imploring eyes, and sees in every face but ours the face of an enemy. Prove to me now that harsh rebuke, indignant denunciation, scathing sarcasm, and pitiless ridicule are wholly and always unjustifiable; else we dare not, in so desperate a case, throw away any weapon which ever broke up the crust of an ignorant prejudice, roused a slumbering conscience, shamed a proud sinner, or changed, in any way, the conduct of a human being. Our aim is to alter public opinion. Did we live in a market, our talk should be of dollars and cents, and we would seek to prove only that slavery was an unprofitable investment. Were the nation one great, pure church, we would sit down and reason of "righteousness, temperance, and judgment to come." Had slavery fortified itself in a college, we would load our cannons with cold facts, and wing our arrows with arguments. But we happen to live in the world,—the world made up of thought and impulse, of self-conceit and self-interest, of weak men and wicked. To conquer, we must reach all. Our object is not to make every man a Christian or a philosopher, but to induce every one to aid in the abolition of slavery. We expect to accomplish our object long before the nation is made over into saints or elevated into philosophers. To change public opinion, we use the very tools by which it was formed. That is, all such as an honest man may touch.

All this I am not only ready to allow, but I should be ashamed to think of the slave, or to look into the face of my fellow-man, if it were otherwise. It is the only thing which justifies us to our own consciences, and makes us able to say we have done, or at least tried to do, our duty.

So far, however you distrust my philosophy, you will not doubt my statements. That we have denounced and rebuked with unsparing fidelity will not be denied. Have we not also addressed ourselves to that other duty, of arguing our question thoroughly?—of using due discretion and fair sagacity in endeavoring to promote our cause? Yes, we have. Every statement we have made has been doubted. Every principle we have laid down has been denied by overwhelming majorities against us. No one step has ever been gained but by the most laborious research and the most exhausting argument. And no question has ever, since Revolutionary days been so thoroughly investigated or argued here, as that of slavery. Of that research and that argument, of the whole of it, the old-fashioned, fanatical, crazy Garrisonian antislavery movement has been the author. From this band of men has proceeded every important argument or idea which has been broached on the antislavery question from 1830 to the present time [Cheers.] I am well aware of the extent of the claim I make. I recognize, as fully as any one can, the ability of the new laborers,—the eloquence and genius with which they have recommended this cause to the nation, and flashed conviction home on the conscience of the community. I do not mean, either, to assert that they have in every instance borrowed from our treasury their facts and arguments. Left to themselves, they would probably have looked up the one and originated the other. As a matter of fact, however, they have generally made use of the materials collected to their hands. But there are some persons about us, sympathizers to a great extent with "Ion," who pretend that the antislavery movement has been hitherto mere fanaticism, its only weapon angry abuse. They are obliged to assert this, in order to justify their past indifference or hostility. At present, when it suits their purpose to give it some attention, they endeavor to explain the change by alleging that now it has been taken up by men of thoughtful minds, and its claims are urged by fair discussion and able argument. My claim, then, is this: that neither the charity of the most timid of sects, the sagacity of our wisest converts, nor the culture of the ripest scholars, though all have been aided by our twenty years' experience, has yet struck out any new method of reaching the public mind, or originated any new argument or train of thought, or discovered any new fact bearing on the question. When once brought fully into the struggle, they have found it necessary to adopt the same means, to rely on the same arguments, to hold up the same men and the same measures to public reprobation, with the same bold rebuke and unsparing invective that we have used. All their conciliatory bearing, their painstaking moderation, their constant and anxious endeavor to draw a broad line between their camp and ours, have been thrown away. Just so far as they have been effective laborers, they have found, as we have, their hands against every man, and every man's hand against them. The most experienced of them are ready to acknowledge that our plan has been wise, our course efficient, and that our unpopularity is no fault of ours, but flows necessarily and unavoidably from our position. "I should suspect," says old Fuller, "that his preaching had no salt in it, if no galled horse did wince." Our friends find, after all, that men do not so much hate us as the truth we utter and the light we bring. They find that the community are not the honest seekers after truth which they fancied, but selfish politicians and sectarian bigots, who shiver, like Alexander's butler, whenever the sun shines on them. Experience has driven these new laborers back to our method. We have no quarrel with them,—would not steal one wreath of their laurels. All we claim is, that, if they are to be complimented as prudent, moderate, Christian, sagacious, statesmanlike reformers, we deserve the same praise; for they have done nothing that we, in our measure, did not attempt before. [Cheers.]

I claim this, that the cause, in its recent aspect, has put on nothing but timidity. It has taken to itself no new weapons of recent years; it has become more compromising,—that is all! It has become neither more persuasive, more learned, more Christian, more charitable, nor more effective than for the twenty years preceding. Mr. Hale, the head of the Free Soil movement, after a career in the Senate that would do honor to any man,—after a six years' course which entitles him to the respect and confidence of the anti-slavery public,—can put his name, within the last month, to an appeal from the city of Washington, signed by a Houston and a Cass, for a monument to be raised to Henry Clay! If that be the test of charity and courtesy, we cannot give it to the world. [Loud cheers.] Some of the leaders of the Free Soil party of Massachusetts, after exhausting the whole capacity of our language to paint the treachery of Daniel Webster to the cause of liberty, and the evil they thought he was able and seeking to do,—after that, could feel it in their hearts to parade themselves in the funeral procession got up to do him honor! In this we allow we cannot follow them. The deference which every gentleman owes to the proprieties of social life, that self-respect and regard to consistency which is every man's duty,—these, if no deeper feelings, will ever prevent us from giving such proofs of this newly-invented Christian courtesy. [Great cheering.] We do not *play* politics; antislavery is no half-jest with us; it is a terrible earnest, with life or death, worse than life or death, on the issue. It is no lawsuit, where it matters not to the good feeling of opposing counsel which way the verdict goes, and where advocates can shake hands after the decision as pleasantly as before. When we think of such a man as Henry Clay, his long life, his mighty influence cast always into the scale against the slave,—of that irresistible fascination with which he moulded every one to his will; when we remember that, his conscience acknowledging the justice of our cause, and his heart open on every other side to the gentlest impulses, he could sacrifice so remorsely his convictions and the welfare of millions to his low ambition; when we think how the slave trembled at the sound of his voice, and that, from a multitude of breaking hearts there went up nothing but gratitude to God when it pleased him to call that great sinner from this world,—we cannot find it in our hearts, we could not shape our lips to ask any man to do him honor. [Great sensation.] No amount of eloquence, no sheen of official position, no loud grief of partisan friends, would ever lead us to ask monuments or walk in fine processions for pirates; and the sectarian zeal or selfish ambition which gives up, deliberately and in full knowledge of the facts, three million of human beings to hopeless ignorance, daily robbery, systematic prostitution, and murder, which the law is neither able nor undertakes to prevent or avenge, is more monstrous, in our eyes, than the love of gold which takes a score of lives with merciful quickness on the high seas. Haynau on the Danube is no more hateful to us than Haynau on the Potomac. Why give mobs to one, and monuments to the other?

If these things be necessary to courtesy, I cannot claim that we are courteous. We seek only to be honest men, and speak the same of the dead as of the living. If the grave that hides their bodies could swallow also the evil they have done and the example they leave, we might enjoy at least the luxury of forgetting them. But the evil that men do lives after them, and example acquires tenfold authority when it speaks from the grave. History, also, is to be written. How shall a feeble minority, without weight or influence in the country, with no jury of millions to appeal to,—denounced, vilified, and contemned,—how shall we make way against the overwhelming weight of some colossal reputation, if we do not turn from the idolatrous present, and appeal to the human race? saying to your idols of to-day, "Here we are defeated; but we will write our judgment with the iron pen of a century to come, and it shall never be forgotten, if we can help it, that you were false in your generation to the claims of the slave!" [Loud cheers.]

At present, our leading men, strong in the support of large majorities, and counting safely on the prejudices of the community, can afford to despise us. They know they can overawe or cajole the Present; their only fear is the judgment of the Future. Strange fear, perhaps, considering how short and local their fame! But however little, it is their all. Our only hold upon them is the thought of that bar of posterity, before which we are all to stand. Thank God! there is the elder brother of the Saxon race across the water,—there is the army of honest men to come! Before that jury we summon you. We are weak here,—out-talked, out-voted. You load our names with infamy, and shout us down. But our words bide their time. We warn the living that we have terrible memories, and that their sins are never to be forgotten. We will gibbet the name of every apostate so black and high that his children's children shall blush to bear it. Yet we bear no malice,— cherish no resentment. We thank God that the love of fame, "that last infirmity of noble mind," is shared by the ignoble. In our necessity, we seize this weapon in the slave's behalf, and teach caution to the living by meting out relentless justice to the dead. How strange the change death produces in the way a man is talked about here! While leading men live, they avoid as much as possible all mention of slavery, from fear of being thought Abolitionists. The moment they are dead, their friends rake up every word they ever contrived to whisper in a corner for liberty, and parade it before the world; growing angry, all the while, with us, because we insist on explaining these chance expressions by the tenor of a long and base life. While drunk with the temptations of the present hour, men are willing to bow to any Moloch. When their friends bury them, they feel what bitter mockery, fifty years hence, any epitaph will be, if it cannot record of one living in this era some service rendered to the slave! These, Mr. Chairman, are the reasons why we take care that "the memory of the wicked shall rot."

I have claimed that the antislavery cause has, from the first, been ably and dispassionately argued, every objection candidly examined, and every difficulty or doubt anywhere honestly entertained treated with respect. Let me glance at the literature of the cause, and try not so much, in a brief hour, to prove this assertion, as to point out the sources from which any one may satisfy himself of its truth.

I will begin with certainly the ablest and perhaps the most honest statesman who has ever touched the slave question. Any one who will examine John Quincy Adams's speech on Texas, in 1838, will see that he was only seconding the full and able exposure of the Texas plot, prepared by Benjamin Lundy, to one of whose pamphlets Dr. Channing, in his "Letter to Henry Clay," has confessed his obligation. Every one acquainted with those years will allow that the North owes its earliest knowledge and first awakening on the subject to Mr. Lundy, who made long journeys and devoted years to the investigation. His labors have this attestation, that they quickened the zeal and strengthened the hands of such men as Adams and Channing. I have been told that Mr. Lundy prepared a brief for Mr. Adams, and furnished him the materials for his speech on Texas.

Look next at the right of petition. Long before any member of Congress had opened his mouth in its defence, the Abolition presses and lecturers had examined and defended the limits of this right with profound historical research and eminent constitutional ability. So thoroughly had the work been done, that all classes of the people had made up their minds about it long before any speaker of eminence had touched it in Congress. The politicians were little aware of this. When Mr. Adams threw himself so gallantly into the breach, it is said he wrote anxiously home to know whether he would be supported in Massachusetts, little aware of the outburst of popular gratitude which the Northern breeze was even then bringing him, deep and cordial enough to wipe away the old grudge Massachusetts had borne him so long. Mr. Adams himself was only in favor of receiving the petitions, and advised to refuse their prayer, which was the abolition of slavery in the District. He doubted the power of Congress to abolish. His doubts were examined by Mr. William Goodell, in two letters of most acute logic, and of masterly ability. If Mr. Adams still retained his doubts, it is certain at least that he never expressed them afterward. When Mr. Clay paraded the same objections, the whole question of the power of Congress over the district was treated by Theodore D. Weld in the fullest manner, and with the widest research,—indeed, leaving nothing to be added: an argument which Dr. Channing characterized as "demonstration," and pronounced the essay "one of the ablest pamphlets from the American press." No answer was ever attempted. The best proof of its ability is, that no one since has presumed to doubt the power. Lawyers and statesmen have tacitly settled down into its full acknowledgement.

The influence of the Colonization Society on the welfare of the colored race was the first question our movement encountered. To the close logic, eloquent appeals, and fully sustained charges of Mr. Garrison's Letters on that subject no answer was ever made. Judge Jay followed with a work full and able, establishing every charge by the most patient investigation of facts. It is not too much to say of these two volumes, that they left the Colonization Society hopeless at the North. It dares never show its face before the people, and only lingers in some few nooks of sectarian pride, so secluded from the influence of present ideas as to be almost fossil in their character.

The practical working of the slave system, the slave laws, the treatment of slaves, their food, the duration of their lives, their ignorance and moral condition, and the influence of Southern public opinion on their fate, have been spread out in a detail and with a fulness of evidence which no subject has ever received before in this country. Witness the works of Phelps, Bourne, Rankin, Grimke, the "Antislavery Record," and, above all, that encyclopaedia of facts and storehouse of arguments, the "Thousand Witnesses" of Mr. Theodore D. Weld. He also prepared that full and valuable tract for the World's Convention called "Slavery and the Internal Slave-Trade in the United States," published in London, 1841. Unique in antislavery literature is Mrs. Child's "Appeal," one of the ablest of our weapons, and one of the finest efforts of her rare genius.

The Princeton Review, I believe, first challenged the Abolitionists to an investigation of the teachings of the Bible on slavery. That field had been somewhat broken by our English predecessors. But in England, the pro-slavery party had been soon shamed out of the attempt to drag the Bible into their service, and hence the discussion there had been short and somewhat superficial. The proslavery side of the question has been eagerly sustained by theological reviews and doctors of divinity without number, from the halfway and timid faltering of Wayland up to the unblushing and melancholy recklessness of Stuart. The argument on the other side has come wholly from the Abolitionists; for neither Dr. Hague nor Dr. Barnes can be said to have added anything to the wide research, critical acumen, and comprehensive views of Theodore D. Weld, Beriah Green, J. G. Fee, and the old work of Duncan.

On the constitutional questions which have at various times arisen,—the citizenship of the colored man, the soundness of the "Prigg" decision, the constitutionality of the old Fugitive Slave Law, the true construction of the slave-surrender clause,—nothing has been added, either in the way of fact or argument, to the works of Jay, Weld, Alvan Stewart, E. G. Loring, S. E. Sewall, Richard Hildreth, W. I. Bowditch, the masterly essays of the Emancipator at New York and the Liberator at Boston, and the various addresses of the Massachusetts and American Societies for the last twenty years. The idea of the antislavery character of the Constitution,—the opiate with which Free Soil quiets its conscience for voting under a proslavery government,— I heard first suggested by Mr. Garrison in 1838. It was elaborately argued that year in all our antislavery gatherings, both here and in New York, and sustained with great ability by Alvan Stewart, and in part by T. D. Weld. The antislavery construction of the Constitution was ably argued in 1836, in the "Antislavery Magazine," by Rev. Samuel J. May, one of the very first to seek the side of Mr. Garrison, and pledge to the slave his life and efforts,— a pledge which thirty years of devoted labors have nobly redeemed. If it has either merit or truth, they are due to no legal learning recently added to our ranks, but to some of the old and well-known pioneers. This claim has since received the fullest investigation from Mr. Lysander Spooner, who has urged it with all his unrivalled ingenuity, laborious research, and close logic. He writes as a lawyer, and has no wish, I believe, to be ranked with any class of antislavery men.

The influence of slavery on our government has received the profoundest philosophical investigation from the pen of Richard Hildreth, in his invaluable essay on "Despotism in America,"—a work which deserves a place by the side of the ablest political disquisitions of any age.

Mrs. Chapman's survey of "Ten Years of Antislavery Experience," was the first attempt at a philosophical discussion of the various aspects of the antislavery cause, and the problems raised by its struggles with sect and party. You, Mr. Chairman, [Edmund Quincy, Esq.,] in the elaborate Reports of the Massachusetts Antislavery Society for the last ten years, have followed in the same path, making to American literature a contribution of the highest value, and in a department where you have few rivals and no superior. Whoever shall write the history either of this movement, or any other attempted under a republican government, will find nowhere else so clear an insight and so full an acquaintance with the most difficult part of his subject.

Even the vigorous mind of Rantoul, the ablest man, without doubt, of the Democratic party, and perhaps the ripest politician in New England, added little or nothing to the storehouse of antislavery argument. The grasp of his intellect and the fulness of his learning every one will acknowledge. He never trusted himself to speak on any subject till he had dug down to its primal granite. He laid a most generous contribution on the altar of the antislavery cause. His speeches on our question, too short and too few, are remarkable for their compact statement, iron logic, bold denunciation, and the wonderful light thrown back upon our history. Yet how little do they present which was not familiar for years in our antislavery meetings!

Look, too, at the last great effort of the idol of so many thousands, Mr. Senator Sumner,—the discussion of a great national question, of which it has been said that we must go back to Webster's Reply to Hayne, and Fisher Ames on the Jay Treaty, to find its equal in Congress,—praise which we might perhaps qualify, if any adequate report were left us of some of the noble orations of Adams. No one can be blind to the skilful use he has made of his materials, the consummate ability with which he has marshalled them, and the radiant glow which his genius has thrown over all. Yet, with the exception of his reference to the antislavery debate in Congress, in 1817, there is hardly a train of thought or argument, and no single fact in the whole speech, which has not been familiar in our meetings and essays for the last ten years.

Before leaving the halls of Congress, I have great pleasure in recognizing one exception to my remarks, Mr. Giddings. Perhaps he is no real exception, since it would not be difficult to establish his claim to be considered one of the original Abolition party. But whether he would choose to be so considered or not, it is certainly true that his long presence at the seat of government, his wholesouled devotedness, his sagacity and unwearied industry, have made him a large contributor to our antislavery resources.

*   *   *

Many of these services to the slave were done before I joined his cause. In thus referring to them, do not suppose me merely seeking occasion of

eulogy on my predecessors and present co-laborers. I recall these things only
to rebut the contemptuous criticism which some about us make the excuse
for their past neglect of the movement, and in answer to "Ion's" representation of our course as reckless fanaticism, childish impatience, utter lack of
good sense, and of our meetings as scenes only of excitement, of reckless and
indiscriminate denunciation. I assert that every social, moral, economical,
religious, political, and historical aspect of the question has been ably and
patiently examined. And all this has been done with an industry and ability
which have left little for the professional skill, scholarly culture, and historical learning of the new laborers to accomplish. If the people are still in
doubt, it is from the inherent difficulty of the subject, or a hatred of light,
not from want of it.

*   *   *

Mr. "Ion" thinks, also, that we have thrown away opportunities, and
needlessly outraged the men and parties about us. Far from it. The antislavery
movement was a patient and humble suppliant at every door whence any
help could possibly be hoped. If we now repudiate and denounce some of
our institutions, it is because we have faithfully tried them, and found them
deaf to the claims of justice and humanity. Our great Leader, when he first
meditated this crusade, did not

At once, like a sunburst, his banner unfurl.

O no! he sounded his way warily forward. Brought up in the strictest reverence for church organizations, his first effort was to enlist the clergymen of
Boston in the support of his views. On their aid he counted confidently in
his effort to preach immediate repentance of all sin. He did not go, with
malice prepense, as some seem to imagine, up to that "attic" where Mayor
Otis with difficulty found him. He did not court hostility or seek exile. He
did not sedulously endeavor to cut himself off from the sympathy and
countenance of the community about him. O no! A fervid disciple of the
American Church, he conferred with some of the leading clergy of the city,
and laid before them his convictions on the subject of slavery. He painted
their responsibility, and tried to induce them to take from his shoulders the
burden of so mighty a movement. He laid himself at their feet. He recognized
the colossal strength of the Clergy; he knew that against their opposition
it would be almost desperate to attempt to relieve the slave. He entreated
them, therefore, to take up the cause. But the Clergy turned away from him!
They shut their doors upon him! They bade him compromise his convictions,—smother one half of them, and support the colonization movement,

making his own auxiliary to that, or they would have none of him. Like Luther, he said: "Here I stand; God help me; I can do nothing else!" But the men who joined him were not persuaded that the case was so desperate. They returned, each to his own local sect, and remained in them until some of us, myself among the number,—later converts to the antislavery movement, —thought they were slow and faltering in their obedience to conscience, and that they ought to have cut loose much sooner than they did. But a patience, which old sympathies would not allow to be exhausted, and associations, planted deeply in youth, and spreading over a large part of manhood, were too strong for any mere argument to dislodge them. So they still persisted in remaining in the Church. Their zeal was so fervent, and their labors so abundant, that in some towns large societies were formed, led by most of the clergymen, and having almost all the church-members on their lists. In those same towns now you will not find one single Abolitionist, of any stamp whatever. They excuse their falling back by alleging that we have injured the cause by our extravagance and denunciation, and by the various other questions with which our names are associated. This might be a good reason why they should not work with us, but does it excuse their not working at all? These people have been once awakened, thoroughly instructed in the momentous character of the movement, and have acknowledged the rightful claim of the slave on their sympathy and exertions. It is not possible that a few thousand persons, however extravagant, could prevent devoted men from finding some way to help such a cause, or at least manifesting their interest in it. But they have not only left us, they have utterly deserted the slave, in the hour when the interests of their sects came across his cause. Is it uncharitable to conjecture the reason? At the early period, however, to which I have referred, the Church was much exercised by the persistency of the Abolitionists in not going out from her. When I joined the antislavery ranks, sixteen years ago, the voice of the clergy was: "Will these *pests* never leave us? Will they still remain to trouble us? If you do not like us, there is the door!" When our friends had exhausted all entreaty, and tested the Christianity of that body, they shook off the dust of their feet, and came out of her.

At the outset, Mr. Garrison called on the head of the Orthodox denomination,—a man compared with whose influence on the mind of New England that of the statesman whose death you have just mourned was, I think, but as dust in the balance,—a man who then held the Orthodoxy of Boston in his right hand, and who has since taken up the West by its four corners, and given it so largely to Puritanism,—I mean the Rev. Dr. Lyman Beecher. Mr. Garrison was one of those who bowed to the spell of that matchless

eloquence which then fulmined over our Zion. He waited on his favorite
divine, and urged him to give to the new movement the incalculable aid of
his name and countenance. He was patiently heard. He was allowed to unfold
his plans and array his facts. The reply of the veteran was, "Mr. Garrison, I
have too many irons in the fire to put in another." My friend said, "Doctor,
you had better take them all out and put this one in, if you mean well either
to the religion or to the civil liberty of our country." [Cheers.]

The great Orthodox leader did not rest with merely refusing to put another iron in his fire; he attempted to limit the irons of other men. As
President of Lane Theological Seminary, he endeavored to prevent the students from investigating the subject of slavery. The result, we all remember,
was a strenuous resistance on the part of a large number of the students, led
by that remarkable man, Theodore D. Weld. The right triumphed, and
Lane Seminary lost her character and noblest pupils at the same time. She
has languished ever since, even with such a President. Why should I follow
Dr. Beecher into those ecclesiastical conventions where he has been tried,
and found wanting, in fidelity to the slave? He has done no worse, indeed
he has done much better, than most of his class. His opposition has always
been open and manly.

*　　*　　*

Sir, when a nation sets itself to do evil, and all its leading forces, wealth,
party, and piety, join in the career, it is impossible but that those who offer
a constant opposition should be hated and maligned, no matter how wise,
cautious, and well planned their course may be. We are peculiar sufferers
in this way. The community has come to hate its reproving Nathan so bitterly,
that even those whom the relenting part of it is beginning to regard as
standard-bearers of the antislavery host think it unwise to avow any connection or sympathy with him. I refer to some of the leaders of the political
movement against slavery. They feel it to be their mission to marshal and
use as effectively as possible the present convictions of the people. They
cannot afford to encumber themselves with the odium which twenty years of
angry agitation have engendered in great sects sore from unsparing rebuke,
parties galled by constant defeat, and leading men provoked by unexpected
exposure. They are willing to confess, privately, that our movement produced
theirs, and that its continued existence is the very breath of their life. But,
at the same time, they would fain walk on the road without being soiled by
too close contact with the rough pioneers who threw it up. They are wise
and honorable, and their silence is very expressive.

When I speak of their eminent position and acknowledged ability, another thought strikes me. Who converted these men and their distinguished associates? It is said we have shown neither sagacity in plans, nor candor in discussion, nor ability. Who, then, or what, converted Burlingame and Wilson, Sumner and Adams, Palfrey and Mann, Chase and Hale, and Phillips and Giddings? Who taught the Christian Register, the Daily Advertiser, and that class of prints, that there were such things as a slave and a slaveholder in the land, and so gave them some more intelligent basis than their mere instincts to hate William Lloyd Garrison? [Shouts and laughter.] What magic wand was it whose touch made the toadying servility of the land start up the real demon that it was, and at the same time gathered into the slave's service the professional ability, ripe culture, and personal integrity which grace the Free Soil ranks? We never argue! These men, then, were converted by simple denunciation! They were all converted by the "hot," "reckless," "ranting," "bigoted," "fanatic" Garrison, who never troubled himself about facts, nor stopped to argue with an opponent, but straightway knocked him down! [Roars of laughter and cheers.] My old and valued friend, Mr. Sumner, often boasts that he was a reader of the Liberator before I was. Do not criticise too much the agency by which such men were converted. That blade has a double edge. Our reckless course, our empty rant, our fanaticism, has made Abolitionists of some of the best and ablest men in the land. We are inclined to go on, and see if even with such poor tools we cannot make some more. [Enthusiastic applause.] Antislavery zeal and the roused conscience of the "godless come-outers" made the trembling South demand the Fugitive Slave Law, and the Fugitive Slave Law "provoked" Mrs. Stowe to the good work of "Uncle Tom." That is something! [Cheers.] Let me say, in passing, that you will nowhere find an earlier or more generous appreciation, or more flowing eulogy, of these men and their labors, than in the columns of the Liberator. No one, however feeble, has ever peeped or muttered, in any quarter, that the vigilant eye of the Pioneer has not recognized him. He has stretched out the right hand of a most cordial welcome the moment any man's face was turned Zionward. [Loud cheers.]

I do not mention these things to praise Mr. Garrison, I do not stand here for that purpose. You will not deny—if you do, I can prove it—that the movement of the Abolitionists converted these men. Their constituents were converted by it. The assault upon the right of petition, upon the right to print and speak of slavery, the denial of the right of Congress over the District, the annexation of Texas, the Fugitive Slave Law, were measures which the antislavery movement provoked, and the discussion of which has made all the Abolitionists we have. The antislavery cause, then, converted these men; it gave them a constituency; it gave them an opportunity to speak, and it gave them a public to listen. The antislavery cause gave them their votes, got them their offices, furnished them their facts, gave them their audience. If you tell me they cherished all these principles in their own breasts before Mr. Garrison appeared, I can only say, if the antislavery movement did not give them their ideas, it surely gave the courage to utter them.

In such circumstances, is it not singular that the name of William Lloyd Garrison has never been pronounced on the floor of the United States Congress linked with any epithet but that of contempt! No one of those men who owe their ideas, their station, their audience, to him, have ever thought it worth their while to utter one word in grateful recognition of the power which called them into being. When obliged, by the course of their argument, to treat the question historically, they can go across the water to Clarkson and Wilberforce,—yes, to a safe salt-water distance. [Laughter.] As Daniel Webster, when he was talking to the farmers of Western New York, and wished to contrast slave labor and free labor, did not dare to compare New York with Virginia,—sister States, under the same government, planted by the same race, worshipping at the same altar, speaking the same language,— identical in all respects, save that one in which he wished to seek the contrast; but no; he compared it with Cuba,—[cheers and laughter,]—the contrast was so close! [Renewed cheers.] Catholic—Protestant; Spanish— Saxon; despotism—municipal institutions; readers of Lope de Vega and of Shakespeare; mutterers of the Mass—children of the Bible! But Virginia is too near home! So is Garrison! One would have thought there was something in the human breast which would sometimes break through policy. These noble-hearted men whom I have named must surely have found quite irksome the constant practice of what Dr. Gardiner used to call "that despicable virtue, prudence"! [Laughter.] One would have thought, when they heard that name spoken with contempt, their ready eloquence would have leaped from its scabbard to avenge even a word that threatened him with insult. But it never came,—never! [Sensation.]

* * *

If all I have said to you is untrue, if I have exaggerated, explain to me this fact. In 1831, Mr. Garrison commenced a paper advocating the doctrine of immediate emancipation. He had against him the thirty thousand churches and all the clergy of the country,—its wealth, its commerce, its press. In 1831, what was the state of things? There was the most entire ignorance and apathy on the slave question. If men knew of the existence of slavery, it was only as a part of picturesque Virginia life. No one preached, no one talked, no one wrote about it. No whisper of it stirred the surface of the political sea. The Church heard of it occasionally, when some colonization agent asked funds to send the blacks to Africa. Old school-books tainted with some antislavery selections had passed out of use, and new ones were compiled to suit the times. Soon as any dissent from the prevailing faith appeared, every one set himself to crush it. The pulpits preached at it; the press denounced it; mobs tore down houses, threw presses into the fire and the stream, and shot the editors; religious conventions tried to smother it; parties arrayed themselves against it. Daniel Webster boasted in the Senate, that he had never introduced the subject of slavery to that body, and never would. Mr. Clay, in 1839, makes a speech for the Presidency, in which he says, that to discuss the subject of slavery is moral treason, and that no man has a right to introduce the subject into Congress. Mr. Benton, in 1844, laid down his platform, and he not only denies the right, but asserts that he never has and never will discuss the subject. Yet Mr. Clay, from 1839 down to his death, hardly made a remarkable speech of any kind, except on slavery. Mr. Webster, having indulged now and then in a little easy rhetoric, as at Niblo's and elsewhere, opens his mouth in 1840, generously contributing his aid to both sides, and stops talking about it only when death closes his lips. Mr. Benton's six or eight speeches in the United States Senate have all been on the subject of slavery in the Southwestern section of the country, and form the basis of whatever claim he has to the character of a statesman, and he owes his seat in the next Congress somewhat, perhaps, to antislavery pretensions! The Whig and Democratic parties pledged themselves just as emphatically against the antislavery discussion,—against agitation and free speech. These men said: "It sha'n't be talked about, it won't be talked about!" These are *your statesmen!*—men who understand the present, that is, and mould the future! The man who understands his own time, and whose genius moulds the future to his views, he is a statesman, is he not? These men devoted themselves to banks, to the tariff, to internal improvements, to constitutional and financial questions. They said to slavery: "Back! no entrance here! We pledge ourselves against you." And then there came up a humble printer-boy, who whipped them into the traces, and made them talk, like Hotspur's starling, nothing BUT slavery. He scattered all these gigantic shadows,—tariff, bank, constitutional questions, financial questions,— and slavery, like the colossal head in Walpole's romance, came up and filled the whole political horizon! [Enthusiastic applause.] Yet you must remember he is not a statesman; he is a "fanatic." He has no discipline,—Mr. "Ion" says so; he does not understand the "discipline that is essential to victory"!

This man did not understand his own time,—he did not know what the future was to be,—he was not able to shape it,—he had no "prudence,"—he had no "foresight"! Daniel Webster says, "I have never introduced this subject, and never will,"—and died broken-hearted because he had not been able to talk enough about it. Benton says, "I will never speak of slavery," and lives to break with his party on this issue! Mr. Clay says it is "moral treason" to introduce the subject into Congress, and lives to see Congress turned into an antislavery debating-society, to suit the purpose of one "too powerful individual"!

These were statesmen, mark you! Two of them have gone to their graves covered with eulogy; and our national stock of eloquence is all insufficient to describe how profound and far-reaching was the sagacity of Daniel Webster! Remember who it was that said, in 1831, "I am in earnest,—I will not equivocate,—I will not excuse,—I will not retreat a single inch,—*and I will be heard!*" [Repeated cheers.] That speaker has lived twenty-two years, and the complaint of twenty-three millions of people is, "Shall we never hear of anything but slavery?" [Cheers.] I heard Dr. Kirk, of Boston, say in his own pulpit, when he returned from London,—where he had been as a representative to the "Evangelical Alliance,"—"I went up to London, and they asked me what I thought of the question of immediate emancipation. They examined us all. Is an American never to travel anywhere in the world but men will throw this troublesome question in his face?" Well, it is all HIS fault [pointing to Mr. Garrison]. [Enthusiastic cheers.]

Now, when we come to talk of statesmanship, of sagacity in choosing time and measures, of endeavor, by proper means, to right the public mind, of keen insight into the present and potent sway over the future, it seems to me that the Abolitionists, who have taken—whether for good or for ill, whether to their discredit or to their praise—this country by the four corners, and shaken it until you can hear nothing but slavery, whether you travel in railroad or steamboat, whether you enter the hall of legislation or read the columns of a newspaper,—it seems to me that such men may point to the present aspect of the nation, to their originally avowed purpose, to the pledges and efforts of all your great men against them, and then let you determine to which side the credit of sagacity and statesmanship belongs. Napoleon busied himself, at St. Helena, in showing how Wellington ought not to have conquered at Waterloo. The world has never got time to listen to the explanation. Sufficient for it that the Allies entered Paris. In like manner, it seems hardly the province of a defeated Church and State to deny the skill of measures by which they have been conquered.

It may sound strange to some, this claim for Mr. Garrison of a profound statesmanship. Men have heard him styled a mere fanatic so long, that they are incompetent to judge him fairly. "The phrases men are accustomed," says Goethe, "to repeat incessantly, end by becoming convictions, and ossify the organs of intelligence." I cannot accept you, therefore, as my jury. I appeal from Festus to Caesar; from the prejudice of our streets to the common sense of the world, and to your children.

Every thoughtful and unprejudiced mind must see that such an evil as slavery will yield only to the most radical treatment. If you consider the work we have to do, you will not think us needlessly aggressive, or that we dig down unnecessarily deep in laying the foundations of our enterprise. A money power of two thousand millions of dollars, as the prices of slaves now range, held by a small body of able and desperate men; that body raised into a political aristocracy by special constitutional provisions; cotton, the product of slave labor, forming the basis of our whole foreign commerce, and the commercial class thus subsidized; the press bought up, the pulpit reduced to vassalage, the heart of the common people chilled by a bitter prejudice against the black race; our leading men bribed, by ambition, either to silence or open hostility;—in such a land, on what shall an Abolitionist rely? On a few cold prayers, mere lip-service, and never from the heart? On a church resolution, hidden often in its records, and meant only as a decent cover for servility in daily practice? On political parties, with their superficial influence at best, and seeking ordinarily only to use existing prejudices to the best advantage? Slavery has deeper root here than any aristocratic institution has in Europe; and politics is but the common pulse-beat, of which revolution is the fever-spasm. Yet we have seen European aristocracy survive storms which seemed to reach down to the primal strata of European life. Shall we, then, trust to mere politics, where even revolution has failed? How shall the stream rise above its fountain? Where shall our church organizations or parties get strength to attack their great parent and moulder, the Slave Power? Shall the thing formed say to him that formed it, Why hast thou made me thus? The old jest of one who tried to lift himself in his own basket, is but a tame picture of the man who imagines that, by working solely through existing sects and parties, he can destroy slavery. Mechanics say nothing but an earthquake, strong enough to move all Egypt, can bring down the Pyramids.

Experience has confirmed these views. The Abolitionists who have acted on them have a "short method" with all unbelievers. They have but to point to their own success, in contrast with every other man's failure. To waken the nation to its real state, and chain it to the consideration of this one duty, is half the work. So much we have done. Slavery has been made the question of this generation. To startle the South to madness, so that every step she takes, in her blindness, is one step more toward ruin, is much. This we have done. Witness Texas and the Fugitive Slave Law. To have elaborated for the nation the only plan of redemption, pointed out the only exodus from this "sea of troubles," is much. This we claim to have done in our motto of IMMEDIATE, UNCONDITIONAL EMANCIPATION ON THE SOIL. The closer any statesmanlike mind looks into the question, the more favor our plan finds with it. The Christian asks fairly of the infidel, "If this religion be not from God, how do you explain its triumph, and the history of the first three centuries?" Our question is similar. If our agitation has not been wisely planned and conducted, explain for us the history of the last twenty years! Experience is a safe light to walk by, and he is not a rash man who expects success in future from the same means which have secured it in times past.

Part III
Black Abolitionists

Black speakers for antislavery tended to be followers of the Garrisonian tradition of agitation. Garrison was on good terms with the leading communities of free blacks in the Northeast, and they supplied the bulk of the readers for *The Liberator*. Two of the speakers represented here, Remond and Douglass, were protegés of Garrison and participated in the rhetoric of agitation in their early careers.

That black speakers need not necessarily be of the Garrison persuasion was demonstrated when Frederick Douglass moved to Rochester, New York, toward the close of 1847 to establish his paper, *The North Star*. In Rochester Douglass came under the influence of the evangelical wing as represented by Gerrit Smith and William Goodell. By 1851, Douglass no longer viewed the Constitution as a proslavery compromise, no longer believed in strict reliance on moral suasion, and no longer subscribed to the Garrisonian doctrine of nonresistance. Douglass also came to believe in working within the political system to utilize the ballot box to achieve reforms and assumed a leading role in the new Republican party.

The three speeches presented here, however, carry the earmarks of the rhetoric of agitation. They are presented chronologically, with Henry Highland Garnet's "An Address To the Slaves of the United States of America," which was delivered at the National Convention of Colored Citizens in Buffalo, New York, in 1843, coming first. Foner called the speech the "most savage indictment of slavery delivered by a Negro since David Walker's *Appeal*...."[1] Frederick Douglass took issue with Garnet on the grounds that

[1]Philip S. Foner, *Frederick Douglass* (New York: The Citadel Press, 1964), p. 110. The speech was printed first in the *Minutes of the National Convention of Colored Citizens, Buffalo, New York, August, 1843*, pp. 8, 10, 13–15 and subsequently published by Garnet along with Walker's *Appeal* as *Walker's Appeal, With a Brief Sketch of His Life; and, also, Garnet's Address to the Slaves of the United States of America* (New York: J. H. Tobitt, 1848). The speech has been anthologized several times and can be found in Carter G. Woodson, *Negro Orators and Their Orations* (Washington, D. C.: The Associated Publishers, Inc.), 1925, pp. 150–157.

the latter's position was too militant and might lead to slave insurrections. The final vote was nineteen to eighteen against the measure.

The second speech is one given by Frederick Douglass before the American Anti-Slavery Society in 1847 and entitled "The Right to Criticize American Institutions."[2] The speech is less famous than Douglass's 5th of July speech given in Rochester in 1852, which has been widely anthologized. "The Right to Criticize American Institutions" illustrates Douglass's ability to make his audience laugh by means of sarcasm, ridicule, and irony. In the 1847 speech Douglass takes the typical position of the rhetoric of agitation on the matters of disunion and the proslavery character of the Constitution.

The third speech is by Charles Lenox Remond and was given in favor of a resolution recommending the dissolution of the Union, before the New England Anti-Slavery Convention in 1854.[3] In the speech, Remond indicts American society as racist and argues for the breaking up of the Union. He makes considerable reference to the case of Anthony Burns, a fugitive slave arrested in Boston in May, 1854, and put into irons. United States Commissioner Edward G. Loring returned a verdict in favor of Burns's master. The abolitionists made the case a rhetorical symbol, and when the fugitive was taken from the courthouse to the wharf to be put on a boat to Virginia, fifty-thousand spectators witnessed the procession.

Henry Highland Garnet

Henry Highland Garnet was born a slave in Maryland. When he was about nine years old, his father, the son of an African Mandingo chief, escaped with his wife and children, and Henry was enrolled in the African Free School in New York City when he was eleven. He left when he was about fourteen to serve as a cabin boy on a ship with regular runs between New York and Cuba. In two years, he returned to the city to find that his family had been harassed by slave-catchers, barely escaping being sent back to slavery. Garnet was enraged. From then on, his crusade to abolish slavery was determined.

With several other black students, Garnet attempted to attend school at Canaan, New Hampshire; they were accepted by the school but not by the townspeople, who surrounded the school as a mob, demanding that the black students leave. Garnet, fearing for the lives of all the students bar-

[2]*National Anti-Slavery Standard*, May 20, 1847.
[3]*The Liberator*, June 23, 1854.

ricaded in the building, secured guns, molded bullets, and fired once through the window. Other students agreed that his one shotgun blast was sufficient, for the townspeople retreated and the students' lives were saved. They did then leave the school, however.

Garnet was welcomed at Oneida Institute (see B. Green and T. Weld biographies) from which he graduated with honors in 1840. He then taught school in Troy, edited a weekly newspaper, married Julia Williams, a student he had met earlier at Canaan, began to study theology, and in 1843, when he was twenty-seven, he was ordained a Presbyterian minister with his first parish in Troy.

That same year, Garnet went to Buffalo for the first national Negro convention in some years. Another ex-slave, Frederick Douglass, was also attending this convention for the first time. When Garnet's speech (which follows) turned into an exhortation for massive slave uprisings, Douglass was shocked. The convention did not endorse Garnet's speech, but it had lasting effects anyway. It was talked about, written about, published, circulated, and read. This was black militancy in 1843.

Garnet continued to speak out against slavery, but he became more minister and less activist. He lectured in Europe; he was a missionary; he gave some support to the colonization idea in the 1850's, though he had opposed it earlier, and he was active in recruiting Negro troops for the Union Army during the Civil War and helped gather relief supplies for the freed slaves. In 1865, when the abolition of slavery had become a fact, Garnet was invited to address the House of Representatives. This was the first time a Negro had been in the House in any other than a menial capacity, and Henry Highland Garnet made the most of his opportunity, reminding the Congressmen that more had yet to be done: much prejudice would have to be erased, black men must vote, job promotions must be based on ability, not color, all people of this country must have equal social opportunity.

Garnet returned to the duties of being a minister in New York. In 1881, he was invited to be U. S. Minister Resident and Consul-General to Liberia. To return to the land his fathers had helped rule was a dream he had had all his life, but he was already ill with chronic asthma. He lived to arrive in Liberia and be welcomed and honored, but he died there two months later.

Garnet was a tall, thin man, his face handsome and trimmed with an elegant side beard; he limped because of a wooden leg, his leg having been amputated after an injury that never completely healed. During the speech that follows, a reporter who was present said that Garnet had the audience and himself laughing, shouting, weeping when he willed, so stinging was his attack and so compelling his style of fervent delivery. It is an irony, indeed, that the mood of the black abolitionists had changed enough that, four years later when the same convention was held, the speech was republished and this time there was much less fear of his radical demands. Douglass himself later came to hope for actual slave uprisings in the South.

born in 1815, in Maryland
died February, 1882, in Liberia

An Address to the Slaves of the United States of America

Brethren and Fellow Citizens: Your brethren of the North, East, and West have been accustomed to meet together in National Conventions, to sympathize with each other, and to weep over your unhappy condition. In these meetings we have addressed all classes of the free, but we have never, until this time, sent a word of consolation and advice to you. We have been contented in sitting still and mourning over your sorrows, earnestly hoping that before this day your sacred liberties would have been restored. But, we have hoped in vain. Years have rolled on, and tens of thousands have been borne on streams of blood and tears to the shores of eternity. While you have been oppressed, we have also been partakers with you; nor can we be free while you are enslaved. We, therefore, write to you as being bound with you.

Many of you are bound to us, not only by the ties of a common humanity, but we are connected by the more tender relations of parents, wives, husbands, and sisters, and friends. As such we most affectionately address you.

Slavery has fixed a deep gulf between you and us, and while it shuts out from you the relief and consolation which your friends would willingly render, it afflicts and persecutes you with a fierceness which we might not expect to see in the fiends of hell. But still the Almighty Father of mercies has left to us a glimmering ray of hope, which shines out like a lone star in a cloudy sky. Mankind are becoming wiser, and better—the oppressor's power is fading, and you, every day, are becoming better informed, and more numerous. Your grievances, brethren, are many. We shall not attempt, in this short address, to present to the world all the dark catalogue of the nation's sins, which have been committed upon an innocent people. Nor is it indeed necessary, for you feel them from day to day, and all the civilized world looks upon them with amazement.

Two hundred and twenty-seven years ago the first of our injured race were brought to the shores of America. They came not with glad spirits to select their homes in the New World. They came not with their own consent, to find an unmolested enjoyment of the blessings of this fruitful soil. The first dealings they had with men calling themselves Christians exhibited to them the worst features of corrupt and sordid hearts: and convinced them that no cruelty is too great, no villainy and no robbery too abhorrent for even enlightened men to perform, when influenced by avarice and lust. Neither did they come flying upon the wings of Liberty to a land of freedom. But they came with broken hearts, from their beloved native land, and were doomed to unrequited toil and deep degradation. Nor did the evil of their bondage end at their emancipation by death. Succeeding generations inherited their chains, and millions have come from eternity into time, and have returned again to the world of spirits, cursed and ruined by American slavery.

The propagators of the system, or their immediate successors, very soon discovered its growing evil, and its tremendous wickedness, and secret promises were made to destroy it. The gross inconsistency of a people holding slaves, who had themselves "ferried o'er the wave" for freedom's sake, was too apparent to be entirely overlooked. The voice of Freedom cried, "Emancipate your slaves." Humanity supplicated with tears for the deliverance of the children of Africa. Wisdom urged her solemn plea. The bleeding captive plead his innocence, and pointed to Christianity who stood weeping at the cross. Jehovah frowned upon the nefarious institution, and thunderbolts, red with vengeance, struggled to leap forth to blast the guilty wretches who maintained it. But all was vain. Slavery had stretched its dark wings of death over the land, the Church stood silently by—the priests prophesied falsely, and the people loved to have it so. Its throne is established, and now it reigns triumphant.

Nearly three millions of your fellow-citizens are prohibited by law and public opinion (which in this country is stronger than law) from reading the Book of Life. Your intellect has been destroyed as much as possible, and every ray of light they have attempted to shut out from your minds. The oppressors themselves have become involved in the ruin. They have become weak, sensual, and rapacious—they have cursed you—they have cursed themselves—they have cursed the earth which they have trod.

The colonies threw the blame upon England. They said that the mother country entailed the evil upon them, and they would rid themselves of it if they could. The world thought they were sincere, and the philanthropic pitied them. But time soon tested their sincerity. In a few years the colonists grew strong, and severed themselves from the British Government. Their independence was declared, and they took their station among the sovereign powers of the earth. The declaration was a glorious document. Sages admired it, and the patriotic of every nation reverenced the Godlike sentiments which it contained. When the power of Government returned to their hands, did they emancipate the slaves? No; they rather added new links to our chains. Were they ignorant of the principles of Liberty? Certainly they were not. The sentiments of their revolutionary orators fell in burning eloquence upon their hearts, and with one voice they cried, LIBERTY OR DEATH. Oh, what a sentence was that! It ran from soul to soul like electric fire, and nerved the arms of thousands to fight in the holy cause of Freedom. Among the diversity of opinions that are entertained in regard to physical resistance, there are but a few found to gainsay the stern declaration. We are among those who do not.

SLAVERY! How much misery is comprehended in that single word. What mind is there that does not shrink from its direful effects? Unless the image of God be obliterated from the soul, all men cherish the love of liberty. The nice discerning political economist does not regard the sacred right more than the untutored African who roams in the wilds of Congo. Nor has the one more right to the full enjoyment of his freedom than the other. In every man's mind the good seeds of liberty are planted, and he who brings his fellow down so low, as to make him contented with a condition of slavery, commits the highest crime against God and man. Brethren, your oppressors aim to do this. They endeavor to make you as much like brutes as possible. When they have blinded the eyes of your mind—when they have embittered the sweet waters of life—when they have shut out the light which shines from the word of God—then, and not till then, has American slavery done its perfect work.

TO SUCH DEGRADATION IT IS SINFUL IN THE EXTREME FOR YOU TO MAKE VOLUNTARY SUBMISSION. The divine commandments you are in duty bound to reverence and obey. If you do not obey them, you will surely meet with the displeasure of the Almighty. He requires you to love Him supremely, and your neighbor as yourself—to keep the Sabbath day holy—to search the Scriptures—and bring up your children with respect for His laws, and to worship no other God but Him. But slavery sets all these at nought, and hurls defiance in the face of Jehovah. The forlorn condition in which you are placed does not destroy your obligation to God. You are not certain of heaven, because you allow yourselves to remain in a state of slavery, where you cannot obey the commandments of the Sovereign of the universe. If the ignorance of slavery is a passport to heaven, then it is a blessing, and no curse, and you should rather desire its perpetuity than its abolition. God will not receive slavery, nor ignorance, nor any other state of mind, for love and obedience to Him. Your condition does not absolve you from your moral obligation. The diabolical injustice by which your liberties are cloven down, NEITHER GOD NOR ANGELS, OR JUST MEN, COMMAND YOU TO SUFFER FOR A SINGLE MOMENT. THEREFORE IT IS YOUR SOLEMN AND IMPERATIVE DUTY TO USE EVERY MEANS, BOTH MORAL, INTELLECTUAL, AND PHYSICAL, THAT PROMISES SUCCESS. If a band of heathen men should attempt to enslave a race of Christians, and to place their children under the influence of some false religion, surely Heaven would frown upon the men who would not resist such aggression, even to death. If, on the other hand, a band of Christians should attempt to enslave a race of heathen men, and to entail slavery upon them, and to keep them in heathenism in the midst of Christianity, the God of heaven would smile upon every effort which the injured might make to disenthral themselves.

Brethren, it is as wrong for your lordly oppressors to keep you in slavery as it was for the man thief to steal our ancestors from the coast of Africa. You should therefore now use the same manner of resistance as would have been just in our ancestors when the bloody foot-prints of the first remorseless soul-thief was placed upon the shores of our fatherland. The humblest peasant is as free in the sight of God as the proudest monarch that ever swayed a sceptre. Liberty is a spirit sent out from God, and like its great Author, is no respecter of persons.

Brethren, the time has come when you must act for yourselves. It is an old and true saying that, "if hereditary bondmen would be free, they must themselves strike the blow." You can plead your own cause, and do the work of emancipation better than any others. The nations of the Old World are moving in the great cause of universal freedom, and some of them at least will, ere long, do you justice. The combined powers of Europe have placed their broad seal of disapprobation upon the African slave-trade. But in the slaveholding parts of the United States the trade is as brisk as ever. They buy and sell you as though you were brute beasts. The North has done much —her opinion of slavery in the abstract is known. But in regard to the South, we adopt the opinion of the *New York Evangelist*—"We have advanced so far, that the cause apparently waits for a more effectual door to be thrown open than has been yet." We are about to point you to that more effectual door. Look around you, and behold the bosoms of your loving wives heaving with untold agonies! Here the cries of your poor children! Remember the stripes your fathers bore. Think of the torture and disgrace of your noble mothers. Think of your wretched sisters, loving virtue and purity, as they are driven into concubinage and are exposed to the unbridled lusts of incarnate devils. Think of the undying glory that hangs around the ancient name of Africa—and forget not that you are native-born American citizens, and as such you are justly entitled to all the rights that are granted to the freest. Think how many tears you have poured out upon the soil which you have cultivated with unrequited toil and enriched with your blood; and then go to your lordly enslavers and tell them plainly, that you *are determined to be free*. Appeal to their sense of justice, and tell them that they have no more right to oppress you than you have to enslave them. Entreat them to remove the grievous burdens which they have imposed upon you, and to remunerate you for your labor. Promise them renewed diligence in the cultivation of the soil, if they will render to you an equivalent for your services. Point them to the increase of happiness and prosperity in the British West Indies since the Act of Emancipation. Tell them in language which they cannot misunderstand of the exceeding sinfulness of slavery, and of a future judgment, and of the righteous retributions of an indignant God. Inform them that all you desire is FREEDOM, and that nothing else will suffice. Do this, and forever after cease to toil for the heartless tyrants, who give you no other reward but stripes and abuse. If they then commence work of death, they, and not you, will be responsible for the consequences. You had far better all die—*die immediately*, than live slaves, and entail your wretchedness upon your posterity. If you would be free in this generation, here is your only hope. However much you and all of us may desire it, there is not much hope of redemption without the shedding of blood. If you must bleed, let it all come at once—rather *die freemen than live to be the slaves*. It is impossible, like the children of Israel, to make a grand exodus from the land of bondage. The Pharaohs are on both sides of the blood-red waters! You cannot move *en masse* to the dominions of the British Queen—nor can you pass through Florida and overrun Texas, and at last find peace in Mexico. The propagators of American slavery are spending their blood and treasure that they may plant the black flag in the heart of Mexico and riot in the halls of the Montezumas. In language of the Reverend Robert Hall, when addressing the volunteers of Bristol, who were rushing forth to repel the invasion of Napoleon, who threatened to lay waste the fair homes of England, "Religion is too much interested in your behalf not to shed over you her most gracious influences."

You will not be compelled to spend much time in order to become inured to hardships. From the first movement that you breathed the air of heaven, you have been accustomed to nothing else but hardships. The heroes of the American Revolution were never put upon harder fare than a peck of corn and few herrings per week. You have not become enervated by the luxuries of life. Your sternest energies have been beaten out upon the anvil of severe trial. Slavery has done this to make you subservient to its own purposes; but it has done more than this, it has prepared you for any emergency. If you receive good treatment, it is what you can hardly expect; if you meet with pain, sorrow, and even death, these are the common lot of the slaves.

Fellowmen! patient sufferers! behold your dearest rights crushed to the earth! See your sons murdered, and your wives, mothers and sisters doomed to prostitution. In the name of the merciful God, and by all that life is worth, let it no longer be a debatable question, whether it is better to choose *liberty* or *death*.

In 1822, Denmark Veazie, of South Carolina, formed a plan for the liberation of his fellowmen. In the whole history of human efforts to overthrow slavery, a more complicated and tremendous plan was never formed. He was betrayed by the treachery of his own people, and died a martyr to freedom. Many a brave hero fell, but history, faithful to her high trust, will transcribe his name on the same monument with Moses, Hampden, Tell, Bruce, and Wallace, Toussaint L'Ouverture, Lafayette, and Washington. That tremendous movement shook the whole empire of slavery. The guilty soul-thieves were overwhelmed with fear. It is a matter of fact that at this time, and in consequence of the threatened revolution, the slave States talked strongly of emancipation. But they blew but one blast of the trumpet of freedom, and then laid it aside. As these men became quiet, the slaveholders ceased to talk about emancipation: and now behold your condition to-day! Angels sigh over it, and humanity has long since exhausted her tears in weeping on your account!

The patriotic Nathaniel Turner followed Denmark Veazie. He was goaded to desperation by wrong and injustice. By despotism, his name has been recorded on the list of infamy, and future generations will remember him among the noble and brave.

Next arose the immortal Joseph Cinque, the hero of the Amistad. He was a native African, and by the help of God he emancipated a whole ship-load of his fellowmen on the high seas. And he now sings of liberty on the sunny hills of Africa and beneath his native palm-trees, where he hears the lion roar and feels himself as free as the king of the forest.

Next arose Madison Washington, that bright star of freedom, and took his station in the constellation of true heroism. He was a slave on board the brig *Creole*, of Richmond, bound to New Orleans, that great slave mart, with a hundred and four others. Nineteen struck for liberty or death. But one life was taken, and the whole were emancipated, and the vessel was carried into Nassau, New Providence.

Noble men! Those who have fallen in freedom's conflict, their memories will be cherished by the true-hearted and the God-fearing in all future generations; those who are living, their names are surrounded by a halo of glory.

Brethren, arise, arise! Strike for your lives and liberties. Now is the day and the hour. Let every slave throughout the land do this, and the days of slavery are numbered. You cannot be more oppressed than you have been— you cannot suffer greater cruelties than you have already. *Rather die freemen than live to be slaves.* Remember that you are FOUR MILLIONS!

It is in your power so to torment the God-cursed slaveholders that they will be glad to let you go free. If the scale was turned, and black men were the masters and white men the slaves, every destructive agent and element would be employed to lay the oppressor low. Danger and death would hang over their heads day and night. Yes, the tyrants would meet with plagues more terrible than those of Pharaoh. But you are a patient people. You act as though you were made for the special use of these devils. You act as though your daughters were born to pamper the lusts of your masters and overseers. And worse than all, you tamely submit while your lords tear your wives from your embraces and defile them before your eyes. In the name of God, we ask, are you men? Where is the blood of your fathers? Has it all run out of your veins? Awake, awake; millions of voices are calling you! Your dead fathers speak to you from their graves. Heaven, as with a voice of thunder, calls on you to arise from the dust.

Let your motto be resistance! *resistance!* RESISTANCE! No oppressed people have ever secured their liberty without resistance. What kind of resistance you had better make you must decide by the circumstances that surround you, and according to the suggestion of expediency. Brethren, adieu! Trust in the living God. Labor for the peace of the human race, and remember that you are FOUR MILLIONS!

Frederick Douglass

Circumstances, talents, and timing produced the highly effective Negro abolitionist, Frederick Douglass. Actually, Douglass was an active abolitionist

for six years while he was still legally a slave, for he had escaped from
slavery in Maryland and was living in Connecticut when he began to take
an active part in the abolition movement.

Frederick Douglass was the son of a Negro woman slave who was part
Indian and an unknown white father. He worked as a field hand, then was
a house servant in Baltimore, where his mistress taught him to read and
write. He was sent back to the fields after an estate settlement, tried to escape,
was taught a trade, and then did make good an escape to New York City.
There he married Anna Murray, a free black woman he had known previously in Baltimore. They moved to New Bedford, where he worked as a
common laborer.

Drawn to the growing antislavery movement, in 1841, when he was
probably in his midtwenties, Douglass attended a convention of the Massachusetts Anti-Slavery Society in Nantucket. In talking with others there,
he said that he was an escaped slave. There seemed to be a natural eloquence
in the man, and he already was an imposing figure, over six feet tall. He
was invited to address the convention. He stammered, spoke hesitatingly, was
ill at ease, but the conviction and effectiveness of his statements was noted
by those responsible for hiring the agents for the Society, and, much to his
surprise, he was asked to be one thereafter. The first black abolitionist speaker,
Charles Remond, happened to be in England at this time, and, moreover,
the personal tragedy of having been a slave was Douglass's strength even
before he became such an effective speaker. Remond had been born a free
man in Massachusetts and had received a fine education in the Salem schools.
Douglass was the diamond in the rough the abolitionists were wise enough
to recognize, and his talents soon proved their wisdom. In fact, before long,
Douglass's natural self-assuredness, combined with his excellent command
of English, made his listeners question his claim to being a slave.

Wanting to put down his past in written form, Douglass began the first
of several autobiographical works, *The Narrative of the Life of Frederick
Douglass, an American Slave* (1845) and because he was still legally a slave,
Wendell Phillips advised him to burn the document. He did not, but he
did run off to England and Ireland for two years as soon as it was published.
While there, he became such a popular speaker with the Liberals of Great
Britain that he earned enough money to come back to the United States and
buy his freedom. In England he had been treated as an equal, and he grew
in his conviction that freeing the slaves was the first big job for the reformers, and that the next was to insure equality and opportunity to all black
citizens of America as well.

He also brought back enough money to start a newspaper for black people. He established the *North Star* and continued it for seventeen years, though it was not a widely circulated nor financially solvent venture.

Douglass continued lecturing everywhere he could on the problem of slavery; in addition to the usual insults directed at the abolitionists, he had to endure "Jim Crow" limitations and other indignations as well, but he never backed down or wavered in his determination to help abolish slavery. With the advent of the Civil War, he really came forth with speeches thundering that slavery was the real cause of the war. He recruited colored men for Massachusetts regiments, and he conferred with President Lincoln.

After the War, he continued his agitation for suffrage and civil rights for the freedmen; he also was a staunch supporter of women's rights. He later served in various government posts in Washington and finally was U. S. minister to Haiti.

When he was nearly seventy, he married for a second time, a white woman named Helen Pitts. There was much criticism, but he replied with good humor that he was truly impartial; his first wife had been "the color of my mother, and the second, the color of my father."

Excellent first-hand accounts of the power of Douglass as a speaker are available in the first volume of Philip S. Foner's *The Life and Writings of Frederick Douglass*. One reporter who heard him speaking very early in his career as an agent said of him, "He is very fluent in the use of language, choice and appropriate language, too; and talks as well, for all we could see, as men who have spent their lives over books. He is forcible, keen and very sarcastic; and considering the poor advantages he must have had as a slave, he is certainly a remarkable man." And another, "This is an extraordinary man.... A commanding person... and of most manly proportions. ... As a speaker he has few equals. It is not declamation—but oratory, power of debate. He has wit, arguments, sarcasm, pathos—all that first rate men show in their master efforts. His voice is highly melodious and rich, and his enunciation quite elegant...." (pp. 47, 48)

Foner says further (pp. 49, 50) that although Douglass used the stock abolitionist arguments as he started his career, he also brought "variety and freshness," and he "injected into his speeches a sense of humor. He could thrill his listeners with an account of his battle with Covey, at the same time getting them to burst into laughter as he described the expression on the Negro-breaker's face as he went down in the filth of the cowpen. He could bring shouts of glee from the audience as he portrayed his master, Mr. Auld, first being converted, the tears rolling down his cheeks as he worshipped

God, then the same Mr. Auld, on the same day, dispersing a group of slaves who were assembled to worship the same God." Douglass's natural talent for mimicry found full use in these stories, so that his addresses were long but "seldom tedious." (p. 51)

born February, 1817 (?) in Maryland
died February, 1895, Washington, D.C.

The Right
to Criticize
American Institutions

I like radical measures, whether adopted by Abolitionists or slaveholders. I do not know but I like them better when adopted by the latter. Hence I look with pleasure upon the movements of Mr. Calhoun and his party. I rejoice at any movement in the slave States with reference to this system of Slavery. Any movement there will attract attention to the system—a system, as Junius once said to Lord Granby, "which can only pass without condemnation as it passes without observation." I am anxious to have it seen of all men: hence I am delighted to see any effort to prop up the system on the part of the slaveholders. It serves to bring up the subject before the people; and hasten the day of deliverance. It is meant otherwise. I am sorry that it is so. Yet the wrath of man may be made to praise God. He will confound the wisdom of the crafty, and bring to naught the counsels of the ungodly. The slaveholders are now marshalling their hosts for the propagation and extension of the institution—Abolitionists, on the other hand, are marshalling their forces not only against its propagation and extension, but against its very existence. Two large classes of the community, hitherto unassociated with the Abolitionists, have come up so far towards the right as to become opposed to the farther extension of the crime. I am glad to hear it. I like to gaze upon these two contending armies, for I believe it will hasten the dissolution of the present unholy Union, which has been justly stigmatized as "a covenant with death, an agreement with hell." I welcome the bolt, either from the North or the South, which shall shatter this Union; for under this Union lie the prostrate forms of three millions with whom I am identified. In consideration of their wrongs, of their sufferings, of their groans, I welcome the bolt, either from the celestial or from the infernal regions, which shall sever this Union in twain. Slaveholders are promoting it—Abolitionists are doing so. Let it come, and when it does, our land will rise up from an incubus; her brightness shall reflect against the sky, and shall become the beacon light of liberty in the Western world. She shall then, indeed, become "the land of the free and the home of the brave."

For sixteen years, Wm. Lloyd Garrison and a noble army of the friends of emancipation have been labouring in season and out of season, amid smiles and frowns, sunshine and clouds, striving to establish the conviction through this land, that to hold and traffic in human flesh is a sin against God. They have been somewhat successful; but they have been in no wise so successful as they might have been, had the men and women at the North rallied around them as they had a right to hope from their profession. They have had to contend not only with skilful politicians, with a deeply prejudiced and pro-slavery community, but with eminent Divines, Doctors of Divinity, and Bishops. Instead of encouraging them as friends, they have acted as enemies. For many days did Garrison go the rounds of the city of Boston to ask of the ministers the poor privilege of entering their chapels and lifting up his voice for the dumb. But their doors were bolted, their gates barred, and their pulpits hermetically sealed. It was not till an infidel hall was thrown open, that the voice of dumb millions could be heard in Boston.

I take it that all who have heard at all on this subject, are well convinced that the stronghold of Slavery is in the pulpit. Say what we may of politicians and political parties, the power that holds the keys of the dungeon in which the bondman is confined, is the pulpit. It is that power which is dropping, dropping, constantly dropping on the ear of this people, creating and mould-ing the moral sentiment of the land. This they have sufficiently under their control that they can change it from the spirit of hatred to that of love to mankind. That they do it not, is evident from the results of their teaching. The men who wield the blood-clotted cow-skin come from our Sabbath Schools in the Southern States. Who act as slave-drivers? The men who go forth from our own congregations here. Why, if the Gospel were truly preached among us, a man would as soon think of going into downright piracy as to offer himself as a slave-driver.

In Farmington, two sons of members of the Society of Friends are coolly proposing to go to the South and engage in the honourable office of slave-driving for a thousand dollars a year. People at the North talk coolly of uncles, cousins, and brothers who are slaveholders, and of their coming to visit them. If the Gospel were truly preached here, you would as soon talk of having an uncle or brother a brothel keeper as a slaveholder; for I hold that every slaveholder, no matter how pure he may be, is a keeper of a house of ill-fame. Every kitchen is a brothel, from that of Dr. Fuller's to that of James K. Polk's (Applause). I presume I am addressing a virtuous audience—I presume I speak to virtuous females—and I ask you to consider this one feature of Slavery. Think of a million of females absolutely delivered up into the hands of tyrants, to do what they will with them—to dispose of their persons in any way they see fit. And so entirely are they at the disposal of their masters, that if they raise their hands against them, they may be put to death for daring to resist their infernal aggression.

We have been trying to make this thing appear sinful. We have not been able to do so yet. It is not admitted, and I hardly know how to argue against it. I confess that the time for argument seems almost gone by. What do the people want? Affirmation upon affirmation,—denunciation upon denunciation,—rebuke upon rebuke?

We have men in this land now advocating evangelical flogging. I hold in my hand a sermon recently published by Rev. Bishop Meade, of Virginia. Before I read that part in favour of evangelical flogging, let me read a few extracts from another part, relating to the duties of the slave. The sermon, by the way, was published with a view of its being read by *Christian* masters to their slaves. White black birds! (Laughter.)

(*Mr. Douglass here assumed a most grotesque look, and with a canting tone of voice, read as follows.*)

"Having thus shown you the chief duties you owe to your great Master in Heaven, I now come to lay before you the duties you owe to your masters and mistresses on earth. And for this you have one general rule that you ought always to carry in your minds, and that is, to *do all services for them, as if you did it for God himself.* Poor creatures! you little consider when you are idle, and neglectful of your master's business; when you steal, waste, and hurt any of their substance; when you are saucy and impudent; when you are telling them lies and deceiving them; or when you prove stubborn and sullen, and will not do the work you are set about, without stripes and vexation; you do not consider, I say, that what faults you are guilty of towards your masters and mistresses, are faults done against God himself, who hath set your masters and mistresses over you in his own stead, and expects that you will do for them just as you would do for him. And pray, do not think that I want to deceive you, when I tell you that your *masters and mistresses are God's overseers*; and that if you are faulty towards them, God himself will punish you severely for it."

This is some of the Southern religion. Do you not think you would "grow in grace and in the knowledge of the truth." (Applause.)

I come now to evangelical flogging. There is nothing said about flogging

—that word is not used. It is called correction; and that word as it is understood at the North, is some sort of medicine. (Laughter.) Slavery has always sought to hide itself under different names. The mass of the people call it "our peculiar institution." There is no harm in that. Others call it (they are the more pious sort), "our Patriarchal institution." (Laughter.) Politicians have called it "our social system"; and people in social life have called it "our domestic institution." Abbot Lawrence has recently discovered a new name for it—he calls it "unenlightened labour." (Laughter.) The Methodists in their last General Conference, have invented a new name—"the impediment." (Laughter.) To give you some idea of evangelical flogging, under the name of correction, there are laws of this description,—"any white man killing a slave shall be punished as though he shall have killed a white person, unless such a slave die under *moderate* correction." It commences with a plain proposition.

"Now when correction is given you, you either deserve it, or you do not deserve it." (Laughter.)

That is very plain, almost as safe as that of a certain orator:—"Ladies and Gentlemen, it is my opinion, my deliberate opinion, after a long consideration of the whole matter, that as a general thing, all other things being equal, there are fewer persons to be found in towns sparsely populated, than in larger towns more thickly settled." (Laughter.)

The Bishop goes on to say—

"Whether you really deserve it or not," (one would think that would make a difference), "it is your duty, and Almighty God requires that you bear it patiently. You may perhaps think that this is a hard doctrine," (and it admits of little doubt), "but if you consider it right you must needs think otherwise of it." (It is clear as mud. I suppose he is now going to reason them into the propriety of being flogged evangelically.) "Suppose you deserve correction; you cannot but see that it is just and right you should meet with it. Suppose you do not, or at least so much or so severe; you perhaps have escaped a great many more, and are at last paid for all. Suppose you are quite innocent; is it not possible you may have done some other bad thing which was never discovered, and Almighty God would not let you escape without punishment one time or another? Ought you not in such cases to give glory to Him?" (Glory!) (Much laughter.)

I am glad you have got to the point that you can laugh at the religion of such fellows as this Doctor. There is nothing that will facilitate our cause more than getting the people to laugh at that religion which brings its influence to support traffic in human flesh. It has deceived us so long that it has overawed us.

For a long time when I was a slave, I was led to think from hearing such passages as "servants obey, &c." that if I dared to escape, the wrath of God would follow me. All are willing to acknowledge my right to be free; but after this acknowledgement, the good man goes to the Bible and says "after all I see some difficulty about this thing. You know, after the deluge, there was Shem, Ham, and Japhet; and you know that Ham was black and had a curse put upon him; and I know not but it would be an attempt to thwart the purposes of Jehovah, if these men were set at liberty." It is this kind of religion I wish to have you laugh at—it breaks the charm there is about it. If I could have the men at this meeting who hold such sentiments and could hold up the mirror to let them see themselves as others see them, we should soon make head against this pro-slavery religion.

I dwell mostly upon the religious aspect, because I believe it is the religious people who are to be relied on in this Anti-Slavery movement. Do not misunderstand my railing—do not class me with those who despise religion—do not identify me with the infidel. I love the religion of Christianity—which cometh from above—which is pure, peaceable, gentle, easy to be entreated, full of good fruits, and without hypocrisy. I love that religion which sends its votaries to bind up the wounds of those who have fallen among thieves. By all the love I bear to such a Christianity as this, I hate that of the Priest and Levite, that with long-faced Phariseeism goes up to Jerusalem and worships, and leaves the bruised and wounded to die. I despise that religion that can carry Bibles to the heathen on the other side of the globe and withhold them from [the] heathen on this side—which can talk about human rights yonder and traffic in human flesh here. I love that which makes its votaries do to others as they would that others should do to them. I hope to see a revival of it—thank God it is revived. I see revivals of it in the absence of the other sort of revivals. I believe it to be confessed now, that there has not been a sensible man converted after the old sort of way, in the last five years. Le Roy Sunderland, the mesmerizer, has explained all this away, so that Knapp and others who have converted men after that sort have failed.

There is another religion. It is that which takes off fetters instead of binding them on—that breaks every yoke—that lifts up the bowed down. The Anti-Slavery platform is based on this kind of religion. It spreads its table to the lame, the halt, and the blind. It goes down after a long neglected race. It passes, link by link till it finds the lowest link in humanity's chain—

humanity's most degraded form in the most abject condition. It reaches down its arm and tells them to stand up. This is Anti-Slavery—this is Christianity. It is reviving gloriously among the various denominations. It is threatening to supercede those old forms of religion having all of the love of God and none of man in it. (Applause.)

I now leave this aspect of the subject and proceed to inquire into that which probably must be the inquiry of every honest mind present. I trust I do not misjudge the character of my audience when I say they are anxious to know in what way they're contributing to uphold Slavery.

The question may be answered in various ways. I leave the outworks of political parties and social arrangements, and come at once to the Constitution, to which I believe all present are devotedly attached—I will not say all, for I believe I know some, who, however they may be disposed to admire some of the beautiful truths set forth in that instrument, recognize its pro-slavery features, and are ready to form a republic in which there shall be neither tyrant nor slave. The Constitution I hold to be radically and essentially slave-holding, in that it gives the physical and numerical power of the nation to keep the slave in his chains, by promising that that power shall in any emergency be brought to bear upon the slave, to crush him in obedience to his master. The language of the Constitution is you shall be a slave or die. We know it is such, and knowing it we are not disposed to have part nor lot with that Constitution. For my part I had rather that my right hand should wither by my side than cast a ballot under the Constitution of the United States.

Then, again, in the clause concerning fugitives—in this you are implicated. Your whole country is one vast hunting ground from Texas to Maine.

Ours is a glorious land; and from across the Atlantic we welcome those who are stricken by the storms of despotism. Yet the damning facts remain, there is not a rood of earth under the stars and the eagle of your flag, where a man of my complexion can stand free. There is no mountain so high, no plain so extensive, no spot so sacred, that it can secure to me the right of liberty. Wherever waves the star-spangled banner there the bondman may be arrested and hurried back to the jaws of Slavery. This is your "land of the free," your "home of the brave." From Lexington, from Ticonderoga, from Bunker Hill, where rises that grand shaft with its capstone in the clouds, asks, in the name of the first blood that spurted in behalf of freedom, to protect the slave from the infernal clutches of his master. That petition would be denied, and he bid go back to the tyrant.

I never knew what freedom was till I got beyond the limits of the American eagle. When I first rested my head on a British Island I felt that the eagle might scream, but from its talons and beak I was free, at least for a time. No slave-holder can clutch me on British soil. There I could gaze the tyrant in the face and with the indignation of a tyrant in my look, wither him before me. But republican, Christian America will aid the tyrant in catching his victim.

I know this kind of talk is not agreeable to what are called patriots. Indeed, some have called me a traitor. That profanely religious Journal "The Olive Branch," edited by the Rev. Mr. Norris, recommended that I be hung as a traitor. Two things are necessary to make a traitor. One is, he shall have a country. (Laughter and applause.) I believe if I had a country, I should be a patriot. I think I have all the feelings necessary—all the moral material, to say nothing about the intellectual. I do not know that I ever felt the emotion, but sometimes thought I had a glimpse of it. When I have been delighted with the little brook that passes by the cottage in which I was born, —with the woods and the fertile fields, I felt a sort of glow which I suspect resembles a little what they call patriotism. I can look with some admiration on your wide lakes, your fertile fields, your enterprise, your industry, your many lovely institutions. I can read with pleasure your Constitution to establish justice, and secure the blessings of liberty to posterity. Those are precious sayings to my mind. But when I remember that the blood of four sisters and one brother, is making fat the soil of Maryland and Virginia,—when I remember that an aged grandmother who has reared twelve children for the Southern market, and these one after another as they arrived at the most interesting age, were torn from her bosom,—when I remember that when she became too much racked for toil, she was turned out by a professed Christian master to grope her way in the darkness of old age, literally to die with none to help her, and the institutions of this country sanctioning and sanctifying this crime, I have no words of eulogy, I have no patriotism. How can I love a country where the blood of my own blood, the flesh of my own flesh, is now toiling under the lash?—America's soil reddened by the stain from woman's shrinking flesh.

No, I make no pretension to patriotism. So long as my voice can be heard on this or the other side of the Atlantic, I will hold up America to the lightning scorn of moral indignation. In doing this, I shall feel myself discharging the duty of a true patriot; for he is a lover of his country who rebukes and does not excuse its sins. It is righteousness that exalteth a nation while sin is a reproach to any people.

But to the idea of what you at the North have to do with Slavery. You furnish the bulwark of protection, and promise to put the slaves in bondage. As the American Anti-Slavery Society says, "if you will go on branding, scourging, sundering family ties, trampling in the dust your down trodden victims, you must do it at your own peril." But if you say, "we of the North will render you no assistance: if you still continue to trample on the slave, you must take the consequences," I tell you the matter will soon be settled.

I have been taunted frequently with the want of valour: so has my race, because we have not risen upon our masters. It is adding insult to injury to say this. You belong to 17,000,000 with arms, with means of locomotion, with telegraphs. We are kept in ignorance three millions to seventeen. You taunt us with not being able to rescue ourselves from your clutch. Shame on you! Stand aside—give us fair play—leave us with the tyrants, and then if we do not take care of ourselves, you may taunt us. I do not mean by this to advocate war and bloodshed. I am not a man of war. The time was when I was. I was then a slave: I had dreams, horrid dreams of freedom through a sea of blood. But when I heard of the Anti-Slavery movement, light broke in upon my dark mind. Bloody visions fled away, and I saw the star of liberty peering above the horizon. Hope then took the place of desperation, and I was led to repose in the arms of Slavery. I said, I would suffer rather than do any act of violence—rather than that the glorious day of liberty might be postponed.

Since the light of God's truth beamed upon my mind, I have become a friend of that religion which teaches us to pray for our enemies—which, instead of shooting balls into their hearts, loves them. I would not hurt a hair of a slaveholder's head. I will tell you what else I would not do. I would not stand around the slave with my bayonet pointed at his breast, in order to keep him in the power of the slaveholder.

I am aware that there are many who think the slaves are very well off, and that they are very well treated, as if it were possible that such a thing could be. A man happy in chains! Even the eagle loves liberty.

> Go, let a cage, with grates of gold,
> And pearly roof, the eagle hold;
> Let dainty viands be his fare,
> And give the captive tenderest care;
> But say, in luxury's limits pent,
> Find you the king of birds content?
> No, oft he'll sound the startling shriek,
> And dash the grates with angry beak.
> Precarious freedom's far more dear,
> Than all the prison's pampring cheer!
> He longs to see his eyrie's seat,
> Some cliff on ocean's lonely shore,
> Whose old bare top the tempests beat,
> And round whose base the billows roar,
> When tossed by gales, they yawn like graves,—

He longs for joy to skim those waves;
Or rise through tempest-shrouded air,
And thick and dark, with wild winds swelling,
To brave the lightning's lurid glare,
And talk with thunders in their dwelling.

As with the eagle, so with man. No amount of attention or finery, no dainty dishes can be a substitute for liberty. Slaveholders know this, and knowing it, they exclaim,—"The South are surrounded by a dangerous population, degraded, stupid savages, and if they could but entertain the idea that immediate, unconditional death would not be their portion, they would rise at once and enact the St. Domingo tragedy. But they are held in subordination by the consciousness that the whole nation would rise and crush them." Thus they live in constant dread from day to day.

Friends, Slavery must be abolished, and that can only be done by enforcing the great principles of justice. Vainly you talk about voting it down. When you have cast your millions of ballots, you have not reached the evil. It has fastened its root deep into the heart of the nation, and nothing but God's truth and love can cleanse the land. We must change the moral sentiment. Hence we ask you to support the Anti-Slavery Society. It is not an organization to build up political parties, or churches, nor to pull them down, but to stamp the image of Anti-Slavery truth upon the community. Here we may all do something.

In the world's broad field of battle,
In the bivouac of life,
Be not like dumb driven cattle—
Be a hero in the strife.

Charles Lenox Remond

If Frederick Douglass had not appeared, Charles Remond would be the black man most remembered as an abolitionist speaker. In fact, Douglass's success, which began while Remond was enjoying himself in England, so hurt and enraged him on his return that he was never again the activist he had been prior to 1840.

Remond had been born a free man in Salem, Massachusetts, a mulatto whose father had been born in Curaçao, and had attended the local schools and received an excellent education. While still very young, he became the first Negro to speak publicly against slavery. He was a man of natural eloquence, and he joined the Massachusetts Anti-Slavery Society as an agent in 1838 when he was twenty-eight, though he had been speaking in public some time before that. For the next two years Remond spoke for the abolitionists, all over Massachusetts, Rhode Island, and Maine, and then went to London as a convention delegate to the 1840 World Anti-Slavery Convention.

Forced to travel to England in steerage because of his color, he was hurt and bitter, and when he began to address the convention, the intensity of his feelings completely won the English liberals. He became a favorite guest and speaker, and he remained in England and Ireland over a year after the convention had ended.

When Remond returned to Boston in 1841, he brought along a strong statement against slavery signed by sixty thousand Irishmen, addressed to their kinsmen in America, urging them to join the abolitionists, an irony considering the competition that grew later between free blacks and immigrant Irish for the unskilled jobs in the Northeast. Anyway, Remond felt personally gratified at the response shown him in Great Britain, and he was expecting a hero's welcome, only to find that Frederick Douglass had taken the spotlight while he was away. His jealousy, coupled with continuing problems with chronic asthma, gradually reduced his participation, though he did write and speak for the cause until slavery was abolished.

Charles Remond was a small, wiry man; his face was long and deeply lined; he had an aquiline nose, bushy eyebrows, and a tall, brushed-up hairdo. Whereas Douglass is said to have had a "commanding" appearance, Remond is said to have been "distinguished" looking but in a "somewhat curious fashion." In his later years, he served as clerk in the Boston custom house.

Remond's speaking is said to have been highly effective; he used pertinent facts, argued well and wisely, and because of his own extreme sensitivity to the prejudices he himself had been subjected to, his eloquence and fire made his speeches all the more real and compelling.

born February, 1810, Salem, Mass.
died December, 1873, Boston, Mass.

Speech
Before the New England
Anti-Slavery Convention

Fellow-Countrymen: I cannot begin by saying "Fellow-citizens," for that would be an unwarrantable assumption, under the circumstances of the case. I do not, Mr. Chairman, intend to speak at length; but I feel this evening, as I have felt on former occasions, that the testimony of colored persons was wanted on this platform, and especially at this time.

I do not presume, either, Mr. Chairman, on rising to speak, that I can hope to entertain the audience long upon the resolution now under consideration, in favor of a dissolution of the Union. I need not remind those who are present, that this subject is by no means a new one to a New England Anti-Slavery Convention. But while, sir, it may be old, and even trite, still, it may be worthy of our consideration at the present time; and I may say, as our esteemed friend Samuel J. May said this afternoon, that in the few remarks I have to make I shall not address myself to abolitionists, but to those who stand in the distance, or sit in the distance, and have yet, like Mr. Furness, of Philadelphia, to "take sides" in this enterprise; and if I shall succeed in interesting but one new mind upon this subject, that shall be honor enough in the humble effort I am to make.

It seems to me, Mr. Chairman, that we have enough of intellect, enough of respectability, in a word, sufficient of social influence, to carry this glorious cause in our own State, if we cannot carry it further. If it is true, that there was a time when Napoleon Bonaparte feared the pen and the voice of a single woman more than all the power of Russia, certainly we may feel the force of the remark I have made. [Cheers.] [Miss Stone had just left the platform.]

Now, sir, I am not among the number of those who despond for the success of this movement for the dissolution of this Union; I am among the number hopeful of that glorious event; and that, too, while I feel that the remark may sound strange, coming from one of my complexion. I regret that it is necessary for a colored man, for a black man or a red man, ever to refer to his complexion on the anti-slavery platform; but it does unfortunately happen that everything hinges upon that circumstance. It is the gist of this matter; and if I could feel fully satisfied that every man and every woman within the hearing of my voice was free from that feeling, I should feel that there was a moral certainty of the liberation of Anthony Burns in the city of Boston. [Cheers.]

We have been told here this evening, Mr. Chairman, that the great trouble with Massachusetts men is to be found in their pockets or their purses. This is true to a certain extent; but is it not also true, that, outside of their pockets and their purses, there is a want of interest in the real, bona fide victims of American slavery? In other words, do we not need to have the complexion of the slave population of our country changed, at least in imagination, in order that the work may be done? I know, Sir, that men do not argue upon this question as they would then argue; I know that they do not write as they would then write; I know that they do not believe as they would then believe; I know that they do not preach as they would then preach; I know that they do not pray as they would pray, with this change of complexion.

Now, since my friend Prince, of Essex, called attention this afternoon to the character of the colored people, allow me to ask you to look in that direction for a moment; for while men live in Boston, go upon 'Change, walk up and down the public streets, all the while coming in contact with colored people, they do not understand their character; they do not know that, notwithstanding the constant pressure, from the commencement of our nation's history, which has been exerted upon their manhood, their morality, upon all that is noble, magnanimous and generous in their characters, they have exhibited as many instances of noble manhood, in proportion to their number, as have been displayed by their more favored brethren of a white complexion. It was said here by Mr. Prince that the colored race is at once morally and physically brave. Do not consider me, Mr. Chairman, in alluding to this subject, as feeling vain in regard to it; I only ask that the whole truth respecting my people may be known, and there I will leave the success of their cause. But I ask the people not to act blindly with regard to it; not to make up their opinions with this great weight of prejudice on their minds. I ask them to look upon this question impartially, generously, magnanimously, patriotically, and I believe they will be converted to our movement.

Sir, I have taken note, for the last eighteen years, of the course pursued by colored people in anti-slavery meetings, for there was a time when the number of colored people present was greater than at the present time; and yesterday, I had evidence that there was some courage left with them yet. I refer to this incident only as an illustration of the character of this people generally in our country. There was a meeting of anti-slavery friends in the basement of Tremont Temple, and a call was made for persons to come forward and give in their names, that they might be called upon, at any moment, to discharge not only a responsible, but dangerous duty; and my heart has not been so much encouraged for many a long day as when I witnessed a large number of the colored men present walk up to that stand, with an unfaltering step, and enroll their names. [Applause.]

Why is it that the anti-slavery cause should recommend itself to every well-wisher of his country? Because there are men, white men, who have never been deprived of their citizenship, nor subjected to persecution, outrage and insult, who are honored for the patriotism they have exhibited; and if the demonstration of that feeling, or principle, or sentiment, or whatever you may please to call it, is worthy of honor in the white man, then it is also worthy of honor in the colored man; and the last evening that I had the privilege of speaking in this house, I endeavored, briefly, to make it clear that, on every occasion where manhood and courage have been required in this country, the number of colored people volunteering their services has been equal to that of white people, in proportion to their number, from the earliest moment of our nation's existence. [Cheers.]

Why is it that men stand aloof from this subject? Why do they look coldly upon the discussion of the question of the dissolution of the Union? I think I may safely say, Sir, that the courage and patriotism of the colored man is of a higher character than that of the white man. There is not a man of fair complexion before me who has not something in this country to protect which the colored man does not possess; and, Sir, when I see them, in the moment of danger, willing to discharge their duty to the country, I have a proof that they are the friends, and not the enemies of the country. Then, why are they treated in this manner? Why are the people not ready to go for a dissolution of the Union? If they were white, the people would say, without hesitation, "Let this Union be dissolved!"

But there is another consideration. I ask white men of what value the American Union is to them, north of Mason and Dixon's line, and I find some of them have considerable trouble in making answer. I know there is a more potent influence than money, and that is the social influence south of Mason and Dixon's line. But what have the citizens of Boston to gain from it to-night? I am glad that one of our popular city papers has to-day asked, although indirectly, of what value is the American Union to the citizens of Boston and of the Commonwealth of Massachusetts, if they must perform such work as is being performed in and around the Court House at the present time? Look at it, gentlemen, carefully, and tell me, if you please, citizens of Boston,—white as you are, educated, as you are, wealthy, as you may be, influential, as you may be,—tell me what reward you are receiving for this almost idolatrous advocacy and defense of the American Union. Has the South honored you? When and where? Has she given you office? When? All I can gather from this whole matter is, that it is the work of education. If the editors of newspapers in Boston would right-about-face to-morrow, and recommend a different course of policy from that which has been hitherto pursued, you would soon discover a change. If the popular lyceum lecturers, instead of ridiculing the black man and traducing the black man's friends, would come up and speak in their behalf, you would find public sentiment changing in this matter. It is immaterial whether we have one organization or a hundred in this part of our country. I am satisfied that all we require to secure the success of the anti-slavery enterprise is right deeds and right words upon this subject. We want the sympathies of men on the side of the slave; we want men understanding their own rights, and daring to defend them.

I went into State Street to-day, and I heard a man say—"The black niggers would do well enough in this community; the great difficulty is with the d—d white niggers." What sort of negro hatred could prompt a man to say more? I heard a poor ignorant Irishman say, within the last forty-eight hours —"Hustle the niggers out of Court Square." I heard others say, "Kick the niggers!" "Drive them out of the country," etc. And these Irishmen are in the city of Boston, and in the United States, only on sufferance. I cannot but settle down in the conviction, that were it not for this spirit of Negro hate, we should not hear them say these things. I therefore call upon this audience, in the name of their country, their principles and their professions, to forget the arguments of Stephen S. Foster, to forget the appeals of my beloved friends, Wendell Phillips and William Lloyd Garrison, to shut their eyes to the character of the gentlemen who sit before and around me, and to go back to revolutionary times, and study the character of old John Adams, and Samuel Adams, and John Hancock, and tell me what there is in the character of these men to warrant the position which you, as citizens of Massachusetts, occupy to slavery and to this slaveholding Union at the present time. Can any man deny that, if John Adams, and Samuel Adams, and John Hancock, were alive to-day, they would, in view of the transactions in the city of Boston, demand the immediate dissolution of the Union? [Applause.] I believe in my soul they would. And why? Because they would hold in too high estimation their own liberties to submit to such outrages. I have said before, and I repeat it again, even in view of the humble position I occupy as a black man in the State of Massachusetts, I would rather be ten thousand times blacker than I am than to be the proudest pale face that walks State Street to-day, doing the bidding of the slaveholder. [Loud cheers.]

Am I asked, Mr. Chairman, why I made this rough remark? If I am, I will answer. It has become not only a part of our education, but almost part and parcel of our nature, to look upon the colored man in this country as born to the vile inheritance of slavery, from his cradle to his grave; to have the word slave written on his brow; to do the bidding of the pale face; to go and come at his call. He must not presume to imitate the white man; if he shall, away with him to Africa on the one hand, or banish him from the

State on the other. But the white man, he can go to Bunker Hill, and look upon that stone which commemorates the noble deeds of his fathers; he can go to Lexington, and bow before the memory of men who fought and bled for liberty; and from that place, he can go to Cambridge, and there be educated under the most favorable auspices; and then he can come to Boston, and live on Beacon Street or Park Street, and he can go up and down the streets, and be everywhere treated with respect and honor; and when he goes upon a steamboat, the officers do not tell him he cannot have a berth to sleep in; when he goes to a hotel he is not told that that is no place for "niggers"; when he goes before a Court, he does not find that none of his own color can sit in the jury box; but every white man is presumed to be a sovereign in this country, and qualified to meet any man in the world. But where is their manhood to-day? Men are found ready to be, here, what the most contemptible man disdains to be in South Carolina or Virginia— a negro catcher. The Southerner will not perform such devilish work; but men born in Boston, and educated at Cambridge, volunteer to do it! Why? Simply because it is the custom of the times.

I ask men to throw themselves back upon their manhood; women to throw themselves back upon their womanhood, and go into the Court House,—if it must be that Anthony Burns is to be delivered up,—I do not believe that it will be necessary for any man to shoulder a musket, or carry a dagger in his bosom. Let them go there to-morrow; and then, if the victim is brought out, let some one cry out, "Rescue that man!" and I believe, as if by magic, he will be rescued. [Loud cheers.] All that is wanted is the right voice, at the right time, and in the right place, and the work will be done. In God's name, cannot that spirit be infused into the people?

Friends! God has made us men. If you will recognize us as such, we will conduct ourselves in a manner worthy your regard and protection. All we want is a fair chance; and just in proportion as this is granted will this recognition be made. I ask no man for his sympathy. I am simply asking of the majority, because we are in a minority, an opportunity to develop the faculties which the Creator has given us. I tell you, my friends, if we were equal in numbers to-morrow, we should not ask your aid; into our own hands we would take the vindication of our rights.

The friend who preceded me (Miss Wright) wanted to know what was to be done, in case the Union was dissolved,—she could not see what was to be gained by it. Sir, if the Union should be dissolved, leave this whole question with the slave population, and they will take care of it. [Applause.] It is the North that practically keeps them in slavery; and hence I say, that the work is with Boston men, with Massachusetts men, with New England men. When New England shall be right, then the work will be accomplished.

If you could only be black, friends, for eight and forty hours, how would you reason on this question? [Cheers.] Talk about the eloquence of the colored man! We should not have a chance to get up, with our poor speech, so many would be eager to occupy the platform. We should have a whole host of eloquent speakers. I met Mr. Choate in the street to-day, and having a stranger friend with me, I pointed him out to him; and I could not but think, as I passed him, that if Mr. Choate would come to this New England Convention, and speak as he is qualified to speak on this subject, and admit that he had been mistaken—mistaken long ago—it would do more to immortalize his name than all the victories he ever gained upon the public forum. [Cheers.]

I would say, in conclusion, Mr. Chairman, to our friends present, do not go away from this meeting feeling prejudiced against it, but go from here and resolve what you will do when that poor fugitive is taken away. One statement I wish to make. The reports are various respecting the proceedings in the court-room. The audience are undoubtedly every one of them aware that there has been some testimony presented to-day going to show a discrepancy in the time when the slaveholders and their counsel say Burns left Virginia and the time when he was actually seen in Boston; and I have since heard, from persons interested in that direction, that considerable confidence is felt that he will be discharged. I have heard that the man claiming to be Burns's master now offers to sell him for four hundred dollars. I hope that he will not have the privilege of taking four hundred cents. I hope that if there is a Commissioner in Boston mean enough to be willing to give up Burns, he will not be purchased: for a lesson will be read from that circumstance, which will do more to aid the cause of the three and a half millions in bonds than any purchase could do. I remember reading, when I was a boy, an account of a British general, who, many years ago, was wounded three times in a battle, yet he would not consent to be taken from his horse; but, receiving a fresh wound, he fell from his horse, and just before he expired, he heard the shout—"They fly!—they fly!" "Who fly?" he asked. "Our enemies," was the reply. "Then," said he, "I die happy." I hope that in this case we may hear the cry—"They fly!" And when we ask, "Who fly?" that we may hear the answer, "The slaveholders!" That shall be glory enough, and a shout shall go up that Massachusetts is redeemed. [Loud cheers.]

I am reminded of another report, which comes from a good source, that in the event of Commissioner Loring giving Burns his freedom, or whether he shall or not, the slaveholder and his friends have determined to carry him off in the face of the purchase money, and the remonstrances and wishes of the people. I hope, therefore, that the friends will be prepared to meet any exigency that may arise, and to vindicate the laws of eternal justice and right.

I know, Mr. Chairman, that I am not, as a general thing, a peacemaker. I am irritable, excitable, quarrelsome—I confess it, Sir, and my prayer to God is, that I may never cease to be irritable, that I may never cease to be excitable, that I may never cease to be quarrelsome, until the last slave shall be made free in our country, and the colored man's manhood acknowledged. [Loud applause.]

Part IV
Female Antislavery Speakers

Maria W. Stewart's speech delivered at the African Masonic Hall in Boston on February 27, 1833, is remarkable in that it is not only one of the first public speeches delivered in the United States by a woman but also because the speaker was black. Benjamin Quarles refers to her as "the deeply religious Maria W. Stewart, the first native-born American woman to speak in public and leave extant texts of her addresses."[1] Mrs. Stewart delivered four adddresses in Boston in 1832–33. Three of the speeches were printed in *The Liberator*. The one included here is representative of the others and illustrative of Mrs. Stewart's speaking style at its best.[2]

Angelina Grimké has left few speech texts relating to her antislavery speaking. Gerda Lerner, the biographer of the Grimké sisters, was able to find only two verbatim accounts of Angelina's speeches.[3] The two extant texts are included here. The first is only the introduction to Angelina's testimony before the legislative committee of the Massachusetts Legislature on February 21, 1838. Angelina's appearance before the committee was unprecedented, but *The Liberator* printed only the exordium.[4]

The second selection is a transcript of Angelina's speech in Pennsylvania Hall in Philadelphia on May 16, 1838.[5] The speech was given during the stormy meetings of antislavery forces in the newly dedicated Pennsylvania Hall. Reformers had decided to solve the problem of finding a suitable place for meetings by erecting their own hall. The building was to be a symbol of free speech and to be open to spokesmen for all opinions.

Angelina Grimké Weld faced one of her most dramatic moments as a

[1]*Black Abolitionists* (New York: Oxford University Press, 1969), p. 7.
[2]*The Liberator*, April 27, 1833.
[3]Gerda Lerner, *The Grimké Sisters from South Carolina: Rebels Against Slavery* (Boston: Houghton Mifflin Company, 1967), p. 438.
[4]*The Liberator*, March 2, 1838.
[5]Reprinted in Elizabeth C. Stanton, Susan B. Anthony, and Matilda J. Gage, *History of Woman Suffrage*, Vol. 1 (New York: Fowler & Wells, Publishers, 1881), pp. 334–36.

speaker when as a bride of two days she was introduced to the audience; accompanied by the sound of the outside mob and the crash of bricks coming through the windows, she gave the speech included here. The outbreak of mob violence occasioned by the antislavery conventions resulted in the destruction of the new building by fire a few days later.

When Angelina finished speaking, a young Quaker woman was so moved by the occasion and the speech that she gained the floor and said:

> I ask permission to say a few words. I have never before addressed a promiscuous assembly; nor is it now the maddening rush of those voices, which is the indication of a moral whirlwind; nor is it the crashing of those windows, which is the indication of a moral earthquake, that calls me before you. No, these pass unheeded by me. But it is the "still small voice within," which may not be withstood, that bids me open my mouth for the dumb; that bids me plead the cause of God's perishing poor; aye, *God's* poor.
>
> The parable of Lazarus and the rich man we may well bring home to our-selves. The North is that rich man. How he is clothed in purple and fine linens, and fares sumptuously! Yonder, YONDER, at a little distance, is the gate where lies the Lazarus of the South, full of sores and desiring to be fed with the crumbs that fall from our luxurious table. Look! see him there! even the dogs are more merciful than we. Oh, see him where he lies! We have long, very long, passed by with averted eyes. Ought not we to raise him up; and is there one in this hall who sees nothing for himself to do?[6]

The speaker was Abby Kelley of Lynn, Massachusetts, and her brief remarks so impressed Theodore Weld that he urged her to become an aboli-tion speaker. She took his advice and became one of the leading female speakers for antislavery in the 1840's.

In the winter of 1861, just after the election of Abraham Lincoln to the presidency and shortly after the start of the Civil War, the Garrisonian abolitionists, aware that the Republican party had absorbed all the political abolitionists into its ranks, and opposed to all compromise, felt the time was ripe to arouse the people and to hold the Republicans to their declared principles. The third selection is representative of the die-hard agitators of the Garrisonian stamp at the start of the war.[7] The speaker, Susan B. Anthony, was a young woman in her prime as an antislavery agent and destined to become one of the greatest speakers for women's rights in American history. The speech is entitled "No Union with Slaveholders," and it was given a number of times during the campaign of 1861 when Miss Anthony was directing the agents for the abolitionists in western New York.

The speech was developed at the period when Miss Anthony was working

---

[6]Stanton, Anthony, and Gage, *History of Woman Suffrage*, pp. 336–37.

[7]Reprinted in Harriet E. Grim, "Susan B. Anthony, Exponent of Freedom," un-published doctoral dissertation, University of Wisconsin, 1938, Part 3, pp. 37–44.

closely with Mrs. Henry B. Stanton. Folklore has it that Elizabeth Cady Stanton wrote the speeches and Susan B. Anthony delivered them. Mrs. Stanton described the preparation of the speeches as follows:

> In writing we did better work together than either could alone. While she is slow and analytical in composition, I am rapid and synthetic. I am the better writer, she the better critic. She supplied the facts and statistics, I the philosophy and rhetoric, and together we have made arguments that have stood unshaken by the storms of thirty long years: arguments that no man has answered. Our speeches may be considered the united product of our two brains.[8]

The women's rights movement of the nineteenth century grew out of the antislavery reform. Many women were moved to help free the slaves, and when they discovered their way blocked because they were women, they drew the analogy between their situation and that of the slaves. The abolitionists also furnished them with a precedent and rhetorical models for their subsequent campaigns, and many of them, including the two leading rhetoricians of women's rights, Elizabeth Cady Stanton and Susan B. Anthony, worked for both abolition and women's rights.

Frances Maria W. Stewart

Mrs. Stewart, sometimes called Steward, sometimes called Frances Stewart, is noted as Mrs. Maria W. Stewart in *The Liberator,* which published three of her four public speeches.

Mrs. Stewart was born in Hartford, Connecticut, a free black, but she was bound out to the family of a minister when she was five years old and remained there until she was fifteen. Although she was denied a formal education, it is evident from these speeches that she received a highly religion-oriented education and a regard for the written and spoken word during the ten years she was surrounded by the family and life of the clergyman.

She married at twenty-three but was widowed three years later, in 1829, and it was three years after that that she began her brief but noteworthy career as an antislavery lecturer. One of her prime contentions was that slavery in the South was but one step worse than the slave-like status of the Northern Negro. She did not support the colonization movement to send blacks back to Africa, but rather felt that America was the land in which

[8]Stanton, Anthony, and Gage, *History of Woman Suffrage,* p. 459.

the blacks could flourish if given the chance. She was adamant that Christian educational opportunities be made available for all black children, and felt that as blacks proved their intellectual and moral worth, whites would have to accept them, that the chains of slavery and prejudice would disappear.

Public pressure probably explains why Maria Stewart spoke only four times. The fact that others in the black community began to hold her in contempt was the final blow which led to her retirement. Although she defended the right of women to speak out, and gave abundant historical evidence, largely Biblical, to show precedents for her right to speak, she nonetheless felt compelled to give in to what must have been great pressures from all sides to cease her campaign.

born 1803, Hartford, Conn.

no dates given for year or place of death

An Address Delivered
at the African Masonic Hall

African rights and liberty is a subject that ought to fire the breast of every free man of color in these United States, and excite in his bosom a lively, deep, decided and heart-felt interest. When I cast my eyes on the long list of illustrious names that are enrolled on the bright annals of fame amongst the whites, I turn my eyes within, and ask my thoughts, "Where are the names of our illustrious ones?" It must certainly have been for the want of energy on the part of the free people of color that they have been long willing to bear the yoke of oppression. It must have been the want of ambition and force that has given the whites occasion to say, that our natural abilities are not as good, and our capacities by nature inferior to theirs. They boldly assert, that, did we possess a natural independence of soul, and feel a love for liberty within our breasts, some one of our sable race, long before this, would have testified it, notwithstanding the disadvantages under which we labor. We have made ourselves appear altogether unqualified to speak in our own defence, and are therefore looked upon as objects of pity and commiseration. We have been imposed upon, insulted and derided on every side; and now, if we complain, it is considered as the height of im-pertinence. We have suffered ourselves to be considered as dastards, cowards, mean, faint-hearted wretches; and on this account, (not because of our complexion,) many despise us and would gladly spurn us from their presence.

These things have fired my soul with a holy indignation, and compelled me thus to come forward, and endeavor to turn their attention to knowledge and improvement; for knowledge is power. I would ask, is it blindness of mind, or stupidity of soul, or the want of education, that has caused our men who are 60 or 70 years of age, never to let their voices be heard nor their hands be raised in behalf of their color? Or has it been for the fear of offending the whites? If it has, O ye fearful ones, throw off your fearfulness, and come forth in the name of the Lord, and in the strength of the God of Justice, and make yourselves useful and active members in society; for they admire a noble and patriotic spirit in others—and should they not admire it in us? If you are men, convince them that you possess the spirit of men; and as your day, so shall your strength be. Have the sons of Africa no souls? feel they no ambitious desires? shall the chains of ignorance forever confine them? shall the insipid appellation of "clever negroes," or "good creatures," any longer content them? Where can we find amongst ourselves the man of science, or a philosopher, or an able statesman, or a counsellor at law? Show me our fearless and brave, our noble and gallant ones. Where are our lecturers on natural history, and our critics in useful knowledge? There may be a few such men amongst us, but they are rare. It is true, our fathers bled and died in the revolutionary war, and others fought bravely under the command of Jackson, in defence of liberty. But where is the man that has distinguished himself in these modern days by acting wholly in the defence of African rights and liberty? There was one—although he sleeps, his memory lives.

I am sensible that there are many highly intelligent gentlemen of color in these United States, in the force of whose arguments, doubtless, I should discover my inferiority; but if they are blest with wit and talent, friends and fortune, why have they not made themselves men of eminence, by striving to take all the reproach that is cast upon the people of color, and in endeavoring to alleviate the woes of their brethren in bondage? Talk, without effort, is nothing; you are abundantly capable, gentlemen, of making yourselves men of distinction; and this gross neglect, on your part, causes my blood to boil within me. Here is the grand cause which hinders the rise and progress of the people of color. It is their want of laudable ambition and requisite courage.

Individuals have been distinguished according to their genius and talents, ever since the first formation of man, and will continue to be whilst the world stands. The different grades rise to honor and respectability as their merits may deserve. History informs us that we sprung from one of the most learned nations of the whole earth—from the seat, if not the parent of science; yes, poor, despised Africa was once the resort of sages and legislators of other nations, was esteemed the school for learning, and the most illustrious men in Greece flocked thither for instruction. But it was our gross sins and abominations that provoked the Almighty to frown thus heavily upon us, and give our glory unto others. Sin and prodigality have caused the downfall of nations, kings and emperors; and were it not that God in wrath remembers mercy, we might indeed despair; but a promise is left us; "Ethiopia shall again stretch forth her hands unto God."

But it is of no use for us to boast that we sprung from this learned and enlightened nation, for this day a thick mist of moral gloom hangs over millions of our race. Our condition as a people has been low for hundreds of years, and it will continue to be so, unless, by the true piety and virtue we strive, to regain that which we have lost. White Americans, by their prudence, economy and exertions, have sprung up and become one of the most flourishing nations in the world, distinguished for their knowledge of the arts and sciences, for their polite literature. Whilst our minds are vacant and starving for want of knowledge, theirs are filled to overflowing. Most of our color have been taught to stand in fear of the white man from their earliest infancy, to work as soon as they could walk, and call "master" before they scarce could lisp the name of mother. Continual fear and laborious servitude have in some degree lessened in us that natural force and energy which belong to man; or else, in defiance of opposition, our men, before this would have nobly and boldly contended for their rights. But give the man of color an equal opportunity with the white, from the cradle to manhood, and from manhood to the grave, and you would discover the dignified statesman, the man of science, and the philosopher. But there is no such opportunity for the sons of Africa, and I fear that our powerful ones are fully determined that there never shall be. Forbid, ye Powers on High, that it should any longer be said that our men possess no force. O ye sons of Africa, when will your voices be heard in our legislative halls, in defiance of your enemies, contending for equal rights and liberty? How can you, when you reflect from what you have fallen, refrain from crying mightily unto God, to turn away from us the fierceness of his anger, and remember our transgressions against us no more forever. But a God of infinite purity will not regard the prayers of those who hold religion in one hand, and prejudice, sin and pollution in the other; he will not regard the prayers of self-righteousness and hypocrisy. Is it possible, I exclaim, that for the want of knowledge, we have labored for hundreds of years to support others, and been content to receive what they chose to give us in return? Cast your eyes about—look as far as you can see—all, all is owned by the lordly white, except here and there a lowly dwelling which the man of color, midst deprivations, fraud and opposition, has been scarce able to procure. Like king Solomon, who put neither nail nor hammer to the temple, yet received the praise; so also have the white Americans gained themselves a name, like the names of the great men that are in the earth, whilst in reality we have been their principal foundation and support. We have pursued the shadow, they have obtained the substance; we have performed the labor, they have received the profits; we have planted the vines, they have eaten the fruits of them.

I would implore our men, and especially our rising youth, to flee from the gambling board and the dance hall; for we are poor, and have no money to throw away. I do not consider dancing as criminal in itself, but it is astonishing to me that our young men are so blind to their own interest and the future welfare of their children, as to spend their hard earnings for this frivolous amusement; for it has been carried on among us to such an unbecoming extent that it has become absolutely disgusting. "Faithful are the wounds of a friend, but the kisses of an enemy are deceitful." Had those men amongst us, who have had an opportunity, turned their attention as assiduously to mental and moral improvement as they have to gambling and dancing, I might have remained quietly at home, and they stood contending in my place. These polite accomplishments will never enrol your names on the bright annals of fame, who admire the belle void of intellectual knowledge, or applaud the dandy that talks largely on politics, without striving to assist his fellow in the revolution, when the nerves and muscles of every other man forced him into the field of action. You have a right to rejoice, and to let your hearts cheer you in the days of your youth; yet remember that for all these things God will bring you into judgment. Then, O ye sons of Africa, turn your mind from these perishable objects, and contend for the cause of God and the rights of man. Form yourselves into temperance societies. There are temperate men amongst you; then why will you any longer neglect to strive, by your example, to suppress vice in all its abhorrent forms? You have been told repeatedly of the glorious results arising from temperance, and can you bear to see the whites arising in honor and respectability, without endeavoring to grasp after that honor and respectability also?

But I forbear. Let our money, instead of being thrown away as heretofore, be appropriated for schools and seminaries of learning for our children and youth. We ought to follow the example of the whites in this respect. Nothing would raise our respectability, add to our peace and happiness and reflect so much honor upon us, as to be ourselves the promoters of temperance, and the supporters, as far as we are able, of useful and scientific knowledge. The rays of light and knowledge have been hid from our view; we have been taught to consider ourselves as scarce superior to the brute creation; and have performed the most laborious part of American drudgery. Had we as people received one half the early advantages the whites have received, I would defy the government of these United States to deprive us any longer of our rights.

I am informed that the agent of the Colonization Society has recently formed an association of young men, for the purpose of influencing those of us to go to Liberia who may feel disposed. The colonizationalists are blind to their own interest, for should the nations of the earth make war with America, they would find their forces much weakened by our absence; or should we remain here, can our "brave soldiers" and "fellow citizens," as they were termed in time of calamity, condescend to defend the rights of the whites, and be again deprived of their own, or sent to Liberia in return? O, if the colonizationists are real friends to Africa, let them expend the money which they collect in erecting a college to educate her injured sons in this land of gospel light and liberty; for it would be most thankfully received on our part, and convince us of the truth of their professions, and save time, expense and anxiety. Let them place before us noble objects, worthy of pursuit, and see if we prove ourselves to be those unambitious negroes they term us. But ah! methinks their hearts are so frozen towards us, they had rather their money should be sunk in the ocean than to administer it to our relief; and I fear, if they dared, like Pharoah king of Egypt, they would order every male child amongst us to be drowned. But the most high God is still as able to subdue the lofty pride of these white Americans, as He was the heart of that ancient rebel. They say though we are looked upon as things, yet we sprang from a scientific people. Had our men the requisite force and energy, they would soon convince them, by their efforts both in public and private, that they were men, or things in the shape of men. Well may the colonizationists laugh us to scorn for our negligence; well may they cry, "Shame to the sons of Africa." As the burden of the Israelites was too great for Moses to bear, so also is our burden too great for our noble advocate to bear. You must feel interested, my brethren, in what he undertakes, and hold up his hands by your good words, or in spite of himself his soul will become discouraged, and his heart will die within him; for he has, as it were, the strong bulls of Bashan to contend with.

It is of no use for us to wait any longer for a generation of well educated men to arise. We have slumbered and slept too long already; the day is far spent; the night of death approaches; and you have sound sense and good judgment sufficient to begin with, if you feel disposed to make a right use of it. Let every man of color throughout the United States, who possesses the spirit and principles of a man, sign a petition to Congress to abolish slavery in the District of Columbia, and grant you the rights and privileges of common free citizens; for if you had had faith as a grain of mustard seed, long before this the mountains of prejudice might have been removed. We are all sensible that the Anti-Slavery Society has taken hold of the arm of our whole population, in order to raise them out of the mire. Now all we have to do is, by a spirit of virtuous ambition to strive to raise ourselves; and I am happy to have it in my power thus publicly to say that the colored inhabitants of this city, in some respects, are beginning to improve. Had the free people of color in these United States nobly and boldly contended for their rights, and showed a natural genius and talent, although not so brilliant as some; had they held up, encouraged and patronized each other; nothing could have hindered us from being a thriving and flourishing people. There has been a fault amongst us. The reason why our distinguished men have not made themselves more influential is, because they fear that the strong current of opposition through which they must pass, would cause their downfall and prove their overthrow. And what gives rise to this opposition? Envy. And what has it amounted to? Nothing. And who are the cause of it? Our whited sepulchres, who want to be great, and don't know how; who love to be called of men "Rabbi, Rabbi," who put on false sanctity, and humble themselves to their brethren, for the sake of acquiring the highest place in the synagogue, and the uppermost seats at the feast. You, dearly beloved, who are the genuine followers of our Lord Jesus Christ, the salt of the earth and the light of the world, are not so culpable. As I told you, in the very first of my writing, I tell you again, I am but as one drop in the bucket—as one particle of the small dust of the earth. God will surely raise up those amongst us who will plead the cause of virtue, and the pure principles of morality, more eloquently than I am able to do.

It appears to me that America has become like the great city of Babylon, for she has boasted in her heart,—"I sit a queen, and am no widow, and shall see no sorrow." She is indeed a seller of slaves and the souls of men; she has made the Africans drunk with the wine of her fornication; she has put them completely beneath her feet, and she means to keep them there; her right hand supports the reins of government, and her left hand the wheel of power, and she is determined not to let go her grasp. But many powerful sons and daughters of Africa will shortly arise, who will put down vice and immorality amongst us, and declare by Him that sitteth upon the throne, that they will have their rights; and if refused, I am afraid they will spread horror and devastation around. I believe that the oppression of injured Africa has come up before the majesty of Heaven; and when our cries shall have reached the ears of the Most High, it will be a tremendous day for the people of this land; for strong is the arm of the Lord God Almighty.

Life has almost lost its charms for me; death has lost its sting and the grave its terrors; and at times I have a strong desire to depart and dwell with Christ, which is far better. Let me entreat my white brethren to awake and save our sons from dissipation, and our daughters from ruin. Lend the hand of assistance to feeble merit, and plead the cause of virtue amongst our sable race; so shall our curses upon you be turned into blessings; and though you shall endeavor to drive us from these shores, still we will cling to you the more firmly; nor will we attempt to rise above you; we will presume to be called equals only.

The unfriendly whites first drove the native American from his much loved home. Then they stole our fathers from their peaceful and quiet dwellings, and brought them hither and made bond men and bond women of them and their little ones; they have obliged our brethren to labor, kept them in utter ignorance, nourished them in vice and raised them in degradation; and now that we have enriched their soil, and filled their coffers, they say that we are not capable of becoming like white men, and that we never can rise to respectability in this country. They would drive us to a strange land. But before I go, the bayonet shall pierce me through. African rights and liberty is a subject that ought to fire the breast of every free man of color in these United States, and excite in his bosom a lively, deep, decided and heartfelt interest.

Angelina Emily Grimké

By far the most dramatic story among the many fascinating lives of the American abolitionists is the story of the two Grimké sisters, Sarah and Angelina. Sarah was thirteen years old when Angelina was born; there were many brothers and sisters, and Sarah asked to be the new baby's godmother. Her parents consented, probably never aware of the depth of feeling and purpose already imbedded in the character of the young Sarah, for Sarah

took her commitment to Angelina most seriously, vowing to find her own
road in life so that she could, in turn, direct the path of her beloved baby
sister, Angelina.

The Grimké family was large, wealthy, socially prominent, and intelligent.
Judge Grimké (of the Supreme Court of South Carolina) allowed his girls
to acquire a "suitable" education, but he did not encourage them to use it,
of course. Sarah adored her older brother, Thomas, and studied his books.
The family owned slaves, and each child had her own slave, who was to be
a constant companion, doing whatever the child wanted. Sarah became extremely fond of her slave playmate, however, and always treated her as an
equal. She even began teaching her to read, which was against South Carolina
law and subject to a fine. Her father, finding out about this, gave her a stern
lecture. After an illness, the young slave girl died. Thomas went off to Yale,
and Sarah's aggressive eagerness began to turn inward as all the interesting
doors she had found seemed to be closed to her. Thus it was a rather chastened
but smoldering Sarah who, at thirteen, took on the sponsorship of the baby
Angelina. The seeds of her hatred of slavery and her resentment of the
restrictions placed on girls and women were well entrenched, and her lifetime
of efforts to reform both evils followed, not immediately, but steadily. As
their reform efforts became more public later in New England, their family
in South Carolina simply could not understand why two attractive, loved
daughters of such a fine family would leave all they had known and live what
must have seemed to the Southerners a truly alien existence.

Both girls were bright, and both seem to have been tenderhearted even
as young children. Sarah was often at Thomas's elbow during debates, which
her father encouraged, but she was not allowed to receive much more than
the young lady's education in the niceties of life, though her father did have
all the children learn to work with their hands, at times in the fields as well
as in the home. All the while, young Sarah's active mind turned over the
elements of her life, which increasingly upset her.

Both girls began to dislike the formalism of the Episcopal church, and so
they joined the Presbyterian church. Still dissatisfied, Sarah visited Philadelphia when she was twenty-seven and decided to become a Quaker. Later,
when Angelina was twenty-five, she too moved to Philadelphia, becoming
in time a member of the Society of Friends, a very formal and governed
group whose members were held to a strict discipline. She began a life of
charitable works as defined by the Quakers, but she still felt stifled by all the
restrictions of the Society, and she thought of becoming a teacher. They
disapproved of this too. She then wrote to Garrison, having read *The*

Liberator, to tell him how much she valued his work and supported the abolitionists. To her surprise, he published the letter. Then, as Sarah had led Angelina away from Charleston and their former life, Angelina began to be more involved with the abolitionists, and sometime later Sarah too left the Friends and joined Angelina in her commitment to antislavery.

At first, Angelina agreed to speak to small groups of women in homes, but from the beginning it was obvious that many women wanted to hear her, so the meeting was held in a church hall. Subsequent "lectures" found men in attendance, first a few, and then more, as the news spread of these rather frail, gentle Southern ladies, former slaveholders, who were growing increasingly effective as they talked with earnestness, conviction, and the authority of those who had known the system first-hand, about the evils of slavery and the need for abolition. The audiences were sometimes unfriendly. The opposition to women speaking in public appears in many newspaper accounts of their speeches, so it became a natural matter for them to take up the cause of women's rights as well, feeling increasingly, as they did, that the two went hand-in-hand, that the guilt of slavery had to be borne by the women of the country as well, and that the reforms needed had to be fought for by the women also. Deeds and words, they demanded, from men and women.

After Angelina's letter to Garrison, she wrote a thirty-six page pamphlet addressed to Southern women urging them to oppose slavery, "this horrible system of oppression and cruelty, licentiousness and wrong," and, in the same fervor with which Northern abolitionists seized the document and welcomed the new crusader, the state of South Carolina threatened Angelina with imprisonment if she came back to Charleston.

The Grimké sisters' reputation for earnestness and eloquence made them popular abolitionist lecturers; their speeches all over New England attracted hundreds, and the response of supporters to the cause was enthusiastic. The man who was supervising the agency of the abolitionists, Theodore Weld, finally felt he had to tell Sarah that Angelina was by far the more effective speaker, and Sarah thereafter confined her activities to writing and teaching.

Angelina Grimké and Theodore Weld were married in May of 1838. She seldom spoke publicly after the marriage; they had two sons, and they ran a liberal school in Belleville, New Jersey, for many years, moving finally to Hyde Park, Massachusetts, where all three died—Weld, Sarah, and Angelina. Sarah never married but lived with the Welds and worked with them throughout her long and busy lifetime.

Of her oratory, Wendell Phillips said of Angelina in tribute: "She swept the chords of the human heart with a power that has never been surpassed and rarely equalled. I well remember, evening after evening, listening to eloquence such as had never then been heard from a woman."[9]

born Feb., 1805, Charleston, S. C.

died October, 1879, Hyde Park, Mass.

Exordium of Speech
Before Legislative Committee
of Massachusetts Legislature,
February 21, 1838

Mr. Chairman—

More than 2000 years have rolled their dark and bloody waters down the rocky, winding channel of Time into the broad ocean of Eternity, since woman's voice was heard in the palace of an eastern monarch, and woman's petition achieved the salvation of millions of her race from the edge of the sword. The Queen of Persia,—if Queen she might be called, who was but the mistress of her voluptuous lord,—trained as she had been in the secret abominations of an oriental harem, had studied too deeply the character of Ahasuerus not to know that the sympathies of his heart could not be reached, except through the medium of his sensual appetites. Hence we find her arrayed in royal apparel, and standing in the inner court of the King's house, hoping by her personal charms to win the favor of her lord. And after the golden sceptre had been held out, and the inquiry was made, "What wilt thou, Queen Esther, and what is thy request? it shall be given thee to the half of the kingdom"—even then she dared not ask either for her own life, or that of her people. She felt that if her mission of mercy was to be success-ful, his animal propensities must be still more powerfully wrought upon— the luxurious feast must be prepared, the banquet of wine must be served up, and the favorable moment must be seized when, gorged with gluttony and intoxication, the king's heart was fit to be operated upon by the pathetic appeal, "If I have found favor in thy sight, O King, and if it please the King, let my life be given at my petition; and my people at my request." It was thus, through personal charms, and sensual gratification, and individual in-

[9]Eleanor Flexnor, *Century of Struggle: The Woman's Rights Movement in the United States* (Cambridge: Harvard University Press, 1959), p. 28.

fluence, that the Queen of Persia obtained the precious boon she craved,—
her own life, and the life of her beloved people. Mr. Chairman, it is my
privilege to stand before you on a similar mission of life and love; but I
thank God that we live in an age of the world too enlightened and too moral
to admit of the adoption of the same means to obtain as holy an end. I feel
that it would be an insult to this Committee, were I to attempt to win their
favor by arraying my person in gold, and silver, and costly apparel, or by
inviting them to partake of the luxurious feast, or the banquet of wine. I
understand the spirit of the age too well to believe that you could be moved
by such sensual means—means as unworthy of you, as they would be beneath
the dignity of the cause of humanity. Yes, I feel that if you are reached at
all, it will not be by me, but by the truths I shall endeavor to present to your
understandings and your hearts. The heart of the eastern despot was reached
through the lowest propensities of his animal nature, by personal influence;
yours, I know, cannot be reached but through the loftier sentiments of the
intellectual and moral feelings.

Let the history of the world answer these queries. Read the denunciations
of Jehovah against the follies and crimes of Israel's daughters. Trace the
influence of woman as a courtezan and a mistress in the destinies of nations,
both ancient and modern, and see her wielding her power too often to
debase and destroy, rather than to elevate and save. It is often said that
women rule the world, through their influence over men. If so, then may we
well hide our faces in the dust, and cover ourselves with sackcloth and ashes.
It has not been by moral power and intellectual, but through the baser
passions of man.—This dominion of women must be resigned—the sooner
the better; "in the age which is approaching, she should be something more
—she should be a citizen; and this title, which demands an increase of knowledge and of reflection, opens before her a new empire."

I stand before you as a southerner, exiled from the land of my birth, by
the sounds of the lash, and the piteous cry of the slave. I stand before you
as a repentant slaveholder. I stand before you as a moral being, endowed
with precious and inalienable rights, which are correlative with solemn
duties and high responsibilities; and as a moral being I feel that I owe it to
the suffering slave, and to the deluded master, to my country and the world,
to do all that I can to overturn a system of complicated crimes, built up
upon the broken hearts and prostrate bodies of my countrymen in chains,
and cemented by the blood and sweat and tears of my sisters in bonds.

[The orator then proceeded to discuss the merits of the petitions.]

Speech in Pennsylvania Hall,
May 16, 1838

Men, brethren and fathers—mothers, daughters and sisters, what came ye out for to see? A reed shaken with the wind? Is it curiosity merely, or a deep sympathy with the perishing slave, that has brought this large audience together? [A yell from the mob without the building.] Those voices without ought to awaken and call out our warmest sympathies. Deluded beings! "they know not what they do." They know not that they are undermining their own rights and their own happiness, temporal and eternal. Do you ask, "what has the North to do with slavery?" Hear it—hear it. Those voices without tell us that the spirit of slavery is *here*, and has been roused to wrath by our abolition speeches and conventions: for surely liberty would not foam and tear herself with rage, because her friends are multiplied daily, and meetings are held in quick succession to set forth her virtues and extend her peaceful kingdom. This opposition shows that slavery has done its deadliest work in the hearts of our citizens. Do you ask, then, "what has the North to do?" I answer, cast out first the spirit of slavery from your own hearts, and then lend your aid to convert the South. Each one present has a work to do, be his or her situation what it may, however limited their means, or insignificant their supposed influence. The great men of this country will not do this work; the church will never do it. A desire to please the world, to keep the favor of all parties and of all conditions, makes them dumb on this and every other unpopular subject. They have become worldly-wise, and therefore God, in his wisdom, employs them not to carry on his plans of reformation and salvation. He hath chosen the foolish things of the world to confound the wise, and the weak to overcome the mighty.

As a Southerner I feel that it is my duty to stand up here tonight and bear testimony against slavery. I have seen it—I have seen it. I know it has horrors that can never be described. I was brought up under its wing: I witnessed for many years its demoralizing influences, and its destructiveness to human happiness. It is admitted by some that the slave is not happy under the *worst* forms of slavery. But I have *never* seen a happy slave. I have seen him dance in his chains, it is true; but he was not happy. There is a wide difference between happiness and mirth. Man cannot enjoy the former while his manhood is destroyed, and that part of the being which is necessary to the making, and to the enjoyment of happiness, is completely blotted out. The slaves, however, may be, and sometimes are, mirthful. When hope is extinguished, they say, "let us eat and drink, for to-morrow we die." [Just then stones were thrown at the windows,—a great noise without, and com-motion within] What is a mob? What would the breaking of every window be? What would the levelling of this Hall be? Any evidence that we are wrong, or that slavery is a good and wholesome institution? What if the mob should now burst in upon us, break up our meeting and commit violence upon our persons—would this be anything compared with what the slaves endure? No, no: and we do not remember them "as bound with them," if we shrink in the time of peril, or feel unwilling to sacrifice our-selves, if need be, for their sake. [Great Noise.] I thank the Lord that there is yet left life enough to feel the truth, even though it rages at it—that con-science is not so completely seared as to be unmoved by the truth of the living God.

Many persons go to the South for a season, and are hospitably entertained in the parlor and at the table of the slaveholder. They never enter the huts of the slaves; they know nothing of the dark side of the picture, and they return home with praises on their lips of the generous character of those with whom they had tarried. Or if they have witnessed the cruelties of slavery, by remain-ing silent spectators they have naturally become callous—an insensibility has ensued which prepares them to apologize even for barbarity. Nothing but the corrupting influence of slavery on the hearts of the Northern people can induce them to apologize for it; and much will have been done for the destruction of Southern slavery when we have so reformed the North that no one here will be willing to risk his reputation by advocating or even excusing the holding of men as property. The South know it, and acknowl-edge that as fast as our principles prevail, the hold of the master must be relaxed. [Another outbreak of mobocratic spirit, and some confusion in the house.]

How wonderfully constituted is the human mind! How it resists, as long as it can, all efforts made to reclaim from error! I feel that all this disturbance is but an evidence that our efforts are the best that could have been adopted, or else the friends of slavery, would not care for what we say and do. The South know what we do. I am thankful that they are reached by our efforts. Many times have I wept in the land of my birth over the system of slavery. I knew of none who sympathized in my feelings—I was unaware that any efforts were made to deliver the oppressed—no voice in the wilderness was heard calling on the people to repent and do works meet for repentance— and my heart sickened within me. Oh, how should I have rejoiced to know that such efforts as these were being made. I only wonder that I had such feelings. I wonder when I reflect under what influence I was brought up, that my heart is not harder than the nether millstone. But in the midst of temptation I was preserved, and my sympathy grew warmer, and my hatred of slavery more inveterate, until at last I have exiled myself from my native land because I could no longer endure to hear the wailing of the slave. I fled to the land of Penn; for here, thought I, sympathy for the slave will surely be found. But I found it not. The people were kind and hospitable, but the slave had no place in their thoughts. Whenever questions were put to me as to his condition, I felt that they were dictated by an idle curiosity, rather than by that deep feeling which would lead to effort for his rescue. I therefore shut up my grief in my own heart. I remembered that I was a Carolinian, from a state which framed this iniquity by law. I knew that throughout her territory was continued suffering, on the one part, and continual brutality and sin on the other. Every Southern breeze wafted to me the discordant tones of weeping and wailing, shrieks and groans, mingled with prayers and blasphemous curses. I thought there was no hope; that the wicked would go on in his wickedness, until he had destroyed both himself and his country. My heart sunk within me at the abominations in the midst of which I had been born and educated. What will it avail, cried I in bitterness of spirit, to expose to the gaze of strangers the horrors and pollutions of slavery, when there is no ear to hear nor heart to feel and pray for the slave. The language of my soul was, "Oh tell it not in Gath, publish it not in the streets of Askelon." But how different do I feel now! Animated with hope, nay, with an assurance of the triumph of liberty and good will to man, I will lift up my voice like a trumpet, and show this people their transgression, their sins of omission towards the slave, and what they can do towards affecting Southern mind, and overthrowing Southern oppression.

We may talk of occupying neutral ground, but on this subject, in its present attitude, there is no such thing as neutral ground. He that is not for us is against us, and he that gathereth not with us, scattereth abroad. If you are on what you suppose to be neutral ground, the South look upon you as on the side of the oppressor. And is there one who loves his country willing to give his influence, even indirectly, in favor of slavery—that curse of nations? God swept Egypt with the besom of destruction, and punished Judea also with a sore punishment, because of slavery. And have we any reason to believe that he is less just now?—or that he will be more favorable to us than to his own "peculiar people?" [Shoutings, stones thrown against the windows, &c.]

There is nothing to be feared from those who would stop our mouths, but they themselves should fear and tremble. The current is even now setting fast against them. If the arm of the North had not caused the Bastille of slavery to totter to its foundation, you would not hear those cries. A few years ago, and the South felt secure, and with a contemptuous sneer asked, "Who are the abolitionists? The abolitionists are nothing?"—Ay, in one sense they were nothing, and they are nothing still. But in this we rejoice, that "God has chosen things that are not to bring to nought things that are." [Mob again disturbed the meeting.]

We often hear the question asked, "What shall we do?" Here is an opportunity for doing something now. Every man and every woman present may do something by showing that we fear not a mob, and, in the midst of threatenings and revilings, by opening our mouths for the dumb and pleading the cause of those who are ready to perish.

To work as we should in this cause, we must know what Slavery is. Let me urge you then to buy the books which have been written on this subject and read them, and then lend them to your neighbors. Give your money no longer for things which pander to pride and lust, but aid in scattering "the living coals of truth" upon the naked heart of this nation,—in circulating appeals to the sympathies of Christians in behalf of the outraged and suffering slave. But, it is said by some, our "books and papers do not speak the truth." Why, then, do they not contradict what we say? They cannot. Moreover the South has entreated, nay commanded us to be silent; and what greater evidence of the truth of our publications could be desired?

Women of Philadelphia! allow me as a Southern woman, with much attachment to the land of my birth, to entreat you to come up to this work. Especially let me urge you to petition. *Men* may settle this and other questions at the ballot-box, but you have no such right; it is only through petitions that you can reach the Legislature. It is therefore peculiarly *your* duty to petition. Do you say, "It does no good?" The South already turns pale at the number sent. They have read the reports of the proceedings of Congress, and there have seen that among other petitions were very many from the women of the North on the subject of slavery. This fact has called the attention of the South to the subject. How could we expect to have done more as yet? Men who hold the rod over slaves, rule in the councils of the nation: and they deny our right to petition and to remonstrate against abuses of our sex and of our kind. We have these rights, however, from our God. Only let us exercise them: and though often turned away unanswered, let us remember the influence of importunity upon the unjust judge, and act accordingly. The fact that the South look with jealousy upon our measures shows that they are effectual. There is, therefore, no cause for doubting or despair, but rather for rejoicing.

It was remarked in England that women did much to abolish Slavery in her colonies. Nor are they now idle. Numerous petitions from them have recently been presented to the Queen, to abolish the apprenticeship with its cruelties nearly equal to those of the system whose place it supplies. One petition two miles and a quarter long has been presented. And do you think these labors will be in vain? Let the history of the past answer. When the women of these States send up to Congress such a petition, our legislators will arise as did those of England, and say, "When all the maids and matrons of the land are knocking at our doors we must legislate." Let the zeal and love, the faith and works of our English sisters quicken ours—that while the slaves continue to suffer, and when they shout deliverance, we may feel the satisfaction of *having done what we could.*

Susan B. Anthony

Susan Brownell Anthony was a young woman who seemed destined to take on the role of reformer because of her Quaker heritage, her very strong father Daniel's characteristics and beliefs, which she inherited and he nurtured, the circumstances of her life, and the times in which she lived. Daniel Anthony was a good friend of Frederick Douglass, and two of his sons accompanied John Brown on his raids into Kansas. Susan's way into the abolition ranks was well paved by Daniel.

Contrary to the notion that many have of the early women suffragettes, Susan did not "come on strong," at least for the most part. The general picture of her as a person is more that of a tenaciously determined and organized woman who, once turned toward a goal, had the energy and purpose to pursue it with more effectiveness than most. She is remembered more for her fight for equal rights and the vote for women, but she was a highly effective agent in the antislavery lecturing campaign, although she did not get directly involved until relatively late, the 1850's, twenty years after the Grimké sisters and others had initiated the public speaking of women reformers. The abolition of slavery was the one reform in which success came during her lifetime.

It was fourteen years after her death that both prohibition and women's suffrage were added as constitutional guarantees; when she died at the age of eighty-six in 1906, she felt that her battles on these reforms might never meet success. She had spent over half a century on the lecture stages of this country, and she was not a particularly good lecturer at that, at least not in the conventional sense that one speaks of a fine orator or a dramatic speaker. She had a storehouse of facts and arguments, which she presented in a clearly articulated and not unpleasant voice that could be heard easily, and she simply talked to her audience, bombarding them steadily in a direct, easy manner.

It was nearly impossible for Susan Anthony to sit down and write a speech, but she found her perfect ghost writer in Mrs. Elizabeth Cady Stanton, wife of Henry, and their collaboration lasted half a century. Actually, when Susan began speaking, it was for the cause of temperance and women's rights. She felt strongly about both, but when she began speaking about slavery, her feelings were far more intense and her rhetoric far more dramatic. She patterned herself after the Garrisonian agitators and used some of the Quaker aggressiveness against sin. If she was ever an "orator," it was during the ten or more years she was an active abolitionist speaker. She seemed to have more stamina than many of the lecturers she was supposed to be scheduling to appear throughout New York State beginning in 1856, so by filling in for others, and by appearing on the platforms with many other experienced speakers, she gained her experience quickly. Miss Anthony first read from manuscripts which Mrs. Stanton wrote (from facts supplied by Susan, whose mind was retentive more than imaginative), but the fire of the campaign to end slavery soon brought her to the point where she had been through the basic speeches so often that she began using only notes. Her gift for speaking on her feet and for making impromptu remarks and repartee was greater than her oratorical skill. Her speeches no doubt became more effective as her feelings came into her words. She used this method of speaking from notes for the rest of her life.

Physical danger seemed not to bother Miss Anthony very much; mobs kept the speakers from being heard in several cities in 1860; she was burned in effigy in Syracuse. At that point, as an abolitionist, Susan B. Anthony was an avenging angel. Unlike the fact-filled, ordered arguments accompanied by amusing sidelights, which were her stock in trade as she battled fifty years for women's suffrage, the abolitionist Miss Anthony had a rousing style and gave passionate, inflammatory speeches. She was, on the abolition platform, a holy terror, absolutely convinced of the rightness of her cause and the destined outcome of her campaign.

born, February, 1820, Adams, Mass.

died, March, 1906, Rochester, N. Y.

No Union
with Slaveholders

What we of the North now need is *Right Action*. True words have been spoken and written from the days of Washington to Jefferson, down to these of Giddings and Sumner.—But words, though piled mountain high, mean nothing to the slave or slave holder.—The action suited to the word is now the one *great* demand.

Washington, the first President of these United States,—canonized the "Father of his Country"—said in a letter to Robert Morris, "there is no man living, who wishes, more sincerely than I do, the adoption of some plan for the abolition of Slavery." And yet, this same Washington,—this "Father of his Country," was the first Slave-Holder, who, under the Fugitive Slave Law of 1783, sent his Slave Minions to the granite hills of New Hampshire to recover his escaped Slave woman Onez.

And Jefferson, author of the *immortal declaration of 1775*, who said, "I tremble for my country when I remember that God is just, and that his justice may not sleep forever;" Jefferson, who said, "One hour of American Slavery is fraught with more misery than *ages* of that which we rose in rebellion to oppose,"—was a slave holder to the day of his death, the *father* of a *slave daughter*, who was sold in the *New Orleans Market for a thousand dollars*. Yes, Jefferson, who uttered so many *noble words* for freedom and so many scathing denunciations against slavery, was the father of a *Slave Mother's Child*,—the father of a *Daughter*, to whom he bequeathed unrequited toil,—hopeless bondage,—outraged person,—violated womanhood;—the father of a Daughter, whom he made heir to the terrible fate of slavery;—*one hour* of which, he had declared, fraught with more misery than *ages* of that which the Revolutionary Fathers rose in rebellion to oppose, and to escape which, they fought, bled and died.—One of Old England's Poets thus records our Country's Shame.

> Can the blood that at Lexington poured o'er her plain,
> When the sons warred with tyrants, their right to uphold,
> Can the tide of Niagara wipe out the stain?—
> No, Jefferson's child has been bartered for gold!
> The Daughter of Jefferson sold for a slave!
> The child of a freeman, for Dollars and Francs!
> The roar of applause, when your Orators rave,
> Is lost in the sound of her chain and its clanks.
> Peace then, ye blasphemers of Liberty's name!
> Though red was the blood by your forefathers spilt,
> Still redder your cheeks should be mantled with shame,
> Till the spirit of freedom shall cancel the guilt.

I need not quote to you the brave words that have fallen from the lips of freedom's veteran Champion, Giddings.—For a century they have fallen like snowflakes and have been wafted on the wings of the wind through the entire length and breadth of this vast Empire.—For a Century have they gone forth from the Legislative Halls of this Nation, to gladden the heart and the home of the Lover of Liberty, and to startle the conscience, and terrify the soul of the oppressor.

And Massachusetts' noble Sumner's living words for freedom need no rehearsal from mortal lips.—Remember the murderous blows, the gaping wounds, the bed of pain,—the sickening months of hope deferred,—the vacant chair,—the senate chamber's blood stained floor,—the electric flash that sent a thrill of anguish to the heart of freedom from Maine to Minnesota, —the barbarous yell of exaltation that went up from the *kennels of slavery,* from Washington to Louisiana, from Virginia to the Carolinas.—*Then Sumner fell!*

> "Then I and you and all of us fell down,
> Whilst bloody treason flourished over us."—

And yet, do Giddings and Sumner, the truest and bravest of American Statesmen, by their position consent to the *existence* and *continuance* of Slavery in Fifteen States of this Union,—and by their *Official Oath*, to support the *United States Constitution*, and the *United States Government*, do promise to protect the Slave-holder in his *Slave Property.*—For both these men admit the fact of the Pro-Slavery Compromises of the *U.S. Constitution* and the ever dominant, Pro-Slavery Political Power of the United States Government.

Giddings, in reply to the question "What was contemplated by that clause in the Constitution, which stipulates for the surrender of fugitive slaves," says—"To secure to the master the same right to pursue and capture his slave in the Free State that he possessed to pursue and capture his horse or mule."—To the question, "*how* is the fugitive to be delivered up," he says, "the Supreme Court of the United States, the *high tribunal* which is *authorized* to give *construction* to the *Constitution*, has distinctly answered, "We are bound to permit the master to take him wherever he finds him.— We must not secrete him from the master.—We must not defend him against the master.—Nor are we to rescue him from the master's custody, after he shall have taken him.—He then adds, they, the slave-holders, the majority of the Supreme Court, have determined *our duties.*—And, I believe them in strict accordance with the intention of those who *framed* the Constitution."—

And yet, with this full concession of the pro-slavery character of the

Constitution, Joshua R. Giddings swears to support it,—swears that he will permit the master to take fugitive slaves wherever he finds them.—Swears that he will not secrete him from the master.—Swears that he will not rescue him from the master's cruelty, after he shall have taken him.—Swears that he will remain a passive looker-on while the "Legrees" hurl their wretched victims back into the hell of slavery. If, as Mr. Giddings asserts, facts do show the characteristics of Slavery to be horrid,—and if facts do prove that slavery "blots out the intellect, and reduces man, created in the image of his God, to the level of brutes, how can he swear to support the United States Constitution?"—How can he, in the presence of his fellow men, the angels, and Jehovah Himself, *swear* that he will *deliver* up to the *cruel task-master,* the *trembling fugitive,* who asks protection at his hands?—Were Giddings' own wife and daughter among the outraged *slave* victims, think you he could be *prevailed* upon to pledge himself by all that is sacred on Earth and in Heaven, to keep inviolate the Pro-Slavery Compromises of the Constitution —including the "Fugitive Slave Law" and "Dred Scott Decision"?

For, according to Mr. Giddings' *own declaration,* that the United States Supreme Court is the high tribunal, authorized to give construction to the Constitution, that abominable Law, and that infamous decision, are as much a part and parcel of the Constitution as any line of the original document. What does Mr. Giddings mean when he, with his hand on the Bible, solemnly swears to support the United States Constitution?

And Charles Sumner says, "It is true that there were compromises at the formation of the Constitution, which were subjects for anxious debate.

> There was a compromise between the small and large states by which equality was secured to all the states, in the Senate.—
>
> There was another compromise, finally carried, under threats from the South, on the motion of a New England Member, by which Slave States were allowed representatives according to the whole number of Free persons and three-fifths of all other persons,

Thus securing political power on account of their slaves, in consideration that *direct taxes* should be apportioned the *same way.*—Direct taxes have been imposed only at *four brief intervals.*—The *political power* has been constant, and at this moment, sends *twenty-one* members to the other House.

"There was a third compromise which cannot be mentioned without Shame. It was the hateful bargain by which Congress was restrained until *1808* from the *prohibition* of the foreign slave trade, thus securing down to that period, *toleration* of *Crime.*"

He finally adds, "Such are the three chief original compromises of the Constitution, and *essential conditions* of the *Union*."

And yet, Charles Sumner swears to support the same Constitution,—consents to the continuance of the same Union, whose *essential conditions* are now, as at the beginning, the Pro-Slavery Compromises;—Consents to the guilty bargain that gives to the Slave States a three-fifths representation for their Slave Property;—consents that every *five slaves* shall be counted as *three votes*, to fasten the chain around the neck of nearly *four millions of human beings!* Were Charles Sumner's own mother a slave on a southern plantation, despoiled of every right sacred to womanhood, would he, by his position as a *loyal citizen* to the United States government,—by his oath to support the United States Constitution,—and by his adherence to the Union, consent, that that Slave Mother should be reckoned in the three-fifths representation, that sends twenty-one members to Congress, to rivet her chains, to sink her still deeper into the dark night of Slavery?—

What we ask of Sumner and Giddings, and *every* United States Citizen, who professes to love freedom for the Slave, as well as himself, is that he shall *cease* to swear allegiance to the United States Constitution, Government and Union, the essential conditions of which are slavery and slavery only.—We ask Giddings and Sumner and all lovers of liberty, that they shall declare to the slave-holding lords of the South and the *whole world* that they are rebels and traitors;—that, henceforth, they will give *no support* to a Slave-holding Constitution,—no allegiance to a Slave-holding government,—no adherence to a Slave-holding Union.

Part V
Establishment Spokesmen
for Antislavery

As the groundswell of support for antislavery grew stronger in the 1840's and 1850's in the North, more and more substantial men of solid reputation joined the ranks of the reformers. The pulpit supplied some of the most famous preachers of the time, including Henry Ward Beecher and Theodore Parker. Among the elected officials of the country were such men as William Seward, governor and senator from New York, John Quincy Adams of Massachusetts, former President and member of the House, Charles Sumner, senator from Massachusetts, and Joshua Giddings, Whig antislavery congressman from Ohio. Perhaps the most famous and one of the more moderate speakers to join the antislavery forces was Abraham Lincoln of Illinois, who came to national prominence in the campaign for the Senate seat from Illinois in 1858.

A number of speeches are illustrative of the established men of important reputation who legitimized the abolition sentiments until they claimed a majority of the votes in the North in the election of 1860. Seward's famous speech "The Irrepressible Conflict" and Sumner's "Crime Against Kansas," which resulted in his being caned by Congressman Brooks from South Carolina, are two. Excerpts from some of Lincoln's speeches in the years from 1858–1860 would also be illustrative. They are widely anthologized and well known.

The speeches included here are by two of the most important of the spokesmen who worked within the system for the emancipation of the slaves. The first is by a clergyman, Theodore Parker, and was one of his early sermons devoted to the subject of slavery. Entitled "A Sermon of Slavery," it was delivered on January 31, 1841, and repeated on June 4, 1843.[1] Parker, one of the foremost scholars of Boston, reveals in the sermon his characteristic ability to step back and analyze a proposition on philosophical

---

[1]Theodore Parker, *Discourses of Slavery* (London: Trubner & Co., 1863), pp. 1–16.

grounds. The sermon also illustrates Parker's considerable skill at denunciation and castigation.

The second selection is from Joshua Giddings' speech on "Relation of the Federal Government to Slavery." In the session of Congress following the presidential election of 1848, some twenty Southern members published an address to the people of the South which complained that their slaves were being permitted to escape, that the people of the North were trying to abolish slavery in the District of Columbia, and that Northerners were trying to prohibit the slave trade on the Southern coast. Attempts were made to write an address answering the Southern protest and to get an equal number of Northern Congressmen to sign it. The attempts failed, but Giddings expressed his personal views in the speech included here, which was delivered in Committee of the whole House, February 17, 1849.[2]

Of all the wars of American history the one with Mexico in the 1840's most resembles the Vietnam war of the 1960's. A large segment of the American people viewed the Mexican war as immoral, and the abolitionists charged it was fought for the imperialistic advantage of the slave power. A leading spokesman against the war was Joshua Giddings, who played a role somewhat similar to that of Senator William Fulbright in the Vietnamese conflict. The ostensible purpose of Giddings' speech of February 17, 1849, was to discuss a bill making appropriations to carry into effect the treaty with Mexico. Giddings also repeated his favorite arguments on the nature of the Constitution and the sinful and wicked character of slavery.

Theodore Parker

If one characteristic runs through the personalities of the abolitionists, it is that of being strong-willed, single-minded, adamant, call it what you will. Though Theodore Parker, the youngest of eleven children, is said to have been a precocious but typical boy, fun-loving and busy, he must have had more than typical determination for the day, for when he was twenty he walked from the home farm at Lexington to Cambridge and, without telling his family, took the entrance examinations to Harvard. He knew there was no money for his tuition, but he passed the exams and somehow was allowed to take the courses on his own (meanwhile working on the farm every day that year and thereafter teaching school) and take the examinations

[2]Joshua R. Giddings, *Speeches in Congress* (Boston: John P. Jewett and Company, 1853), pp. 333–63.

when they were given. He never did get his B.A. degree, but ten years after he began his self-study program, Harvard conferred an honorary Master of Arts degree upon him. He had, in the meantime, with the help of a special fund for poor students and what pennies he had saved from several years of teaching, graduated from Harvard Divinity School and been ordained. From many offers, he chose a parish near Boston so that he could be near good libraries. It was a simple return of favors when, after his death, he bequeathed his very extensive personal library to the Boston Public Library, for he was a man who had loved books since he was a boy, and he wanted to share his discoveries with others.

Theodore Parker was a scholar. He overworked himself, however, those years he was teaching and taking exams at Harvard and trying to prepare himself for Divinity school; he began to feel inordinately upset if any of his ideas were criticized, he had trouble keeping in good spirits and good humor, and he was thereafter always overly sensitive to the opinions of others. This is somewhat ironic because, through the years, he became increasingly critical of the orthodox religious beliefs of his day; he acquired more of a militant disposition himself, attacking any and all things he believed needed changing. He would attack wrongs with great enthusiasm and then suffer deeply when he felt himself ostracized.

Theodore Parker's doubts about the need for divine revelation as a basis for religious beliefs, and about miracles, and about the virgin birth of Christ, increased as he became familiar with European theologists; he read many modern foreign languages as well as the ancient scriptural ones, and he became almost too cosmopolitan for Boston. Although some were liberal and ready for his new theology that man did not need a mediator but could "go" directly to God, that man could fathom the perfection of God, could intellectually comprehend the eternal right, could accept the idea of immortal life, many could not. But when he, with friends, opened a new church in downtown Boston (The Boston Congregational Society), thousands came, and he was a stimulating preacher whose new ideas found many ready ears.

As was usual for him, when Theodore Parker decided to attack slavery, he made a careful study of the economic aspects of it, and in 1850, after the Fugitive Slave Law was passed, he made two passionate speeches in Boston's Faneuil Hall, and he actively participated in efforts to help various escaped slaves as chairman of the Boston Vigilance Committee.

After the Kansas-Nebraska Bill of 1854, Parker gave many more sermons and speeches, some passionately rhetorical, some less dramatic but filled with forceful arguments based on economics, and he publicly stated that he felt civil war was inevitable. He was a member of a secret committee that helped finance a foray by John Brown into the mountains of Virginia.

Theodore Parker had a remarkable mind, evident when he was quite young; he had a retentive memory, a love of beauty, and some natural talents of expression; even as a boy he developed some reputation as an effective declaimer. It was said of Parker, the man, that his voice was unmusical, that he was not an animated speaker, that his bearing was ungraceful and his manner undistinguished, but that despite all this, he dominated his audience with what he had to say. He had facts, he had well reasoned arguments to present, he had high moral idealism and the ability to share with his listeners his own love of God; he felt the world was perfectible and full of beauty, and he exhorted his listeners to share his dreams and go forth and do what was necessary to achieve this even better society.

From 1845, Parker publicly allied himself with the abolition party, and for the next twenty-five years he was a driving force in the North in a steady campaign to awaken and enlighten people of Boston to the evils of slavery.

Theodore Parker married Lydia Cabot the same year he was ordained; he was then twenty-seven. They had no children. When he was forty-seven, after many years of strenuous, exciting life, a life which included journeys, thousands of sermons and speeches, voluminous correspondence, he became ill while on a speaking tour. He had inherited a tendency toward consumption, and his lungs became involved. Two years later he had to end his public life and left for an extended trip; he died in Florence, Italy, before the Civil War and before the fought-for emancipation of slaves took place.

born August, 1810, Lexington, Mass.

died May, 1860, Florence, Italy

A Sermon
of Slavery

Know ye not that to whom ye yield yourselves servants to obey, his servants ye are whom ye obey; whether of sin unto death, or of obedience unto righteousness?—ROM. vi. 16.

In our version of the New Testament the word *servant* often stands for a word in the original, which means *slave*. Such is the case in this passage just read, and the sense of the whole verse is this:—"If a man yields unconditional service to sin, he is the *slave* of sin, and gets death for his reward." Here, however, by a curious figure of speech, not uncommon in this apostle, he uses the word *slave* in a good sense—*slave* of obedience unto righteousness. I now ask your attention to a short sermon of slavery.

A popular definition has sometimes been given of common bodily slavery, that it is the holding of property in man. In a kindred language it is called body-property. In this case, a man's body becomes the possession, property, chattel, tool, or thing of another person, and not of the man who lives in it. This foreign person, of course, makes use of it to serve his own ends, without regard to the true welfare, or even the wishes, of the man who lives in that body, and to whom it rightfully belongs. Here the relation is necessarily that of force on one side and suffering on the other, though the force is often modified and the suffering sometimes disguised or kept out of sight.

Now man was made to be free, to govern himself, to be his own master, to have no cause stand between him and God, which shall curtail his birthright of freedom. He is never in his proper element until he attains this condition of freedom; of self-government. Of course, while we are children, not having reached the age of discretion, we must be under the authority of our parents and guardians, teachers, and friends. This is a natural relation. There is no slavery in it; no degradation. The parents, exercising rightful authority over their children, do not represent human caprice, but divine wisdom and love. They assume the direction of the child's actions, not to do themselves a service, but to benefit him. The father restrains his child, that the child may have more freedom, not less. Here the relation is not of force and suffering, but of love on both sides; of ability, which loves to help, and necessity, which loves to be directed. The child that is nurtured by its parent gains more than the parent does. So is it the duty of the wise, the good, the holy, to teach, direct, restrain the foolish, the wicked, the ungodly. If a man is wiser, better, and holier than I am, it is my duty, my privilege, my exaltation to obey him. For him to direct me in wisdom and love, not for his sake but for my own, is for me to be free. He may gain nothing by this, but I gain much.

As slavery was defined to be holding property in man, so freedom may be defined as a state in which the man does, of his own consent, the best things he is capable of doing at that stage of his growth. Now there are two sorts of obstacles which prevent, or may prevent, men from attaining to this enviable condition of freedom. These are:—

I. Obstacles external to ourselves, which restrict our freedom; and

II. Obstacles internal to ourselves, which restrict our freedom.

A few words may be said on the condition to which men are brought by each of these classes of objects.

I. Of the slavery which arises from a cause external to ourselves. By the blessing of Providence, seconding the efforts, prayers, tears of some good men, there is no bodily, personal slavery sanctioned by the law amongst us in New England. But at the South we all know that some millions of our fellow-citizens are held in bondage; that men, women, and children are bought and sold in the shambles of the national capital; are owned as cattle; reared as cattle; beaten as cattle. We all know that our fathers fought through the War of Independence with these maxims in their mouths and blazoned on their banners: that all men are born free and equal, and that the God of eternal justice will at last avenge the cause of the oppressed, however strong the oppressor may be; yet it is just as well known that the sons of those very fathers now trade in human flesh, separating parent and child, and husband and wife, for the sake of a little gain; that the sons of those fathers eat bread not in the sweat of their own brow, but in that of the slave's face; that they are sustained, educated, rendered rich, and haughty, and luxurious by the labour they extort from men whom they have stolen, or purchased from the stealer, or inherited from the purchaser. It is known to you all, that there are some millions of these forlorn children of Adam, men whom the Declaration of Independence declares "born free and equal" with their master before God and the Law; men whom the Bible names "of the same blood" with the prophets and apostles; men "for whom Christ died," and who are "statues of God in ebony"—that they are held in this condition and made to feel the full burden of a corrupt society, and doomed from their birth to degradation and infamy, their very name a mock-word; their life a retreat, not a progress, —for the general and natural effect of slavery is to lessen the qualities of a man in the slave as he increases in stature or in years,—their children, their wives, their own bones and sinews at the mercy of a master! That these things are so, is known to all of us; well known from our childhood.

Every man who has ever thought at all on any subject, and has at the same time a particle of manhood in him, knows that this state of slavery would be to him worse than a thousand deaths; that set death in one scale, and hopeless slavery for himself and children in the other, he would not hesitate in his choice, but would say, "Give me death, though the life be ground out of me with the most exquisite tortures of lingering agony that malice can invent or tyranny inflict." To the African thus made the victim of American cupidity and crime, the state of slavery, it will be said, may not appear so degrading as to you and me, for he has never before been civilized, and though the untaught instinct of man bid him love freedom, yet Christianity has not revealed to him the truth, that all men are brothers before God, born with equal rights. But this fact is no excuse or extenuation of our crime. Who would justify a knave in plundering a little girl out of a fortune that she inherited, on the ground that she was a little girl "of tender years," and had never enjoyed or even beheld her birthright? The fact, that the injured party was ignorant and weak, would only enhance and aggravate the offence, adding new baseness and the suspicion of cowardice to guilt. If the African be so low, that the condition of slavery is tolerable in his eyes, and he can dance in his chains—happy in the absence of the whip—it is all the more a sin, in the cultivated and the strong, in the Christian (!) to tyrannize over the feeble and defenceless. Men at the South with the Bible in one hand —with the Declaration of Independence in the other hand—with the words of Jesus, "Love your neighbour as yourself," pealing upon them from all quarters, attempt to justify slavery; not to excuse, to cloak, or conceal the thing, but to vindicate and defend it. This attempt, when made by reflecting men in their cool moments, discovers a greater degree of blackness of heart than the kidnapping of men itself. It is premeditated wickedness grown conscious of itself. The plain truth of the matter is this:—Men who wish for wealth and luxury, but hate the toil and sweat, which are their natural price, brought the African to America; they make his chains; they live by his tears; they dance to the piping of his groans; they fatten on his sweat and are pampered by his blood. If these men spoke as plainly as they must needs think, they would say openly; "our sin captured these men on the African sands; our sin fettered them in slavery; and, please God, our sin shall keep them in slavery till the world ends." This has been thought long enough, it is high time it was said also, that we may know what we are about and where we stand.

Men at the North sometimes attempt to gloss the matter over, and hush it up by saying the least possible on the subject. They tell us that some masters are "excellent Christians." No doubt it is so, estimating these masters by the common run of Christians,—you find such on the deck of pirate ships; in the dens of robbers. But suppose some slaveholders are as good Christians as Fenelon or St. Peter; still a sin is sin, though a Christian commit it. Our fathers did not think "taxation without representation" any the less an evil because imposed by "his most Christian Majesty," a King of Christians.

Then, too, it is said, "the slaves are very happy, and it is a great pity to disturb them," that "the whole mass are better fed and clothed, and are troubled with fewer cares, than working men at the North." Suppose this true also, what then? Do you estimate your welfare in pounds of beef; in yards of cloth; in exemption from the cares of a man! If so all appeal to you is vain, your own soul has become servile. The Saviour of the world was worse fed and clothed, no doubt, than many a Georgian slave, and had not where to lay his head, wearied with many cares; but has your Christianity taught you that was an evil, and the slave's hutch at night, and pottage by day, and exemption from a man's cares by night and day, are a good, a good to be weighed against freedom! Then are you unworthy the soil you stand on; you contaminate the air of New England, which free men died to transmit to their children free!

Still further it is said, "the sufferings of slaves are often exaggerated." This may be true. No doubt there have been exaggerations of particular cases. Every slave-owner is not a demon, not a base man. No doubt there are what are called good Christians, men that would be ornaments to a Christian church, among slaveholders. But though there have been exaggerations in details, yet the awful sum of misery, unspeakable wretchedness, which hangs over two millions of slaves is such that eye hath not seen it; nor ear heard it; nor heart conceived of it. It were so if all their masters were Christians in character, in action, still retaining slaves. How much deeper and wilder must swell that wide weltering sea of human agony, when the masters are what we know so many are, hard-hearted and rapacious, insolent and brutal!

This attempt to gloss the matter over and veil the fact, comes from two classes of men.

1. Some make the attempt from a real design to promote peace. They see no way to abate this mischief; they see "the folly and extravagance" of such as propose "dangerous measures," and therefore they would have us say nothing about it. The writhing patient is very sick; the leech more venturesome than skilful; and the friends, fearful to try the remedy, unwilling to summon wiser advice, declare the sick man is well as ever if you will only let him alone! These men mourn that any one should hold another in bondage; they think our fathers were illustrious heroes, for fighting dreadful wars with the parent country rather than pay a little tax against their will, but that this evil of slavery can never be healed; therefore, in the benevolence of their heart, they refuse to believe all the stories of suffering that reach their ears. The imagination of a kind man recoils at the thought of so much wretchedness; still more, if convinced that it cannot be abated. Now these men are governed by the best of motives, but it does not follow that their opinions are so just as their motives are good.

2. But there are others, who are willing to countenance the sin and continue it, well knowing that it is a sin. They would not have it abated. They

tell you of the stupidity of the African; that he is made for nothing but a slave; is allied to the baboon and the ape, and is as much in his place when fettered, ignorant and savage, in a rice field, to toil under a taskmaster's whip, as a New Englander, free and educated, is in his place, when felling forests, planning railroads, or "conducting" a steam-engine. Hard treatment and poor fare, say they, are the black man's due. Besides, they add, there is a natural antipathy between the black race and the white, which only the love of money, or the love of power, on the part of the white is capable of overcoming; that the blacks are an inferior race, and therefore the white Saxons are justified in making them slaves. They think the strong have a right to the services of the weak, forgetting that the rule of reason, the rule of Christianity, is just the other way; "We that are strong ought to bear the infirmities of the weak." They would have us follow the old rule, "that they should get who have the power, and they should keep who can." Of this class nothing further need be said save this: that they are very numerous, and quote the New Testament in support of slavery, thus contriving to pass for Christians, and have made such a stir in the land that it is scarce safe to open one's mouth and strip the veil from off this sin.

If some one should come and tell us that a new race of men had been discovered living at the bottom of the sea, who had a government which declared that all men were "born free," and a religion which laid down these excellent maxims: that all men were brothers; that God was no respecter of persons; and that man's chief earthly duty was to love and serve his fellow-mortals, keeping the law God Himself had made for man; we should say, what an admirable government! what a beautiful religion! what a free, religious, and blessed people they must be! "Happy is the people that is in such a case. Yea, happy is that people whose God is the Lord." But if we were told that a part of that nation had seized certain men weaker than themselves, whom their government had declared "free," whom their religion called "brothers" to the best of men; that they held these men in bondage, making them do all their masters' work, and receive no recompense, but a wretched life which they were to transmit to their children; and that in the mean time the other part of the nation looked on, and said nothing against this shameful wrong; they encouraged the crime and lent their wisdom, their wealth, and their valour to support and perpetuate this infamous institution; what should we say? Certainly that these men were liars! Liars before their government! Liars before their God! Such is the fact. This people does not live at the bottom of the sea, but on the firm land, and boasts the name of Republic, and Christian Commonwealth!

The opinion of good and religious men here amongst us seems to be, that slavery is a great sin and ought to be abolished as soon as possible; that the talent and piety of the nation cannot be better employed than in devising the speediest and most effectual way of exterminating the evil. Such of them as see a way to abolish the wrong cry aloud and publish the tidings; others who see no way state that fact also, not failing to express their dread of all violent measures. Such is the conviction of good and religious men at the North. But there is another opinion a little different, which is held by a different class of men at the North;—they think that slavery is a great sin, and ought to be kept up so long as men can make money by it. But if the suppression of slavery could be effected—not as our fathers won their freedom, by blood and war—so gently as not to ruffle a sleeping baby's eyelid, yet if it diminished the crop of rice, or cotton, or tobacco, or corn, a single quintal a year, it would be a great mistake to free, cultivate, Christianize, and bless these millions of men! No one, I take it, will doubt this is a quite common opinion here in New England. The cause of this opinion will presently be touched upon. To show what baseness was implied in holding such opinions, would be simply a waste of time.

We all know there is at the North a small body of men, called by various names, and treated with various marks of disrespect, who are zealously striving to procure the liberation of slaves, in a peaceable and quiet way. They are willing to make any sacrifice for this end. They start from the maxim, that slavery is sin, and that sin is to be abandoned at once, and for ever, come what will come of it. These men, it is said, are sometimes extravagant in their speech; they do not treat the "patriarchal institution" with becoming reverence; they call slave-holders hard names, and appeal to all who have a heart in their bosoms, and to some who find none there, to join them and end the patriarchal institution by wise and Christian measures. What wonder is it that these men sometimes grow warm in their arguments! What wonder that their heart burns when they think of so many women exposed to contamination and nameless abuse; of so many children reared like beasts, and sold as oxen; of so many men owning no property in their hands, or their feet, their hearts, or their lives! The wonder is all the other side, that they do not go to further extremities, sinful as it might be, and like St John in his youth, pray for fire to come down from heaven and burn up the sinners, or like Paul, when he had not the excuse of youthful blood, ask God to curse them. Yet they do none of these things; never think of an appeal to the strong arm, but the Christian heart. When a man in this land of ours begins to feel this desperate iniquity and sees the deadness of those around him; the silly game played over his head by political parties and political leaders; the game yet sillier played by theological parties and theological leaders, while the land lies overgrown with "tresspasses and sins,"—he may be pardoned if he shrieks over human sufferings and human crime; if he cries out and spares not, but wishes he had a mouth in his hands, and a mouth in his feet, and was speech all over, that he might protest in every limb against this abomination which maketh the heart desolate. There is no doubt that these men are sometimes extravagant! There need be no wonder at that fact. The best of men have their infirmities, but if this extravagance be one of them, what shall we call the deadness of so many more amongst us? An infirmity? What shall we say of the sin itself? An infirmity also? Honest souls engaged in a good work, fired with a great idea, sometimes forget the settled decorum of speech, commonly observed in forum and pulpit, and call sin SIN. If the New Testament tell truth, Paul did so, and it was thought he would "turn the world upside down," while he was only striving to set it right. John the Baptist and Jesus of Nazareth did the same thing, and though one left his head in a charger, and the other his body on a cross, yet the world thinks at this day they did God's great work with their sincerity of speech.

The men who move in this matter encounter opposition from two classes of men; from the moderate, who do not see the wisdom of their measures, and who fear that the slave if set free will be worse off than before, or who think that the welfare of the masters is not sufficiently cared for. These moderate men think "we had better not meddle with the matter at present," but by and by, at a convenient season, they will venture to look into it. Now these moderate men it is not likely would ever think of doing the work until it is all done, yet deserve the gratitude of the public, of the more enthusiastic Abolitionists. A balance wheel is useful to a machine; though it renders more force necessary at first to start the machine, it gives it stability and power when once set a moving. In certain stages of vegetation a chilly day is a most auspicious event.

Then too they encounter opposition from the selfish, who see, or think they see, that the white masters will lose some thousands of millions of dollars, if slavery be abolished! Who has forgotten the men that opposed the introduction of Christianity at Ephesus,—the craftsmen that made silver shrines for Diana!

I know some men say, "we have nothing to do with it. Slavery is the affair of the slave-owners and the slaves, not yours and mine. Let them abate it when they will." A most unchristian saying is this. Slavery! we have something to do with it. The sugar and rice we eat, the cotton we wear, are the work of the slave. His wrongs are imported to us in these things. We eat his flesh and drink his blood. I need not speak of our political connection with slavery. You all know what that is, and its effect on us here. But socially, individually, we are brought into contact with it every day. If there is a crime in the land known to us, and we do not protest against it to the extent of our ability, we are partners of that crime. It is not many years since it was said, temperate men had nothing to do with the sin of drunkenness; though they paid for it out of their purse! When they looked they found they had much to do with it, and sought to end it. I have no doubt, to go back to the Hebrew mythical tale, that when God called Cain, "Where is Abel?" he said, "I have nothing to do with it; that is Abel's affair. Am I my brother's keeper?" If the Law of Moses made it the duty of a Hebrew to lift up the beast of a public enemy which had stumbled in the street, how much more does the Law of God make it a Christian's duty to tell his brother of his sin, and help him out of it; how much more to rescue the oppressed,—"to bind up the broken-hearted; to proclaim liberty to the captives, the opening of the prison to them that are bound?"

Such then is slavery at the South; such the action of men at the North to attack or to defend it. But look a moment at the cause of this sin, and of its defence. It comes from the desire to get gain, comfort, or luxury; to have power over matter, without working or paying the honest price of that gain, comfort, luxury, and power; it is the spirit which would knowingly and of set purpose injure another for the sake of gaining some benefit to yourself. Such a spirit would hold slaves everywhere, if it were possible. Now when the question is put to any fair man,—Is not this spirit active at the North as well as the South? there is but one answer. The man who would use his fellow-man as a tool merely, and injure him by that use; who would force another in any way to bend to his caprice; who would take advantage of his ignorance, his credulity, his superstition, or his poverty, to enrich and comfort himself; in a word, who would use his neighbour to his neighbour's hurt,—that man has the spirit of slave-holding, and were circumstances but different, he would chain his brethren with iron bonds. If you, for your own sake, would unjustly put any man in a position which degrades him in your eyes, in his own eyes, in the eyes of his fellow-men, you have the spirit of the slave-holder. There is much of this spirit with us still. This is the reason that slavery finds so many supporters amongst us; that we deliver up the fugitives, and "bewray him that wandereth," sheltering ourselves under the plea, that we keep the law of the land, written by man on parchment, half a century ago, while we violate the law of nature, written everlastingly by God on the walls of the world. It was through this spirit,—so genial to our Anglo-Saxon blood,—that our fathers slew the Indians, who would not work, and the Southern planter enslaves the African, who will work. Both acted from the same motives, at North and South; killing or enslaving. That spirit is still with us, and shows itself in many shapes that need not be touched on now. It is not owing so much to our superior goodness, perhaps, as to a fortunate accident, that we have no slaves here at this day. They are not profitable. The shrewd men of our land discerned the fact long ago, and settled the question. Doubtless we have still social institutions which eyes more Christian than ours shall one day look upon as evils, only less than that of slavery itself. But it is gradually that we gain light; he that converts it to life as fast as it comes, does well.

II. Let a word be said on the other kind of slavery; that which comes from a cause internal to ourselves. This is common at the North, and South, and East, and West. In this case the man is prevented from doing what is best for him, not by some other man who has bound him, but by some passion or prejudice, superstition or sin. Here the mischief is in his own heart. If you look around you, you find many that bear the mark of the beast; branded on the forehead and the right hand; branded as slaves. "He that committeth sin is the slave of sin." The avaricious man is a slave. He cannot think a thought but as his master bids. He cannot see a truth if a dollar intervene. He cannot relieve the poor, nor sympathize with the distressed, nor yield to the humane impulse of his natural heart. If he sees in the newspaper a sentence on the wastefulness or the idleness of the poor, he remembers it for ever; but a word in the Bible to encourage charity,—he never finds that.

The passionate man is a slave; he lies at the mercy of the accidents of a day. If his affairs go well he is calm and peaceful; but if some little mistake arise he is filled with confusion, and the demon that rules him draws the chain. This master has many a slave under his yoke. He is more cruel than any planter in Cuba or Trinidad. He not only separates friend from friend, parent from child, and husband from wife, but what is worse yet, prevents their loving one another while they are together. This makes man a tyrant, not a husband; woman a fiend, not an angel, as God made her to be. This renders marriage a necessary evil, and housekeeping a perpetual curse, for it takes the little trifles which happen everywhere, except between angels, and makes them very great matters; it converts mistakes into faults, accidents into vices, errors into crimes; and so rends asunder the peace of families, and in a single twelvemonth disturbs more marriages than all the slave-holders of Carolina in a century.

So the peevish man is a slave. His ill humour watches him like a demon. Ofttimes it casteth him into the fire, and often into the water. In the morning he complains that his caprice is not complied with; in the evening that it is. He is never peaceful except when angry; never quiet but in a storm. He is free to do nothing good; so he acts badly, thinks badly, feels badly,—three attributes of a devil. A yoke of iron and fetters of brass were grievous to bear, no doubt; the whip of a task-master makes wounds in the flesh; but God save us from the tyranny of the peevish, both what they inflict and what they suffer.

The intemperate man also is a slave; one most totally subjugated. His vice exposes him to the contempt and insult of base men, as well as to the pity of the good. Not only this, but his master strips him of his understanding; takes away his common sense, conscience, his reason, religion,—qualities that make a man differ from a beast; on his garments, his face, his wife and child, is written in great staring letters, so that he may read that runs—This man also has sold his birthright and become a slave. The jealous planter forbids his slave to learn; but he cannot take from him the understanding he has got. This refinement of torture it was left for intemperance to exercise, levelling at once the distinctions between rude and polished.

* * *

Body-slavery is so bad that the sun might be pardoned if it turned back, refusing to shine on such a sin; on a land contaminated with its stain. But soul-slavery, what shall we say of that? Our fathers bought political freedom at a great price; they sailed the sea in storms; they dwelt here aliens on a hostile soil, the world's outcasts; in cold and hunger, in toil and want they dwelt here; they fought desperate wars in freedom's name! Yet they bought it cheap. You and I were base men, if we would not give much more than they paid, sooner than lose the inheritance.

But freedom for the soul to act right, think right, feel right, you cannot inherit; that you must win for yourself. Yet it is offered you at no great price. You may take it who will. It is the birthright of you and me and each of us; if we keep its conditions it is ours. Yet it is only to be had by the religious man—the man true to the nature God gave him. Without His Spirit in your heart you have no freedom. Resist His law, revealed in nature, in the later scripture of the Bible, in your own soul; resist it by sin, you are a slave, you must be a slave. Obey that law, you are Christ's freeman; nature and God are on your side. How strange it would be that one man should be found on all the hills of New England, of soul so base, of spirit so dastardly, that of his own consent took on him the yoke of slavery; went into the service of sin; toiled with that leprous host, in hopeless unrecompensed misery, without God, without heaven, without hope. Strange, indeed, that in this little village there should be men who care not for the soul's freedom, but consent to live, no, to die daily, in the service of sin.

Joshua Reed Giddings

Joshua Giddings was a militant antislavery congressman from the Western Reserve of Ohio for twenty years. When he first tried to speak against slavery in the House of Representatives, in 1838, he was stopped with the use of the "gag-rule." This rule denying the right to speak was later repealed largely as a result of his efforts stemming from the incident. Giddings would not be kept silent, for he was an avid campaigner to end slavery, and he used every opportunity to work for its abolition through Congress. Giddings boarded at the same place as did Abraham Lincoln in 1847 and 1848, and some people believe he not only helped Lincoln evolve his own ideas about the institution of slavery, but also helped prepare public opinion with his own efforts, so that when Lincoln did assume the mantle for abolition, Giddings' efforts up to that time had had some effects in encouraging people to accept Lincoln's leadership.

Born in Pennsylvania, Giddings moved to Ohio with his family when he was ten. His father had bought a large amount of land, and all the family had to work hard to make it profitable. His education, therefore, was irregular, though he studied some languages. He began studying law in a Canfield, Ohio, office and passed the Ohio bar examination in 1821 when he was twenty-six. He married two years before that, was happily married and became a loving, companionable father to several children. His law practice thrived.

Giddings spent one term in the Ohio House before being elected to Congress when he was forty-three; he spent most of the rest of his public life there. He threw himself into the aging John Quincy Adams's struggle to allow antislavery petitions to be admitted to Congress, he crusaded to allow freedom of debate regarding slavery in Congress, and fought the taxation of free states for the support of slave states. He was relentless in his attack on slaveholders; his speeches were filled with exaggeration and bitterness. His attitude in all his antislavery speeches was severe and un-compromising. He was so in earnest and felt so strongly the moral necessity for the end to slavery that he was inflexible on the matter.

He was a tall man, said to be the most muscular in Congress during the years he was a member, and he delivered his speeches with such force and enthusiasm that other members would tend to gather around him when he rose to speak, listening attentively, arguing, agreeing. He was a forceful man, unpleasant only on the one subject, and was definitely a focal point in Congress in the national stirrings to abolish slavery.

Many in Washington hated and feared Joshua Giddings. At one point when he visited jailed slaves who had attempted to escape in the schooner *Pearl*, some slaveholders in Congress demanded that he be hanged. Another time, charges were trumped up by plotters saying that he had stolen valuable mail documents; he was cleared by a congressional investigating committee and thoroughly supported by his constituency back home in Ohio.

Once in 1856, and then again two years later, Giddings was speaking when he was suddenly stricken by a seizure, falling to the floor of the House. After the second episode, he retired from Congress. Lincoln appointed him to be consul general to Canada, where he died in 1864, not living to see the actual end to slavery but perhaps able to feel it would be accomplished, and to know that his efforts had been of use.

born, October, 1795, Tioga Point, Penna.

died, May, 1864, Montreal, Canada

Relation
of the Federal Government
to Slavery

Mr. Chairman,—A treaty of peace has been entered into between this government and Mexico; and we are called on to grant the necessary means to carry it into effect. For that purpose, the bill under consideration has been presented. The subject is one of a comprehensive character, and opens up a wide field of debate. Gentlemen who have preceded me have availed them-selves of this latitude of remark. But some of them have refused to be cor-rected on matters of fact and of law, when other members believed them in error. I regard speeches made in this body profitable, only so far as they elicit truth; and will thank any gentleman to correct me upon matters of fact or of law, as I pass along in my remarks. If I labor under error, I desire to be set right at the earliest moment, before I impress that error upon any other human being.

The bill before us has presented to us the important question of the relation which this government holds to the institution of slavery. The exclusion of that institution from our new territories, sustaining it in this district, and the maintenance of the slave-trade here, have all been ably and eloquently debated. I have no hope of bringing any new views before the committee, although I may perhaps present those already advanced in a connection different from those who have gone before me.

On that ill-fated day, when this House adopted the war which had been commenced by the Executive, I saw, or thought I clearly saw, the present difficulties into which we have been precipitated. These difficulties I pointed out in an humble speech which I had the honor of delivering to this body on the day following. During the whole period of hostilities, we were conscious that it was the design of the Executive to acquire territory, principally for the purpose of spreading the curse of human bondage over it. Gentlemen of the two great political parties then united in sustaining and continuing the war, with our present position in full view before them. During the progress of the war, we constantly cautioned our southern friends, we assured them that, if territory were obtained, we should not consent to abolish freedom therein. They now speak of the amount of southern blood shed in that war. It was their own folly. They knew that our army was fighting for the purpose of bringing these questions before us for decision. They now talk of its dangers. Sir, they should have reflected on that before the declaration of war; they should have listened to our advice, and avoided the dangers which we so distinctly pointed out. If our maintenance of liberty be dangerous, that danger has now become unavoidable. We hope to meet it in a manner as becomes freemen.

In the arguments of southern gentlemen, there seems to be a fundamental error common to them all. They assume that this government was founded for the support of slavery. They insist that southern oppression is as much entitled to the encouragement and fostering care of the National Government as are the liberties of the people for whom we legislate. They seem to have overlooked the great object which the founders of our institutions had in view. That design stands recorded on every page of our history; they left perpetual monuments on every battle field of the Revolution, proclaiming, in unmistakable language, their hostility to oppression, and their devotion to freedom. No class of men, at any period of the world, were more inveterately opposed to slavery than were the founders of this government. In setting forth the reasons which induced them to separate from the mother country, and to found an independent sovereignty, they declared that the objects of government were to secure the *lives* and *liberties* of the people. It was hostility to slavery of every description which impelled them to action.

Every argument, therefore, based on the assumption that we are, to any extent or in any manner, to shape our legislation for the encouragement or maintenance of slavery, must of course be erroneous. If we carry out in good faith the intentions of those who framed our institutions, we shall devote our energies to the support and encouragement of freedom, limiting our efforts in this respect by the Constitution, so as not to interfere with slavery within the States. But to encourage its existence even there, would be a violation of every principle which controlled the action of those who achieved our independence, as well as of those who framed our Constitution.

Here, then, is the precise point on which the advocates of slavery and the supporters of liberty differ. We demand that our whole legislation shall be in favor of freedom, of justice and humanity; they insist that we are to place slavery, injustice, and crime upon the same level, and to bestow upon each the same attention and encouragement. Differing thus as to the essential elements of our compact, it were impossible for us to arrive at the same conclusions in our arguments. The controversy is therefore radical. It involves the most vital principles of our association.

Of all the erroneous sayings common to our country, none is more unfounded than the very common assertion that "slavery is guaranteed by the Federal Constitution." We hear it repeated in this hall, and we read it in official documents, and gentlemen appear to regard it as an established maxim, by which we are to guide our legislation. I have often requested those who repeat this assertion, to point me to the article, section, or clause of the Constitution, which *guarantees slavery*. I most respectfully made the inquiry, in the presence of the House, of the gentleman from Virginia (Mr. Meade) who sits opposite; but he failed to name the clause, or section, or article.

Now, Sir, I desire to elicit truth, and to expose error. I am surrounded by the ablest statesmen of the South, by men who insist that slavery is thus guaranteed to them. I therefore respectfully desire any one of them now to inform this body and the country on what clause of the Constitution they rely to sustain the assertion to which I have alluded. To enable any one to do that, I now proffer to him the floor.

[Mr. Giddings here paused for some moments, and then resumed.]

Mr. Chairman, here is a most important error, either on my part, or on the part of those who assert that the Constitution guarantees slavery. If wrong,

I desire to be corrected now, before this body, and before the American people. I call on gentlemen, in respectful terms, to show the grounds of their faith on this point. They sit in silence. No one is willing to hazard his reputation by attempting it. Sir, there is no such guaranty. The pretence is entirely without foundation. I therefore repeat, that the proper constitutional attitude of this government is in favor of liberty, and opposed to every form of oppression.

The doctrine, that we are bound to encourage and perpetuate slavery, is of recent origin. It was never asserted until 1843. Prior to that period, the doctrine which I have laid down was admitted by statesmen from all portions of the Union. An attempt was then made to change the fundamental principles of our government, and to transform it into a slave-holding, a slave-sustaining confederacy. The great apostle of southern slavery stood forth as the advocate of this new theory. He went out of his way to argue the human character of slavery in his official correspondence, and to point out the dangers of freedom to the colored race. He went farther, and endeavored to show that it was the duty of this government to uphold, extend, and perpetuate an institution abhorred by nearly all civilized nations. He, Sir, is a bold and honest statesman. He speaks his thoughts, and leaves no doubts as to his position. For this, I honor him. He was born and educated in a land of slavery. His interest has at all times been identified with that institution. His prejudices are in favor of it. It is interwoven as it were with his very existence. This is his misfortune; for that I will not reproach him. This new doctrine was carried into practice by the annexation of Texas. The war and conquest which followed, and the present efforts to appropriate our Mexican territory to the blighting curse of slavery, has precipitated upon us the important questions now pending. These circumstances have aroused the northern people to examine their rights. Southern aggressions have accomplished a work which northern philanthropy attempted in vain. A portion of our northern people have taken their position distinctly in favor of separating this government from all interference with slavery in the States, and of hostility to it in all places where we have the power to legislate upon the subject.

This position of northern men has called forth a convention of southern statesmen. They have issued an address to the people of the South....

Now, Sir, for a moment, let us look into this address, and ascertain why dissatisfaction exists among our southern friends.

The general cause of complaint is, that this National Government has failed to secure and encourage oppression; that under its administration men are rending the chains that have bound them for ages; that they are rising from a state of degradation, and resuming the rights with which God endowed them.

We of the free States regard this as the best of all possible arguments in favor of the Union. We look upon it as carrying into practice the very objects for which it was formed. These gentlemen, however, evidently think it was formed, not for the purpose of encouraging liberty, but to uphold slavery. Thus I am again brought to this point of divergence, mentioned at the commencement of my remarks. Southern men holding this doctrine shape their legislation to the support of slavery, believing that the legitimate object of our association; while we of the North direct our efforts to the promotion of freedom, believing that to be the design for which our government was instituted. Thus we start in different directions, and while we travel, we shall of course increase the distance between us.

This address will serve in a great degree to inform the country of the true issues between the advocates of slavery and those who are laboring to promote the cause of human rights. We hope that southern men will no longer deal in vague generalities. We rejoice to see them in this address come down to distinct specifications. This enables us to meet them understandingly, and to compare our views on specific points.

They first complain, that we lend them no aid in the arrest of their *fugitive* slaves. They evidently think that by the terms of our compact we are bound to aid the slave-holder in arresting the bondman who flees from oppression. On this point we are not left without definite information of the intention of those who framed the Constitution.

*   *   *

These are our stipulations. We are to pass no law, make no regulation by which the person escaping shall be discharged. Our duty thus far is negative. We are *not* to act; we are to refrain from all action, to leave master and slave to themselves.

The latter part of the clause says, "he shall be delivered up on claim of the person to whom such service or labor may be due." How delivered up? This question is distinctly answered by the Supreme Court of the United States, in the case of Prigg *v.* The Commonwealth of Pennsylvania. They say he is to be delivered up in the same manner that we deliver up our friends to the civil officer in our own State. We are bound to permit the master to take him wherever he finds him. We must not secrete him from the master. We must not defend him against the master; nor are we to rescue him from the master's custody after he shall have taken him. This is the way in which he is to be delivered up, according to the high tribunal which is authorized to give construction to the Constitution; and it is worthy of remark that a majority of the Court making this decision were slave-holders. They have determined our duties; I believe them in strict accordance with the intentions of those who framed the Constitution. These slave-holding judges do not pretend that this government, or the people of the free States, are bound to encourage or sustain slavery; on the contrary, they solemnly declare that our whole duty is to abstain from secreting, defending, or rescuing the slave. These obligations we observe to the very letter. They may have been violated by individuals. I have heard and read of cases where citizens of my own State have been convicted of violating these stipulations, and have suffered the legal penalties attached to such violation.

It is proper, on such occasions as the present, that we should speak with perfect frankness. I therefore remark, that our people consider these obligations as restraining the exercise of our moral duties. They therefore very properly refuse to go farther than is required by the Constitution. Their sympathies are with the slave,—such is the ordained law of the human intellect. We cannot suppress the feelings of our nature; we cannot look with indifference upon the panting fugitive as he flies from bondage; we will not do it. We receive him into our houses, we feed and clothe him, and treat him as a *man*. We inform him, teach him his rights, and point him to that immortality that awaits him. Sir, our people know their constitutional obligations on this subject. It is useless to say to them that it is their duy to assume the character of bloodhounds, and give chase to him who is fleeing from a land of chains and tears. No, Sir, they have neither sympathy nor respect for the slave-catcher. We look upon him as a moral pestilence, a legalized pirate; we will not admit him to our dwellings; we drive him from our premises; we regard him as unworthy to associate with any portion of our race.

* * *

This address further complains that the people of the North discuss the subject of slavery; that debating clubs examine into its demerits; and that members on this floor denounce it as wrong, as destructive to the best interests of mankind; and that the newspaper press is left untrammeled by a censorship.

This feeling did not exist when the framers of the Constitution solemnly declared, "that Congress shall make no law abridging the freedom of speech or of the press." The founders of our government had no idea of rendering the press subservient to slavery. Deeming it one of the bulwarks of liberty, they placed its freedom beyond the power of Congress. They had no thoughts of sealing the lips of freemen, or of members of Congress, in order to uphold and continue the slavery of the South.

Yet it is a lamentable truth, that for a time these rights were surrendered, ingloriously surrendered by northern timidity. Yes, in servile obedience to slave-holding dictation, for a time we established a vitiated state of public sentiment throughout the whole North. Fifteen years since, it was regarded as disreputable to discuss the demerits of slavery in our social circles. Our pulpits were silent in regard to the most heaven-daring crimes when connected with southern oppression. Our presses dared not speak the language of freedom; and here, in this hall, a tyranny more absolute and unrelenting than exists in any deliberative body in the civilized world, held undisputed sway. I speak with some feeling on this subject. I witnessed that tyranny; Sir, I *felt* it. For years I sat here under the inexorable rule of the slave power; reproached, assailed, insulted, and driven from my seat, because I insisted upon my right, as an American statesman, to speak the sincere convictions of my heart.

But, Sir, after years of toil, of solicitude, and of responsibility, we have regained the freedom of speech. Do not gentlemen know that we found our right to speak our thoughts both here and elsewhere upon the Constitution, upon the very rock of our political salvation? Do they desire again to seal our lips? Do they complain that truth spoken here excites their slaves to strive for freedom? I rejoice to hear such tidings. Would that I were able, from this forum, to make every bondman in the nation hear me. I would teach them their rights, and if truth could instantly effect it, I would, before I resume my seat, strike the chains from every slave in the wide universe.

I am perfectly aware that these gentlemen are correct, when they assure the country that these discussions are constantly weakening and relaxing the cords by which the slaves are bound. I rejoice at it. Truth is doing its perfect work. Justice is beginning to assert her rights. The voice of humanity is listened to. Our press of the North is beginning to speak out. The people talk of slavery as they do of other great iniquities. Truth and righteousness are now preached from our pulpits. While Turks and Tartars denounce the sins of slavery, shall Americans keep silence? While the followers of Mohammed are purifying themselves from its crimes, shall Christians uphold and encourage its God-provoking iniquities? Here, in this city, in every street, we meet our brother man, borne down, trampled upon, and held in the most abhorrent degradation. From the windows of this hall, we witness the barracoons, those legalized hells, established by our laws, and now sustained by this body. And shall we keep silence? We possess the moral and constitutional right to speak and print whatever shall conduce to the elevation of our race. Duty to our fellow men, and obedience to God, require the exercise of those rights. They will never be surrendered.

Those gentlemen also complain that we regard slavery as sinful and wicked. I presume at this day it would be superfluous to argue that any act or institution which detracts from the happiness of mankind, or inflicts misery and suffering upon any portion of our race, except as a punishment for crimes, is opposed to the design of our Creator, and in violation of his law. I believe this may be regarded as an admitted principle. How is it with slavery? How does the civilized world regard it? How have we as a nation regarded it? When, in 1804, the semi-barbarians of Tripoli seized and enslaved our people, did we not regard it as sinful?

By the most accurate data we can obtain, the number of human lives sacrificed upon the sugar, cotton, and rice plantations of the South, amounts annually to more than twenty thousand. These murders are effected by driving the slaves so hard as to render their average existence upon those plantations from five to seven years. And will southern gentlemen assert that this worse than savage barbarity is innocent? Does our religion teach this bloody code? Sir, happy would those slaves feel if they could escape from professed Christians, whose hands are dripping with human gore, to the protection of the most unrelenting despotisms of the Old World; or, could they even fall into the hands of the savage Arabs of Morocco, they would regard it as an unspeakable improvement of their condition. Look at the victims of our domestic slave-trade! Mark the agony, the horror, the transports of grief which they suffer! Listen to their sighs, their groans, and wailings! Do you believe that a holy, pure, and righteous God, approves the infliction of such suffering? Sir, these gentlemen are correct, when they assert that we regard slavery as a *sin*. We look upon it not only as wicked and sinful, but as compounded of the worst of crimes. It *robs* men of their labor; it *steals* from them their domestic and intellectual enjoyments; it *degrades, brutalizes, and murders them.* For my own part, I can conceive of no greater crime than that of slavery. It is on that account that the Christian world are opposed to it.

Another and principal cause of complaint set forth in this address, is the expected exclusion of slavery from our newly acquired territory. In establishing a government there, we have an object by which we are guided. What is it? The answer is given in the American Declaration of Independence: "Governments are instituted among men to secure the enjoyment of life and liberty." Northern men are now ready and willing to form such a government in California; but our southern friends insist that a government shall be established there by which a portion of the people may be robbed of those rights, may be brutalized, disrobed of their humanity. We reply, that such an act would be vitally opposed to the objects for which our Union was formed, at war with the principles of justice, of humanity, and the Constitution. This subject, however, has been so fully argued by others, as well as by myself, on former occasions, that I will not detain the committee longer upon it. I will merely add, that the people of the North have examined and considered this subject, and, I think, have made up their judgments in regard to it. Their motto is, "*No slave territory,—no more slave States.*"

I again remark, that this address in its general aspect, and in each and every particular, is founded upon the erroneous assumption that this government is bound to regard slavery with favor, and to uphold and encourage it; while we of the North hold that the ultimate design of our Constitution is unyielding hostility to slavery, and every species of oppression.

It is this error into which southern men have so generally fallen, that leads us to differ in relation to the abolition of slavery in this district. By our law of 1801, we took possession of this territory, and extended over it the laws of Maryland. In that act we declared that the laws of that State then in operation here, *should remain and continue in force.* Among those laws was the entire slave code of that State. This we adopted with the others as laws of the district. By this enactment, they became "*acts of Congress.*" They are to this day sustained and made law by this act of 1801. It is, therefore, solely by virtue of this act of 1801, that slavery exists in this district. It is that which sustains the slave-trade. By force of this Congressional enactment, men are bought and sold, women are made the subjects of traffic, and a commerce in children is carried on within this territory, under the jurisdiction of this Government.

Now, Sir, all that the advocates of freedom ask, is the repeal of that law of 1801. Let that be repealed, and the chains will instantly fall from every slave in the district. This is the doctrine which, for ten years, we have constantly held forth in this hall. We insist that our power to repeal this law of our own enacting is clear and indisputable. I have never been able to find any member of this body willing to deny this position. Yet we sit here and listen to long and eloquent speeches, denouncing us for attempting to interfere with the rights of slave property here. We have heard a most ingenious argument from the gentleman who has just taken his seat, (Mr. Crisfield,) urging that we have not the constitutional power to abolish either slavery or the slave-trade in this district. I had hoped that he would have met this position. While listening to his speech, I greatly desired to ask him whether he denied the power of Congress to repeal its own law to which I have referred. He, however, refused to be interrupted. I see the gentleman is now in his seat. I feel desirous of knowing whether he and I differ on this subject; and in order to determine that question, I respectfully ask him, whether he denies the power of Congress to repeal that law of 1801, to which I have referred? And I tender him the floor to answer that interrogatory.

[Mr. Crisfield said he had not been paying particular attention to what the gentleman from Ohio (Mr. Giddings) was saying. But he had refused to be interrogated, and should refuse answering any questions.]

Mr. Giddings: Yes, Mr. Chairman, that is probably a more convenient mode for gentlemen to get along with this subject. Evasion, Sir, is their only mode of escape. I call on the House and the country to witness, that I desire to meet this question openly and candidly. At the very opening of my remarks, I tendered the floor to any gentleman who deemed me in error, for the purpose of setting me right. I regard it as a favor to me, and an act of friendship in any gentleman who will propound to me questions for the purpose of eliciting truth. That, Sir, is the very object for which I speak. Now, if the gentleman admits our power to repeal our own laws, then there would be no issue between us in regard to our constitutional authority.

The gentleman, and his colleague (Mr. McLane) who spoke the other day, insist that we ought not to abolish slavery here, until Maryland abolishes it in that State. Slavery, as I have already shown, exists by virtue of our own laws. Its existence has no more connection with slavery in Maryland, than it has with that institution in Algiers. We, Sir, the people of Ohio,— of all the free States,—uphold and sustain slavery in this district. Its wrongs, its outrages, its crimes, and its guilt rest on us. To God and to mankind we are responsible. Yet we are told that we must continue involved in all these enormities until the people of Maryland shall awake to the turpitude of slavery. The guilt of sustaining the crimes of that institution, sits heavy upon the consciences of our people. They are deeply anxious to be relieved from it.

Again, Sir, the slave-trade carried on here, forms a part of the institution itself. But the gentleman from Maryland denies that the slave-trade exists in this district, or that slave prisons are to be found in this city, or that persons are brought here from Maryland for sale. Why, Sir, this very day I was applied to for counsel in a case where three persons, said to be legally entitled to their freedom, were brought from Maryland, and during yesterday were sold and taken to Alexandria. At the last session, I was called on for counsel in a case where a large family was brought from that State and sold South, where, if living, they are now dragging out a miserable existence. But the gentleman denies that there are slave prisons in this city. If he will go to either of these front windows, and cast his eye down Maryland avenue as far as Seventh street, he will see a large brick building, standing back from both streets, its outbuildings surrounded by a high brick wall. Sir, I hesitate not to say, that if he will ask any colored person in the city of ten years of age, they will tell him *"that is a slave pen."* I have visited it. I went there to redeem my fellow man with "sordid dust," from the grasp of the soul-driver. On my right, sits my friend from Pennsylvania, (Mr. McIlvaine,) who accompanied me. I leave it for that gentleman to give a full description of the scene which we witnessed on that occasion. I have no language adequate to that purpose. The man whom we redeemed was there some six or seven days. He assured us that every night during his stay, slaves were brought in from the country and confined in that receptacle of suffering humanity.

When gentlemen deny the existence of the slave-trade here, do they intend to charge falsehood upon the venerable Justice Cranch, and ten hundred and sixty-three other respectable citizens of this district, who have assured us that this traffic, with all its horrors and attendant crimes, is continually carried on in this city? There is their petition praying us to deliver them from those painful exhibitions of this slave-trade which your law has authorized. Yet gentlemen say there is no traffic carried on here. Will they deny that in April last, Hope H. Slatter, a noted dealer in slaves, marched fifty-two men, women, and children, victims of this commerce, from the jail in this city, through Pennsylvania avenue, to the railroad depot, thence to Baltimore, for the southern market, where they now pine in bondage? No man will deny these specific facts. They are known to the whole country.

The gentleman from Indiana (Mr. Thompson) said that he had seen nothing of this slave-trade, and sneeringly remarked that "gentlemen who had *looked for it may have seen it.*" Sir, I receive his taunts with all humility. I am one of those who feel it my duty to look around me, and learn the effect of the laws which we enact. I have attended the sale of slaves at auction in this city for this express purpose. I have witnessed the chained coffle as they passed by the very walls of the building in which we are now sitting; where the star-spangled banner which floats over us, threw its shadow in bitter irony upon those victims of your barbarous law, which we now uphold and sustain.

Now, Sir, I repeat, that this government was not formed for the purpose of thus robbing men of their rights,—of degrading and brutalizing them. It was not for such purpose that our fathers of the revolution toiled and bled. They struggled to establish a government that should suppress outrages and crimes like these.

But it is said that this slave-trade causes no suffering; that it produces no distress. There is no doubt that great pains are taken to prevent the promulgation of facts which illustrate the barbarous character of this traffic. Generally, the slaves of the district are sold when they are unconscious of the fact. They are sent by their masters to some place agreed upon with the purchaser; there they are seized, gagged, and instantly taken to the slave-pen, and few, if any, spectators witness the horrid process. Those purchased out of the city, are brought here in the night, and are taken away during the hours of darkness. This caution has increased as the public attention has been turned to the subject, until now but few of its enormities are witnessed by the public.

On a former occasion, I stated that some years since, a man of this city, more white than black, having a wife and several children, was informed by his owner that she had sold him to one of those dealers in our common humanity who hover around this city. The man, in a transport of despair, attempted to cut his throat. He was seized, and the wound was dressed; but no sooner was he released from the grasp of those who held him, than he ran to the bridge over the canal on Seventh street, and threw himself into its turbid waters. In death he sought relief from the barbarity inflicted upon him by your laws. If the gentleman from Indiana wishes to know more of this transaction, I refer him to the then representative from the city of Boston, who saw the body taken from its watery grave the next morning. Nor is it unusual for the victims of this commerce to seek relief in death from those sufferings to which your laws subject them.

At a more recent period, I was told of a young woman who attempted in the day time to escape from the establishment situated on Maryland avenue, to which I have referred. She was making her way back to her home in Virginia, and while on the bridge over the Potomac, was pursued. Those who sought to arrest her gave the alarm to some men who were coming from the other side of the river. She halted, looked forward, then behind her. She saw that escape was impossible. But one appeal was left; that was to her final Judge. She threw herself from the bridge; the waters closed over her body; her spirit ascended to the "Judge of all the earth." Believe you, Sir, that He will hold us guiltless of her blood? Is there no responsibility resting on us, who now maintain these barbarous laws?

A few members are exerting all their efforts to relieve the people of the free States from the stain of such infamy, but all our labors are baffled by those who show themselves anxious to continue these outrages upon humanity. I feel constrained to speak frankly on this subject, to point the people to existing facts.

* * *

Tell me not of the whig party, or of the democratic party, while their hands are dripping with the blood of innocent victims daily hurried to their final account by the barbarity of those laws which they support. Whether those crimes be protected by whig or by democratic votes, I will not participate in the turpitude.

The time has arrived when parties must separate on this absorbing question. Those who support outrage and crime will be politically opposed by those who adhere to the "self-evident truth" of man's equality. On those truths we base our action. Those who are not with us are against us. There can be no neutrals. Every man is in favor of this slave-trade and its attendant crimes, or he is against it. Those with whom I act are opposed to every man and every party who upholds oppression.

We shall put forth our utmost endeavors to strike the chains of bondage from the limbs of mankind, wherever this government has power to legislate. "Free soil, free men, and free speech," is our motto. If General Taylor and his friends unite with us, we shall rejoice to act with them. They may have the offices; we want them not. We desire to extend liberty to the down-trodden, to raise up the bowed-down, to exalt our race. To this object our energies will be directed. And if General Taylor's administration shall be devoted to riveting the chains of servitude upon our fellow man, to the degradation of any portion of our race, then, Sir, we shall be opposed to him. I make these remarks that our position may be distinctly understood.

There is one point on which some gentlemen appear to deceive themselves. They urge the passage of a bill to organize our Mexican territory, in order to silence the agitation in regard to slavery. They should be undeceived. They should distinctly understand that, while the people of the free States are involved in the support of slavery in this district, or of the coastwise slave-trade; while Congress lends its powers and influence to rob a portion of the people of their inalienable rights, northern philanthropy and northern patriotism will make their voices heard in this hall. Nor will they be silenced until this district is rendered *free*, until the nation's flag shall cease to float over cargoes of slaves, and the territories of the United States shall be exempt from the curse of oppression. We wish to deceive no one. We desire all to understand our position. We base our efforts distinctly upon the letter and the spirit of the Constitution. Separation of the Federal Government and the people of the free States from all participation in the support of slavery, constitutes our object. Nor shall we relax our exertions while a slave shall be held as such under the laws of Congress.

But myself and political friends are charged with "agitation." What is intended by this language I do not precisely understand. No man accuses us of bringing irrelevant or improper subjects into discussion, or that we speak upon them at improper times; nor do they charge us with misrepresentation or erroneous statements. If they intend by this language to say that we speak truth without disguise, that we do not attempt to suppress facts, then, Sir, I admit the correctness of their assertion. They do not deny our doctrines. No man, either North or South, will rise here and take issue on any principle embraced in our political creed. I repeat, that I am wholly incapable of understanding the import of this charge of *agitation* made against the free soil members of this House.

Gentlemen have constantly asserted that northern members were invading the rights of the South. The gentleman from Indiana, (Mr. Thompson,) and the gentleman from Pennsylvania, (Mr. Brown,) and my colleague, (Mr. Taylor,) were all understood as imputing to us efforts to interfere with southern rights. For years I have listened to such charges. They seem to be stereotyped. For years I have called on gentlemen to come down from these *general* denunciations, and specify *an instance* in which any proposition was ever made in this body to invade the rights of the South. I have constantly called on them to state *who* made such proposition; to give us the name. When was such proposition made? What was the proposition? To all these questions a respectful silence is the only answer which I have ever been able to obtain.

But gentlemen find fault with northern democrats for voting with us. One gentleman charged them with having changed their course of action on the subject of slavery. And who has not changed on this subject? I well recollect that my late venerable and lamented friend (Mr. Adams) interested me greatly when describing this change in his own mind. We have all changed. But it is said that the democrats are not sincere in their professions. Of that I can only judge by their acts. The voice of inspiration has taught us to show our faith by our works. If men will speak, and act, and vote right, I will leave the examination of their hearts to "Him who searcheth the heart." But those gentlemen who make this complaint will neither speak, nor act, nor vote in favor of freedom; yet they complain of the motives of others. "O! consistency, thou art a jewel." I am constrained to regard these

gentlemen as sincere, when voting against *freedom*, precisely as I feel bound
to believe those sincere who vote against *slavery*.

During the discussions of this body, those with whom I act have been
reproached for having supported for President a man who, in former times,
was opposed to the abolition of slavery in this district. Sir, the charge is
true. Mr. Van Buren, in 1837, like all our public men of both parties at that
time, was undoubtedly opposed to the abolition of slavery in this district.
The subject had undergone no investigation by them. They had not looked
into it. Even John Quincy Adams, the distinguished friend of humanity, was
then opposed to that measure. The gentlemen who now assail us not only
supported the same doctrines at that time, but they now sustain both slavery
and the slave-trade in this city, and assail all who attempt to abolish them.
The difference between these gentlemen and Mr. Van Buren is this: he now
avows our doctrines; they adhere to the slave-trade, with all its turpitude; and
they supported a man for President who made no professions on the subject,
but who is a slave-holder, and whose interest and associations are all in favor
of that institution.

It is also true that Mr. Van Buren, while President, followed the example
of General Jackson, in lending the influence of his office to sustain the coastwise slave-trade. In this he complied with the avowed opinion of the Senate.
That august body adopted resolutions, as late as 1840, unanimously declaring
it to be the duty of this government to protect those who were engaged in
that detestable traffic. Neither whig nor democrat then denied the correctness
of that doctrine. No man who now denounces Mr. Van Buren, *then* even
objected to his policy. Indeed, when I alone, and single-handed, denied its
correctness, not one of them stood by me or sustained me in that denial.
But the Convention at Buffalo which nominated Mr. Van Buren, declared
it the duty of this government, "to relieve itself from all support of slavery
and the slave-trade." In answer to this doctrine, Mr. Van Buren replied, that
"it breathes the right spirit;" and he pledged himself to its support. Before
Heaven I believe the doctrine to be right. I had no doubt of his sincerity,
and I advocated his election cheerfully and cordially. Sir, I would rather have
been the author of that letter than to enjoy all the honors that he has ever
gained in discharging the duties of President.

Several gentlemen have inquired, rather vauntingly, what we have effected
by our labors in the cause of humanity? They will find a very satisfactory
answer to this interrogatory in the address of the southern members to which
I have called attention.

When I first took my seat in this hall, the petitions of our people asking to be relieved from the burden, the guilt, and disgrace of supporting the slave-trade, were not received, nor were they permitted to be read; but they were treated with the most marked contempt. I found here that distinguished statesman whom history will describe as the great champion of popular rights, (Mr. J. Q. Adams); he was laboring to regain the right of petition. His zeal and devotion to that cause were unbounded. His spirit was undaunted, and his energy never relaxed. Who that was then here has forgotten his herculean labors? No difficulties embarrassed, no dangers deterred him. His determination of purpose appeared to be more and more developed as opposition increased. We saw him arraigned at your bar, like a base felon, for no other charge than that of sustaining the right of the people; and as the dark storm of human passions gathered thick, and the tempest raged, and the waves of vituperation and calumny rolled and dashed in wild confusion around him, he stood calm and unmoved in his purpose as the adamantine rock. Who has forgotten the boundless resources of his intellect, or his unrivalled eloquence, or his terrible invective? They were all called forth and exerted in favor of the right of petition. I rejoice that he lived to witness the consummation of his labors. He has now gone to his rest, but the affections of a nation cluster around his memory.

At my first entrance to this hall, no member was allowed to speak irreverently of the slave-trade, or of slavery. A more unrelenting tyranny never existed in a Turkish divan, than reigned here. The gentleman who now fills the Presidential chair then presided over our deliberations, and most effectually did he exercise his authority for the suppression of truth and of liberty. For years my lips were hermetically sealed on the subject of humanity. Often have I listened for hours to language insulting to myself, to my constituents, and to the people of the free States, without the liberty of saying a word in vindication of those whom I represented, or of expressing in any degree the indignant emotions which prompted the utterance of salutary truth. Often have I seen the venerable and world-honored member from Massachusetts (Mr. J. Q. Adams) peremptorily ordered to his seat when he dared even to allude to the slave-trade, or to the slavery which was sustained in this district by laws of our own enactment. But how changed the scene! I can scarcely realize that this is the hall in which I have witnessed the display of deadly weapons, exhibited for the purpose of intimidating northern members to keep silence in regard to the crimes and disgrace of slavery. Here, Sir, in this body has been displayed, in the most striking manner, the power of truth. *The freedom of speech has been regained.*

We now give free utterance to the emotions of the soul in behalf of suffering humanity. We have regained and now enjoy an equality of privileges with southern members. This important reformation has been brought about by toil, and labor, and suffering which never will and never can be appreciated by any person who has not shared in them. It is, however, due to truth that I should say, northern servility, manifested through a venal press, and exhibited to this body in speeches, in a variety of ways, has presented even greater obstacles to the progress of truth than all the opposition of southern men.

* * *

The case of the Creole is fresh in the recollections of all who hear me. On board that ship the slaves, conscious of the rights with which God had endowed them, and true to the noblest impulses of our nature, asserted and maintained in practice the doctrines of our revolutionary fathers. They regained their freedom by their own physical strength. They then navigated the ship to the island of New Providence, and each sought his own happiness. At that time a whig administration controlled the government. Mr. Van Buren, now so much denounced for his favor to the slave power, had retired to Lindenwold. The Executive sent immediate orders to our minister at London to demand compensation of the English government for the loss of these slave merchants who had been unable to control their human cargo.

Sir, I then saw the party with whom I had always acted about to commit itself and the government to the support of a detestable commerce in mankind. I saw the Constitution violated, by a prostitution of our national influence to support a traffic detested by men, and cursed of Heaven; a traffic abhorrent to every feeling of our nature, and at war with every principle of Christianity. I had sworn at your altar faithfully to support that Constitution. I saw no way but to express my views, humble and unpretending as they were. I did so in a series of resolutions, denying the right of this government thus to involve the people of the free States in the expense, disgrace, and crimes of the slave-trade. The effect of that movement upon myself was unimportant—of that I do not speak; but the effect which it exerted upon the government should be known and understood by all. It called public attention to the subject. The press of the North spoke forth the sentiments of the North. Leading men and statesmen denounced the practice of involving the people of the free States in the support of crimes at the contemplation of which humanity shudders.

* * *

When asked what we had effected by our efforts, I answer, that in Congress we have regained the right of petition and the freedom of debate. We have relieved the government from the ostensible support of the coastwise slave-trade. We have called the attention of statesmen and jurists to the investigation of those rights which northern freemen hold under the federal compact. We have rendered northern servility unpopular. Where now are those timid, faltering statesmen of the North who filled these seats ten years since? During the short period of my service in this body, I have seen whole generations, as it were, appear here, avow their detestation of those who maintained the rights of our people and of humanity, meekly bow to the dictates of the slave power, and then depart to that political "bourn from which no traveller returns." Where are now those northern members who, only seven years since, voted to censure me for merely asserting the rights of my constituents to be exempt from the crimes attendant upon the coastwise slave-trade? Why, Sir, three or four of them yet remain, the "spared monuments" of the people's mercy; but I believe not one of them has been reëlected to meet me here in December next. A few days will separate us probably forever. Towards them I feel no unkindness; and I now refer to the fact as showing the progress of that revolution which is going forward.

Look at the other end of the capitol, and you will find unmistakable evidences of the change now going on in the popular mind. Read the proceedings of our State Legislatures. In Ohio, at one vote, they have erased from our statutes the whole code of black laws which have disgraced the State for nearly half a century. In Pennsylvania, they have gone even farther in the cause of justice and freedom; they have very properly rendered it penal for the citizens or officers of that State to aid or assist the slave-catcher in seizing upon the victims of his unrighteous oppression, as they fly from bondage. New York, too, that "Empire State," is assuming a position on this subject worthy of herself.

Of other States I need not speak. The effects of our labors are seen and felt in every free State—in every county, town, and school district of the free States. They are visible in our social circles, in our pulpits, in our literary publications, our newspapers, our debating clubs, our political discussions, and in all departments of society. The foundations of the mighty deep of popular sentiment are broken up. Political parties are disorganized, and party attachments are disregarded.

These are some of the effects of that moral and political revolution now going forward in this nation. I trust it will continue to progress, until this government and the people of the free States shall be fully redeemed and purified from the contagion of slavery and all manner of oppression, and the Constitution and the rights of humanity shall be fully vindicated.

The Abolitionist
Rhetorical Tradition
in Contemporary America

When President Lincoln announced the Emancipation Proclamation and when, after the Civil War, the Thirteenth, Fourteenth, and Fifteenth Amendments to the Constitution were adopted, such leading spokesmen for anti-slavery as William Lloyd Garrison, Theodore Dwight Weld, and Henry B. Stanton retired from the field, assuming that the cause had largely been achieved. Many of the black leaders, such as Frederick Douglass and Henry Highland Garnet, became influential members of the Republican Party. Douglass accepted a post as the Minister-Resident and Consul-General to the Republic of Haiti, and Garnet became Minister Resident and Consul-General to Liberia.

Lincoln had developed a moderate plan for reconstructing the South, which included relatively mild measures of punishment for the soldiers who fought in the Rebellion. When Lincoln was assassinated, the new President, Andrew Johnson, continued the moderate policies of his predecessor. The radical abolitionists within the Republican party, however, led by Thaddeus Stevens and Charles Sumner, took control of the federal government and instituted a much more stringent and punitive form of reconstruction. The new plan divided the South into military districts, and for a decade the Confederacy was governed by an army of occupation which enforced equal rights for the black man.

The freedman was given the vote, and blacks were elected to the state legislatures of every Southern state. The Mississippi legislature elected two black senators; twenty black congressmen served in Washington, D. C., and in Louisiana a black man, P. B. S. Pinchback, became governor.

Although black leaders relied primarily upon political action in the hey-day of radical reconstruction, they also used direct action. Blacks used ride-ins, sit-ins, and walk-ins in New Orleans, Charleston, and several Northern cities to force compliance to federal laws. For example, in 1871, blacks in Louis-ville, Kentucky, began sitting in the white sections of horse-drawn streetcars and, although whites overturned some cars and smashed some windows in others, the action continued until the company instituted integrated seating.

The flow of history is seldom linear. Reform efforts in America have ebbed and risen like a tide. The ebbing of radical reconstruction began with the crucial election of 1876 in which the Republican Rutherford B. Hayes and the Democrat Samuel J. Tilden found themselves so deadlocked in the race for the presidency that the balance of power lay with the disputed electoral votes from South Carolina, Louisiana, and Florida. The compromise that was worked out saw Hayes elected to the presidency and the restoration of "home rule" to the states of the old Confederacy.

The next twenty years were stormy ones in the history of race relations. The white supremacists grew in strength with the removal of the Northern armies, and the black man was systematically disenfranchised. The newly emerged white leadership, composed mainly of rising and aggressive middle-class entrepreneurs and the leaders of the old aristocracy, was quickly challenged by the revolt of the "rednecks" as Populism swept through most of the southern states in the 1890's. The lower middle class fought for control of the state governments to protect its largely rural interests from the exploitation of the monopolies and "interests." The Populist reform sought in its early stages to mobilize both the black and white poor farmer. In the bitter and violent struggles that followed, the specter of black power was used to beat back the Populists in their attempt to start a People's Party.

Frederick Douglass was still alert, influential, and active as a Negro spokesman until 1895. By the turn of the century, however, a new generation of rhetoricians was in the field. Booker T. Washington was active as a speaker and publicist, urging peace and accommodation between the races. Countering Washington were two more militant spokesmen for the black community, William Monroe Trotter and William Edward Burghardt Du Bois.

Active in the early years of the twentieth century were two other black leaders who had inherited the traditions of the old abolitionists in a poignant and personal way and who continued to practice the old rhetoric in the years following World War I. They were both Grimkés from South Carolina, and both were colored.

Archibald H. Grimké and Francis J. Grimké made their way north at the close of the Civil War to seek an education. They both eventually entered Lincoln University in Chester County, Pennsylvania. When Angelina Grimké Weld happened by chance to read an account of a young man named Grimké who had delivered a fine speech at a meeting at Lincoln University, she developed the heart-rending suspicion that he might be the son of one of her brothers who had remained in Charleston, South Carolina.

The Grimké brothers were indeed Angelina and Sarah Grimké's nephews, being the sons of Henry Grimké and Nancy Weston, his slave who joined his household as the children's nurse after the death of his wife. The Welds and Sarah immediately adopted the nephews as members of their family, invited them into their home, and supported them through the remainder of their education.

Francis Grimké went on to Princeton Theological Seminary and became pastor of the 15th Street Presbyterian Church in Washington, D. C. Archibald Grimké graduated from Harvard Law School, edited a Negro journal, *The Hub*, wrote a biography of William Lloyd Garrison, and was active as both a speaker and writer on behalf of Negro rights.

The year 1909 saw the formation of the National Association for the Advancement of Colored People, and the flow of racial reform began to move again toward high tide. The dislocations of World War I and the new opportunities and freedoms resulting from war mobilization brought the effort to a climax in the years immediately following the war.

Archibald Grimké, in a speech entitled "The Shame of America," represented the old abolitionist rhetoric in the roaring twenties. In a style reminiscent of the Garrisonians he pointed out the hypocrisy of the Preamble to the Constitution:

> "We the people!" From the standpoint of the Negro, what grim irony; "establish justice!" What exquisitely cruel mockery; "to insure domestic tranquility!" What height and breadth and depth of political duplicity; "to provide for the common defense!" What cunning paltering with words in a double sense; "to promote the general welfare!" What studied ignoring of an ugly fact....The muse of history, dipping her iron pen in the generous blood of the Negro, has written large across the page of that Preamble, and the face of the Declaration of Independence, the words, "sham, hypocrisy."[1]

Later in the same speech, Grimké traced the history of Negro rights in the United States from the time of the Constitution down to the declaration of war against Germany. When the United States entered the war, the outlook for the Negro was at its darkest, according to Grimké, but the "Republic's program of false promises and hypocritical professions" was revived in order to bring the black man to its aid. The black Americans rallied to the war effort but received only discrimination, ingratitude, and treachery. But once the black soldiers got to France, they saw the truth about the United States, for in France the black American was treated as a brother.

[1]Archibald Grimké, "The Shame of America, or the Negro's Case Against the Republic," in Carter G. Woodson, ed., *Negro Orators and Their Orations* (Washington, D. C.: The Associated Publishers, Inc., 1925), pp. 674–75.

Because of his experience in the war, the black soldier "has come back not as he went but a New Negro. He has come back to challenge injustice in his own land and to fight wrong with a courage that will not fail him in the bitter and perhaps bloody years to come."[2]

In an address delivered at a Harvard University Commencement in 1922, Mordecai Wyatt Johnson analyzed two of the black rhetorics that grew up to sustain the movement for civil rights in the postwar period. Noting that after the war Negro hopes were disappointed, and that efforts to keep the blacks in their place finally culminated in racial violence in the Red Summer of 1919, Johnson went on to say that many blacks took weapons in their hands and fought back with bloody resistance. " 'If we must die,' they said, 'it is well that we die fighting.' "[3]

Of one group of young black men, Johnson said they believed that the United States Government was controlled by selfish capitalists, and they urged the colored man to ally himself with the revolutionary labor movement of America and the world.

Another group believed in religion and in the principles of democracy but not in white religion and white democracy. The blacks of this persuasion believed that the entire nation was tacitly racist and that they had nothing to hope for from white America. The leaders of the group were meeting with representatives from around the Negro world "to lay the foundations of a black empire, a black religion, and a black culture; it has organized the provisional Republic of Africa...."[4]

The introduction of the Marxist rhetoric of the decade following the Russian Revolution was a new development for black persuasion, but the refurbishing of the old colonization schemes was not. One of the most amazing black rhetoricians of American history was active in the latter movement. His name was Marcus Garvey, and in a short time he gained millions of followers and raised large amounts of money to establish a chain of co-operative enterprises and the Black Star Line of steamships. Garvey, at the height of his popularity, announced the formation of an African Republic.

Many of the lines of argument in the rhetoric of the 1920's relating to the hypocrisy of the American dream as represented by the Preamble to the Constitution and the Declaration of Independence are direct inheritances from the nineteenth century rhetoric of the abolitionists. Garvey's adoption

[2]Grimké, pp. 687–88.
[3]Mordecai Wyatt Johnson, "The Faith of the American Negro," in Woodson, p. 660.
[4]Johnson, p. 661.

of the colonization approach added the nuance of African heritage and pride in blackness.

In the late 1920's, repressive counterforces followed the violence of the Red Summer of 1919, and the efforts of black rhetoricians ebbed once again only to flow more strongly with the attack on Pearl Harbor and the mobilization for war.[5] The tide crested in the successful attempts of Asa Philip Randolph, called by Lerone Bennett, Jr., the "Gandhi in Harlem," to integrate the army and open defense industries to black workers.[6] Randolph developed both the rhetoric and the direct action tactic of nonviolence. By a skillful use of the threat of a march of 100,000 on Washington, he got President Franklin Roosevelt to appoint a Fair Employment Committee. Despite the successes of Randolph with his nonviolent approach, discontent boiled up in 1943 in a series of riots during the summer in Harlem, Mobile, and Los Angeles. The worst incident came in June with the "Black Pearl Harbor" in Detroit, where over thirty persons were killed and more than one thousand injured in the rioting.

After 1943, the tide of agitation and direct action ebbed again as efforts turned toward litigation and legal remedies for black grievances. For a contemporary student of black rhetoric, the current persuasive campaign, which looms almost as large from our perspective as did the first big abolition reform of the 1830's and 1840's, began in the mid-1950's with the Supreme Court Decision on school integration, and with the sit-ins, walk-ins, wade-ins, and kneel-ins to integrate public accommodations and service industries. Indeed, some would pinpoint the moment the new movement gained momentum as the Thursday in Montgomery, Alabama, in December, 1955, when Mrs. Rosa Park refused to move from a seat when ordered to do so by a bus driver.[7] Martin Luther King came to national prominence in the Montgomery Bus Boycott and became the symbol of the contemporary black rhetorics in much the same way that William Lloyd Garrison symbolized the abolition movement of the 1830's.

The decade of the 1960's was reminiscent of the 1830's. Martin Luther King won the Nobel Prize for Peace and was martyred. The ghettos of many

---

[5]The Red Summer of 1919 was one of the most violent in American history in terms of racial disorder. A black mob held sway in the nation's capital for one whole day, and for thirteen days Negroes and whites fought in Chicago. In all there were twenty-six race riots that summer. See, for example, Lerone Bennett, Jr., *Confrontation: Black and White* (Chicago: Johnson Publishing Company, Inc., 1965), pp. 142–43.

[6]Bennett, pp. 170–96.

[7]See, for example, Haig A. Bosmajian and Hamida Bosmajian, eds., *The Rhetoric of the Civil Rights Movement* (New York: Random House, 1969), p. 3.

cities erupted into violence. Malcolm X arose as a spokesman for black nationalism and was assassinated. The Black Panthers gained notoriety and served as a rhetorical symbol for black militancy. The leaders of the Student Nonviolent Coordinating Committee, such as Stokely Carmichael and H. Rap Brown, gained a reputation for agitation. Sustaining the true believer, explaining the bewildering and chaotic events, and exhorting the potential converts were several competing black rhetorics.

My purpose here is not to provide an extensive criticism of the persuasion in behalf of black power, integration, black nationalism, and racial justice, which pervade the contemporary scene. Rather I should like to suggest possible ways for you to make your own rhetorical criticisms of important persuasive campaigns.

Now that you have some understanding of the tradition of antislavery rhetoric as analyzed and illustrated by the earlier sections of this book, you are prepared to make your own analysis of current black rhetorics. One good way to do so is to make an analog analysis by comparing the rhetoric of the abolitionists with the rhetoric of contemporary black speakers in such a way that each movement serves as a reference standard for the other. You may use the analog method to achieve several purposes. A careful comparative speech criticism can serve to discover basic features which are common to both rhetorical contexts. Such common features provide earmarks to use for the study and understanding of other American reform rhetorics related to foreign policy, welfare, and economic matters as well as to race relations. Another purpose of an analog criticism of rhetorical movements might be to discover what continuity, if any, there is in reform persuasion dedicated to a problem like race relations in the history of American Public Address. Finally, a comparative analysis can be used to assess the relative effectiveness and the artistic merits of various rhetorics by comparing them to one another.[8]

The similarities between the current movement and the abolition crusade are so strong that you have undoubtedly noted many of them already. I shall only sketch in brief form some of the more striking comparisons and quickly note several of the main differences. My objective is to provide some general guidelines of how an analog criticism of the rhetoric of abolition and of contemporary black rhetorics might proceed.

---

[8]For the term *analog criticism* and, to some extent, for the concept as I use it, I am indebted to Professor Lawrence Rosenfield. See, for example, L. W. Rosenfield, "A Case Study in Speech Criticism: The Nixon-Truman Analog," *Speech Monographs*, 35 (1968), 435–50.

Although in his emphasis on nonviolence, peace, and immediacy, Martin Luther King's rhetoric resembles that of William Lloyd Garrison, in the wider aspects his persuasion was much more like that of the rhetoric of conversion, as exemplified by Theodore Weld, than like agitation.

Most important in the similarity between the persuasion of the Southern Christian Leadership Conference and the evangelicals of the "Great Revival" was the acceptance of the cherished values of the total society. King fitted his movement into the mainstream of American society and sought to purge that society the same way as did the agents for benevolent antislavery. King's rhetorical strategy is symbolized by the key term "integration." Much as the rhetorical symbol of the "melting pot" served the rhetoric of unification for a previous generation trying to create a sense of community and national cohesion for waves of immigrants, the concept of integration was the fulcrum of King's rhetoric. Martin Luther King argued essentially for unification, and his dream, as he put it in his most famous speech, was "...deeply rooted in the American dream that one day this nation will rise up and live out the true meaning of its creed—we hold these truths to be self-evident, that all men are created equal."[9]

Like the evangelicals of an earlier day, the spokesmen for the SCLC emerged from the church. Their rhetoric was couched in the cadences and style of the black preacher. They drew their support from the black churches, and although they attacked elements of the church, they never turned their backs upon the institution. Like Weld, Finney, and the "New Lights," they referred to one another as "brother" and "sister" to indicate their common bond in the movement. In town after town in the South in the last years of the decade of the 1950's, local black ministers led the sit-ins and boycotts and fired up the rank and file in protest meetings in the churches with speeches indistinguishable from the typical evangelical sermon.

Like the abolitionists, the spokesmen for the contemporary movement were impatient. Again the rhetoric of reform was full of reference to immediacy. The slogan of the movement was "Freedom Now!" Martin Luther King told the thousands assembled to hear him during the march on Washington, D. C. in 1963, "We have also come to this hallowed spot to remind America of the fierce urgency of now."[10]

As the rhetoricians of conversion of the earlier day had claimed the cause

[9]Martin Luther King, Jr., "I Have a Dream," in Wil A. Linkugel, R. R. Allen, and Richard L. Johannesen, eds., *Contemporary American Speeches* (Belmont, California: Wadsworth Publishing Company, Inc., 1965), p. 159.

[10]King, "I Have a Dream," p. 158.

had supernatural support, the followers of Martin Luther King sustained and consoled themselves with the theme that they had the sanction of God and were therefore assured of inevitable victory. In King's words, "We will win our freedom because the sacred heritage of our nation and the eternal will of God are embodied in our echoing demands."[11] The anthem of the movement proclaimed the same message:

> We shall overcome, we shall overcome,
> We shall overcome some day,
> Oh, deep in my heart, I do believe
> We shall overcome some day.

The contemporary rhetoric of racial revolt shares a common theme and a common set of rhetorical techniques, as did the rhetoric of agitation and of conversion for the abolitionists. The description of the problem is couched in emotional language and in considerable graphic detail. Comparisons with slavery, incidents of physical violence, murder, psychological bullying, and lack of opportunity are the stock in trade of all styles of black rhetoric. In his "Letter from Birmingham City Jail," Martin Luther King wrote, "...you have seen vicious mobs lynch your mothers and fathers at will and drown your sisters and brothers at whim;...you have seen hate-filled policemen curse, kick, brutalize, and even kill your black brothers and sisters with impunity...."[12]

In general, all black speakers agree upon the causes of the realities that must be fought. The main explanation, they say, is to be found in an essentially racist white society, but a basic weakness in the black community is also a factor. Without Uncle Toms who accept exploitation, the white racists would be frustrated.

Perhaps the greatest distinction between current black rhetorics and the rhetoric of abolition is that the main audience for the latter had to be the white community, because in the 1830's and 1840's the great bulk of the blacks were slaves and could not be reached by the words of the speakers and writers. Today a rhetorician planning a persuasive campaign for reform of race relations can decide to adopt a strategy of unity with the entire society, white and nonwhite, as did Martin Luther King and his followers and as did some leaders of the biracial Congress Of Racial Equality (CORE), or they may choose to adopt a strategy of divisiveness and appeal primarily to the black audience.

---

[11]Martin Luther King, Jr., "Letter from Birmingham City Jail," in Bosmajian and Bosmajian, p. 54.
[12]King, "Letter...", p. 42.

Today's agitator for racial revolt has often made the decision to appeal only to the black audience and has adopted the tactic of a divisive rhetoric. We might argue, of course, that the Black Panther ministers of information, the Carmichaels, H. Rap Browns, and Floyd McKissicks of today are not agitators at all in the sense that Garrison, Foster, and Phillips were, because in terms of their decision to speak primarily to the blacks, their attacks on the cherished values of the total, predominantly white society are irrelevant. Such an analysis has much to commend it. Several factors must, however, be kept in mind before we discredit the claim that they are agitators in the sense of attacking cherished values. The black speakers cannot keep from having a wider audience. The television cameras are ubiquitous, and every major statement is flashed into the living rooms of Indians, Mexicans, Orientals, and Caucasians. Thus the agitation effect, although it may be irrelevant in terms of the speaker's objectives, is not unimportant if we take a broader view of the effects of the persuasion.

The argument that attacking the American dream (as represented by the notion that all men are created equal and that the best society is an open one of equal opportunity) would not necessarily agitate the black community is also suspect. The fact that Martin Luther King could mobilize so many black Americans with an appeal that emphasized the common values of black and white society indicates that, for an important segment of the black audience, the rhetoric of divisiveness and separateness would also be a rhetoric of agitation.

The decision of the agitators to divide American society into the good guys and the bad guys, making a sharp and clear division between blacks and whites, brought with it certain options that the rhetoricians of the Southern Christian Leadership Conference could not exercise. Many of the options have been taken up by one or more of the agitators. Among the more important choices for the agitator was the opportunity to depict the white man as the enemy in sharp and bold outline to arouse hatred and anger in the black audience. Personalizing the abstract enemy as "whitey" or "honky" or "the man," or picturing the enemy as a vicious club-wielding policeman— a fascist pig—was one tactic to implement the strategy of arousing emotions.

Another important option that some agitators employed was to threaten violence and to claim that the riots in the ghetto areas were "rebellions" in support of the movement. The theme of revolution and rebellion led some to talk of guerrilla warfare and push the colonial analogy. Dividing the people of the country into black colonists exploited by white imperialists, the agitators sometimes talked of the movement as a revolutionary effort to achieve liberation from a colonial power.

In general, the contemporary black agitator places his movement outside the mainstream of American society and rejects the American dream. The black speakers discount the content of the unifying rhetoric by charging the white community with hypocrisy and arguing that it does not live by its ostensible creed. The agitators define a new set of values which they assert are the real ideology of the white enemy. The American society, in actuality, they say, is materialist, power hungry, repressive, and racist. The vileness of the enemy is illustrated by the analogy of the Jew in Nazi Germany, a powerful historical allusion for all Americans which was not available to the earlier abolitionists, who tended to get somewhat the same effect by comparing America to the oppressive climate of tyrannized Russia. The agitators who press the German Jewish analogy to its ultimate conclusion call society's treatment of blacks "genocide," as a rhetorical tactic to accuse the whites of conscious or unconscious desires for race murder.

Having turned their backs upon the American heritage, the spokesmen for the rhetoric of agitation cannot adopt the best parts of the American value system for their own rhetoric, as can the evangelicals. The agitators cannot, as Martin Luther King did, dream of a future in which life in America matches its democratic ideology and thus build common ground with those members of the audience who accept the American credo.

The decision to reject the American culture and traditions has forced the agitators to search for other histories and other cultures with which to build a sense of community among their followers and give. meaning and relevance to their movement. Some have identified their efforts with those of the nonwhite peoples of the world, particularly with the African heritage of their ancestors. Black audiences are reminded that as part of the nonwhite population of the globe, they are in the majority, and inevitably the white man will soon face a reversal of his domination of the world by the growing strength of the colored majority.

Much as the abolitionists of the 1840's saw the Mexican War as an immoral effort to extend the institution of slavery and strengthen its hold on the government, the black rhetoricians of the 1960's saw the Vietnam war as part of the white man's vendetta against the colored man and as a defense of white colonialism in Asia.

Another tactic of the agitators to build a sense of community and a strong group self-image within the black audience was symbolized by the slogan "Black is Beautiful." In a speech to black students at Morgan State College, Stokely Carmichael, of the Student Nonviolent Coordinating Committee, ridiculed the students who adopted the life style of middle-class America.

He poked fun at fraternities and sororities and debutante balls. He grew sarcastic about black coeds who tried to appear like white beauties by pinching their noses, straightening their hair, and biting in their thick lips.

Carmichael demonstrated a sophisticated understanding of the importance of rhetoric in building a sense of identity and group pride as he gave the students a lesson in speech criticism. The problem was one of definition, he told the students. "Now then we come to the question of definitions. We will talk about that for a while. It is very, very important because I believe that people who can define are masters."[13] The students, according to Carmichael, were defining a beauty in white terms as a person with a narrow nose, white skin, and thin lips. At Morgan State they were picking their homecoming queen on the basis of white definitions of beauty. The speaker urged the students to develop their own criteria for beauty. Have "guts" enough, he said, to decide "that your nose is boss; your lips are thick, you are black, and you are beautiful."[14]

History does not repeat itself, and Stokely Carmichael and H. Rap Brown are not speaking in precisely the same terms as Frederick Douglass or Henry Highland Garnet. Yet rhetorical situations do fall into analogous patterns. The problems facing the civil rights movement in the 1950's and 1960's and those that will face the black rhetoricians of the future are similar in many respects.

Whenever a movement deals with race relations in the United States, the historical rhetoric continues to intrude into the contemporary campaign. Thus today's agitators make Frederick Douglass a hero to symbolize, in terms of an attractive personality, a laudable tradition of protest, just as they make Booker T. Washington a villain to symbolize the undesirable, submissive black man.

If you know the history of the persuasive campaigns for antislavery in the nineteenth century, you are in a much better position to understand, evaluate, and appreciate the efforts of black and white spokesmen for racial justice today. (You are also in a better position to understand the revolutionary rhetoric of the New Left.) We are in the midst of several great rhetorical campaigns for change, and to be buffeted by the bombardment of television images, print-media messages, and public address without knowledge of the first great reform rhetorics in our history is to fail to understand the full relevance of today's rhetorical battles.

[13]Stokely Carmichael, "Speech at Morgan State College," in Bosmajian and Bosmajian, p. 113.
[14]Carmichael, "Speech," p. 121.

Suggested Reading

Barnes, Gilbert H., *The Antislavery Impulse: 1830–1844*. New York: Appleton-Century Co., 1933.

Bartlett, Irving H., *Wendell Phillips, Brahmin Radical*. Boston: Beacon Press, 1961.

Bennett, Lerone, Jr., *Confrontation: Black and White*. Chicago: Johnson Publishing Company, Inc., 1965.

Bosmajian, Haig A. and Bosmajian, Hamida, eds., *The Rhetoric of the Civil Rights Movement*. New York: Random House, 1969.

Breitman, George, ed., *Malcolm X Speaks*. New York: Grove Press, Inc., 1966.

Curry, Richard O., ed., *The Abolitionists*. New York: Holt, Rinehart and Winston, Inc., 1965.

Filler, Louis, *The Crusade Against Slavery: 1830–1860*. New York: Harper & Row, Publishers, 1960.

Flexner, Eleanor, *Century of Struggle: The Woman's Rights Movement in the United States*. Cambridge: Harvard University Press, 1959.

Foner, Philip, *Frederick Douglass*. New York: The Citadel Press, 1964.

Hill, Roy L., ed., *The Rhetoric of Racial Revolt*. Denver: The Golden Bell Press, 1964.

King, Martin Luther, Jr., *Why We Can't Wait*. New York: Harper & Row, Publishers, 1964.

Lerner, Gerda, *The Grimké Sisters from South Carolina: Rebels Against Slavery*. Boston: Houghton Mifflin Company, 1967.

Lomas, Charles, *The Agitator in American Society*. Englewood Cliffs, N. J.: Prentice-Hall, Inc., 1968.

McPherson, James, *The Struggle for Equality: Abolitionists and the Negro in the Civil War and Reconstruction*. Princeton: Princeton University Press, 1964.

O'Connor, Lillian, *Pioneer Women Orators*. New York: Columbia University Press, 1954.

Quarles, Benjamin, *Black Abolitionists*. New York: Oxford University Press, 1969.

Scott, Robert L. and Brockriede, Wayne, eds., *The Rhetoric of Black Power*. New York: Harper & Row, Publishers, 1969.

Smith, Arthur L., *Rhetoric of Black Revolution*. Boston: Allyn and Bacon, Inc., 1969.

Stanton, Elizabeth Cady, *Eighty Years and More*. London: T. Fisher Unwin, 1898.

Stanton, Elizabeth C., Susan B. Anthony, and Mathilda J. Gage, *History of Woman Suffrage*. 6 vols. New York: Fowler & Wells, 1881–1922.

Thomas, Benjamin P., *Theodore Weld, Crusader for Freedom*. New Brunswick, N. J.: Rutgers University Press, 1950.

Thomas, John L., *The Liberator: A Biography of William Lloyd Garrison*. Boston: Little, Brown & Co., 1963.

Wolf, Hazel, *On Freedom's Altar: The Martyr Complex in the Abolition Movement*. Madison: The University of Wisconsin Press, 1952.

Woodson, Carter G., *Negro Orators and Their Orations*. Washington, D. C.: The Associated Publishers, Inc., 1925.

Index